Globalization, Urbanization, and the State

GLOBALIZATION, URBANIZATION, AND THE STATE

Selected Studies on Contemporary Latin America

Satya R. Pattnayak

University Press of America, Inc.
Lanham • New York • London

Copyright © 1996 by
University Press of America,® Inc.
4720 Boston Way
Lanham, Maryland 20706

3 Henrietta Street
London, WC2E 8LU England

Library of Congress Cataloging-in-Publication Data

Globalization, urbanization, and the state : selected studies in
contemporary Latin America / edited by Satya R. Pattnayak.
p.   cm.
1. Latin America--Economic conditions--1982--Congresses. 2. Latin
America--Economic policy--Congresses. 3. Latin America--Politics
and government-1980--Congresses. 4. Latin America--Foreign
economic relations--Congresses. I. Pattnayak, Satya R.
HC123.G54   1996   338.98--dc20   96-16414 CIP

ISBN 0-7618-0352-1 (cloth: alk. ppr.)
ISBN 0-7618-0353-X (pbk: alk. ppr.)

To Dr. R. Narayanan

for being a great teacher, a true friend, and an insightful guide in the most formative but critical years of my academic life.

Contents

Tables and Figures

Tables

Figures

Preface

Satya R. Pattnayak

Since World War II, states around the globe have become more
interventionist in civil societies. This intervention has assumed many
varying forms. In the case of Latin America, state intervention has
permeated almost all countries through public sector investment,
stimulation of import substituting industrialization programs, and/or
efforts to distort markets to promote domestic capital and industry.

Politically, these statist experiments have been accompanied by
various forms of corporatist arrangements (both inclusionary and
exclusionary) that have sustained workable alliances between segments
of capital and labor. State-led development efforts have created
infrastructure, subsidized the life styles of urban poor and middle-
classes, and in some cases, guaranteed access to minimum health care.
All these economic, political, and social experiments spearheaded by
states ---whether military, semi-military, or civilian--- have required
enormous amounts of public borrowing from international sources
including commercial banks.

Starting with the Mexican debt crisis in 1982, the state-led
experiments have begun to unravel, buffeted by global restructuring,

growing external debt, and declining political legitimacy for the regimes, the latter largely because of their inability to sustain high economic growth. The vulnerability of Latin American economies to fluctuations in the prices of their major export products remains ominous. Furthermore, the scandal-plagued state of secular authorities across this vast region calls for new experiments to instill a sense of life, legitimacy, and hope in the civil society.

In the mid-1990s the whole region of Latin America is engaged in a different kind of economic, political, and social engineering where states play a quantitatively and qualitatively different role than the earlier era. In the euphoria of neoliberalism, there is increasing skepticism about any kind of state activity. The market has been projected as the only viable mechanism for sustaining economic growth, political democracy, and relatively equitable social development. Didn't we hear all of this before in the US in the early 1980s?

The implemented ideology of neoliberalism no doubt has contributed to some aggregate growth, but has also intensified the problems of income distribution and mass suffering. In particular, over the past decade the informal sector growth has become an increasingly important player in political equations. Can the informal sector provide an unique Latin American solution to the problems of growth and development? At a minimum, the authors of this volume believe that a debate on these issues should begin in earnest.

In the dominant political circles, the neoliberal ideology has created a simple but illusory solution to the highly complex problem of market efficiency compatible with relatively egalitarian distribution of income. Already some political groups are crying foul as large public enterprises are sold at throwaway prices to private monopolies and foreign debt is swapped for acquiring equity in state-owned enterprises. As social expenditure is reduced, a major component of the civil society, particularly the lower and middle classes, face a greater crisis of survivability. In the absence of much state support in the social arena, poverty has increased all across Latin America, particularly in the urban areas.

Given the problems of representation faced by much of the vulnerable and under-represented segments of the Latin American society, it is only sensible to ask that both the positive and negative aspects of neoliberal marketization be honestly debated in the academic circles. To address the social impact of the neoliberal economic and political strategies in Latin America, Villanova University sponsored a two-day academic conference in March of 1993 as part of its Sesquicentennial Celebration. Eminent scholars from various disciplines took part in the conference and grappled with the theoretical as well as substantive understanding of the issues. That conference laid the foundation for this volume.

After the conference, many scholars agreed to rewrite their arguments into fully developed chapters. New scholars joined the project and this volume slowly began to emerge in its present shape. It is important to note that all the chapters were written or re-written in 1993 or early 1994. Undoubtedly, some later events have overtaken the projections in the book. With regard to some other developments, the authors' predictions have largely come true. Because of the inevitable time-lag between the time the chapters are written and the release of the book, some discrepancy between the nature of prediction and outcome of events is natural. This discrepancy is inevitable to some extent if one deals with fluid social processes, in particular the forces of neoliberal marketization that are still taking shape and shaping others. But in the process, I, as the editor, have incurred numerous intellectual debts, and would like to acknowledge them at this juncture. First, I must thank the Sesquicentennial Steering Committee of Villanova University for the generous financial support it provided for the conference. In particular, Christine Lysionek deserves my gratitude.

I am also grateful to a number of my colleagues in the Department of Sociology and in the College of Arts and Sciences at Villanova University for constant encouragement. Michael Burke, Lowell Gustafson, William Waegel, Bernard Gallagher, Brian Jones, Lynda Malik, Tom Arvanites, Rick Eckstein, and Peter Knapp must be mentioned as they collaborated at various stages in the conference organization. In the preparation of the manuscript, I credit the invaluable assistance of Rachel Schaller.

I wish to congratulate all the contributors for their assistance in completing this volume. They showed remarkable patience with me over these three years. Finally, I have dedicated this volume to Dr. R. Narayanan, my esteemed teacher, long-time friend, and an incessant source of inspiration during the most formative but critical years of my academic life.

Satya R. Pattnayak, Ph.D.
Villanova
Pennsylvania

1

Latin American Political Economy at a Crossroads: An Introduction[1]

Satya R. Pattnayak

The political economy of Latin American states may be better explained at a level intermediate between larger, global processes and smaller, urban ones. In the present climate of neoliberal marketization, it is particularly important to see the linkage of processes in the national economy to these global and metropolitan processes. Two important issues of popular concern lie at the heart of the linkage: economic growth and social development. By economic growth I refer primarily to the aggregate growth indices in the national economy or in any specific sector within. Social development can be defined in terms of progress in the areas of income distribution, life expectancy, educational attainment, health standards, etc.; all are indicators of a general improvement in the welfare of the majority of inhabitants in a nation.

Economic growth and social development in Latin America have long been major concerns for social scientists.[2] The region, stretching from the U.S-Mexican border to the southern tip of South America, is projected to contain over 527 million people by the year 2000, about twice the projected population size of the United States.[3] As economic growth and social development become more pressing with each passing decade of population explosion, major political strategies affecting these issues come under the scrutiny. But these strategies cannot be adequately understood unless linked on the one hand to global and, on the other hand, to metropolitan processes.

The Background

Several Latin American countries undertook a series of policy reforms to alleviate the problems of growth and development in the wake of the 1982 debt crisis. Because the debt-crisis was so pervasive in its negative impact, immediate steps were taken to stabilize the economy. These were followed by favorable policies towards foreign trade, privatization of some state enterprises, withdrawal of many state regulations considered harmful to competitive capitalism, and changes in the social expenditure patterns. Of course, not all of these measures were undertaken in all the countries of the region at the same time, nor were they all introduced with the same vigor. For example, while dramatic market-oriented reforms, including significant privatization, have indeed occurred in Chile, Mexico, Argentina, Peru, and Bolivia, these have not been undertaken to the same degree in Brazil, Colombia, or Venezuela. But variation within the region notwithstanding, theoretically it is conceivable that a transitional phase has been underway in the direction of *neoliberalism* since the early 1980s, whose major features are clearly not in tune with the earlier policies.[4]

In a general sense, the strategy of Import Substituting Industrialization (ISI) which is aimed at the domestic market (operative in most of the region since the 1930s) has gradually been succeeded by an emphasis on exports to the global market. After the initial period of adjustment (in which economic growth rates suffered throughout the region), changes in favor of economic globalization have resulted in a relatively steady growth in the Gross Domestic Product (GDP) during the late 1980s and early 1990s. According to the World Bank, for example, 14 of the 22 Latin American nations have documented positive overall growth rates in their per capita GDP during 1987-92.[5] Other indicators testify to a greater integration of Latin American economies with the advanced industrial nations, especially in the late 1980s and early 1990s. Several countries, including Argentina, Brazil, Chile, Mexico, and Uruguay, have registered favorable balances of trade during the mid- and late 1980s, a reversal from the heyday of ISI in the 1960s.[6]

These aggregate indicators provide *prima facie* evidence that economic globalization has been beneficial in terms of at least some aggregate growth indicators. So the question is not whether aggregate economic growth has occurred under the neoliberal experiment with economic globalization. Rather, the question should be: Would there be comparable growth *in the absence* of such a strategy? The contributors to this volume argue in the negative and focus on the social and political costs of the neoliberal agenda.[7]

But not all aggregate indicators of growth have been impressive. Many reveal some disturbing trends. For example, the urban minimum (real) wage has declined in Latin America during 1980-89, except in Colombia, Costa Rica, and Paraguay.[8] The general decline in wages suggests a drop in the quality of life.[9] In addition, although exports to advanced industrial nations have increased in the larger economies of the region resulting in favorable balances of trade, many smaller economies still continue to experience negative trade and payments imbalances.[10]

Other indicators paint a bleak picture for Latin America as well. For example, the larger economies of the region, such as Brazil, Mexico, Argentina, Chile, Peru, and Venezuela, have continued to fail in the income redistribution front. The gap between the top 20 and the bottom 20 percent of the population in terms of their respective shares in total household income has continued to increase in favor of the former.[11] At the least these trends raise questions concerning the appropriateness of the neoliberal model of economic growth.[12]

The persistence of these disturbing trends makes it imperative that we re-evaluate the link between economic growth and social development. The experiences of many Latin American countries suggest that the direction of this relationship is not as straightforward as is commonly assumed.[13] Unless political strategies are designed to sustain a positive link between economic growth and social development, a vast majority of the Latin American population appears unlikely to benefit from the current emphasis on economic globalization. This is where the role of the state comes into the consideration. In particular, the changes in the nature of the developmental state is called into question. I take up the theoretical issues involved with the changing nature of the developmental state later in the book.

The issue of political strategies to minimize the detrimental effects of economic growth (or lack of growth) on social development is particularly important as many Latin American countries have also experienced a gradual liberalization of their political systems. The process of political liberalization has facilitated the resurgence of political parties, labor unions, and other popular sector organizations. In some countries political liberalization has accommodated free and fair elections, unthinkable under military regimes just a few years ago.[14] These simultaneous processes of economic and political liberalization have important ramifications for the *state* in Latin America and its role in facilitating social development.

This book, then, is devoted to understanding Latin American political economy through analyses of the recent changes in two key areas crucial for economic growth and social development: Globalization of the economies and the changing urban processes. Despite differences of disciplinary background, ideological preferences, method, and style, the contributors to this volume share thematic compatibility. Chapters 2 through 5 examine the processes of economic globalization and their importance for economic growth. The authors in these chapters argue that economic growth must not be an end in itself. Rather, it must be a vehicle to sustain democratic forces through social development. These authors maintain that "political legitimacy," "political inclusion," and "relative social equality" must accompany economic growth as vital components in the future sustenance of the processes of democratization.

Chapters 6 through 8 focus on the changing urban processes and the sectors in which state policies and actions would prove to be important for sustaining social development. These authors are of the opinion that economic globalization has facilitated certain fundamental changes in the urban landscape. In particular, they notice signs of change in "urban primacy" and the status of "informal sector growth" in many nations of Latin America. These changes have potentially positive as well as negative implications for the democratic process. In Chapter 9, I explore the changing nature of the state in Latin America and its implication for development theory. Finally, in Chapter 10 I further examine the question of political legitimacy of the current neoliberal model of growth and development.

In the remainder of this introduction I address to thematic compatibility in the chapters to follow. As I discuss the themes I situate them in the literature relevant to understanding the processes of economic globalization and change in the urban landscape. I also deal with the political dimension and state'e role in sustaining both processes.

Globalization as an Economic Process

Since economic globalization has more than one meaning in the literature I propose a broader understanding of the term. I define it as a process generally characterized by: (1) a greater emphasis on exports, particularly of the nontraditional variety (e.g., non-agricultural), (2) an added impetus applied to manufacturing in the composition of the industrial sector, (3) an asymmetrical relationship between capital and labor in that capital is more mobile across national borders and uses the least expensive labor available, (4) substantial deregulation of state economic control and some privatization of public sector enterprises, and (5) an alliance of international financial agencies (e.g., IMF and the World Bank), foreign private capital, domestic private capital, and state elites.[15] True, not all of these characteristics have manifested themselves to the same degree across Latin America. But the ideal goal behind economic globalization is a simple one. It is expected to promote high economic growth and, in turn, social development.

To varying degrees, economic globalization has become the official ideology of the democratizing as well as the already democratic states of Latin America. It is also considered an important component of the neoliberal agenda. The earlier experiments of state-led ISI, pursued by the democratic or military regimes, appear to be over.[16]

The movement towards globalization of the economies via increased exports has been deemed to be a natural political reaction to growing skepticism over consistent failure of Latin American states to simultaneously promote economic growth and social development.[17] The optimism of the earlier development theorists in implicitly assuming that states have almost unlimited capacity to intervene in the economy and run it better than can the private sector has been the focus of much scholarly debate and discussion.[18] Several proponents of the neoliberal experiment operate under the assumption that state failure is worse than market failure and, therefore, states should be asked to play a more limited role in the new emphasis on economic globalization.[19] Withdrawing the obstacles to production, accumulation, and export are advocated as the new priority areas of state action. Some theorists in the neoliberal tradition strongly believe that unimpeded competition in the market place will mitigate the counterproductive domestic behaviors encouraged by corrupt state bureaucrats.[20]

I am not a defender of states engaged in wasteful, rent-seeking activities. However, one must take a cautious approach to the suggestion of simply substituting the market in place of the state. As is well established in the academic literature, a mere substitution of market for state oversimplifies the problems of economic growth and social development. Numerous studies have openly questioned the wisdom of a straight substitution policy.[21] An idealized global market, unless accompanied by state action and policies to address the forces of economic and social inequity, is as likely to fail as simple statism.

Not all Latin American nations can benefit equally from the economic globalization efforts. For example, smaller states, purely because of reasons of the economy of scale, are perhaps better advised to seek closer cooperation among the public, private, and labor elites to amass larger bases of capital.

Several economists have argued that the *priori* case for an open or closed economic policy regime can never be fully proved or disproved.[22] In the absence of reliable comparative-historical studies that clearly demonstrate the superiority of an export-oriented, liberalizing economic regime over others, one must modify such policies in light of critical contextual factors. Some of these critical factors include the size of skilled labor force, progressive income distribution, prior level of industrial development, access to relevant technology, and size of the informal sector. In order for a nation to fare well in all these aspects, a capable state is a requirement. In other words, despite the trends in Latin America in the direction of privatization of some state-owned enterprises, one still needs the state to play a critical role in making sure that certain structural limitations are minimized so that market forces can flourish.[23] Put differently, economic globalization policies need the state in order to sustain themselves in the long-run. But this point of view has largely been ignored in several recent attacks on the state.[24]

In the reigning political climate of neoliberalism, the end of the Cold War, the disintegration of the former Soviet Union, and the subsequent systemic liberalization efforts in the former Eastern bloc there is a popular impression that economic globalization in something new. But globalization of the economy is not really a novelty in Latin America. Ever since its discovery the region's economic growth has been largely determined by the external market forces. But despite its long-term incorporation into the world economy, the terms of trade have historically been unfavorable to Latin America.[25] Consistently, attempts to neutralize the unfavorable trade balances have been made in the form of either pushing the sheer volume of all major exports or excessive reliance on borrowed capital.[26] In the past, the emphasis on the former has resulted in many cases in an export boom, creating an enclave of prosperity surrounded by deepening social inequity in the rest of the economy. In many ways, the past reliance on exports has contributed to an intensification of per capita external debt in Latin America.[27] The Latin American state has an important role to play in the form of critical fiscal and monetary policy adjustments so that such experiences are not repeated.

Despite impressive recent strides in the production of technology-intensive products in countries, such as Argentina, Brazil, and Mexico, Latin America remains vulnerable to the fluctuations in the external demand for its priority exports.[28] Why, then, such euphoria over the current economic globalization programs pursued in various countries of Latin America since the 1980s? As James Petras points out in Chapter 2, economic policies pursued by the democratizing countries are primarily designed to instill a false sense of political legitimacy on behalf of the regime.

The Import Substituting Industrialization after World War II was essentially sustained by an economic-political alliance between the emerging state elites and the national bourgeoisie. But the new phase of economic globalization is being vigorously supported by international private capital and its allies in the industrial and service sectors. In addition, austerity programs dictated by international financial agencies and eagerly supported by many domestic elites have had casualties. These programs have already worsened social inequity in the region, more specifically in urban areas.

Although the neoliberal emphasis, mainly shared by the elites, seems to be pro-privatization of the public sector, the state still is an active player. It still directly intervenes in the economy, manipulates monetary instruments, and directs sales of its own property. But a number of these state actions have been enacted by decree. Petras warns that such efforts of privatization of the economy by decree in countries such as Brazil, Argentina, and Chile have already worsened poverty and will most likely continue to do so. In response to deepening poverty, social movements of different types have emerged in various parts of Latin America.[29] The new movements have encompassed the complex mosaic of a modernizing region. They have appeared as *Mothers of the Plaza de Mayo in Buenos Aires, Women's Movement in Chile, Shining Path in Peru, Peasant movements in Michoacan and Chiapas in Mexico, and São Paolo Metal Workers in Brazil.* This list is by no means exhaustive. Although not all of these are the direct products of deregulated capitalism, the economic globalization policies have undoubtedly expedited the emergence and in some cases sustenance of many of these movements.[30] As a result, many unrepresented and under-represented segments of the Latin American population have already begun to question the legitimacy of the policies of economic globalization and their implementors.

The Political Dimension

An understanding of the political dimension to the processes of economic globalization is critical. Thus far I have used economic globalization and political liberalization as parallel terms which perhaps portray them as coextensive. They are not. There are some underlying tensions between the two processes. The experiences of the former Soviet Union and Eastern Bloc nations make that point abundantly clear. Many contributors in the selections to follow maintain that certain consequences of economic globalization, as unintended they may be, have retarded the process of democratization. These unintended consequences, unless abated by smart state policies as well as a more associational civil society, pose a major threat to political democracy in the long run.

Although the new climate of economic globalization has coincided with efforts to open-up the political system, most existing political parties have largely failed thus far to effectively link the needy sectors of society (e.g., labor, urban poor, rural landless, and informal sector workers) to the processes of democratization.[31] Part of the reason behind such failure is the inability to incorporate popular identities which have been ignored in favor of the dominant ideology of the party or class. Popular knowledge about survival, solidarity, and mobilization have been largely abandoned in favor of technical knowledge of the intelligentsia.[32] Democracy has been incorrectly interpreted as synonymous with elections and, therefore, legislators have misinterpreted popular movements that suggest a different recourse (to elections) as undemocratic.[33]

Various factors, both external and internal, have prompted policy makers to embark upon a dual policy of economic globalization and political liberalization. Externally, the emergence of a multi-centered core structure[34] has facilitated much greater competition for financial outlets, markets, and raw materials. The slow decline of the United States as the predominant economic power in the world and the gradual rise of Japan and Germany as well as the death of the Cold War have intensified the economic restructuring at the top of the global economy.[35] The emphasis of multinational corporations (MNCs) on the global servicing scheme has obligated capital to be the most mobile of all factors of production.

Internally, deterioration of the economic situation following the debt crisis in the early 1980s in the largest economies of the region (e.g., Brazil, Mexico, Argentina, Venezuela, and Peru) has called for alternate strategies that would simultaneously provide temporary political respite and a short-term boost in economic growth. As Arthur Schmidt notes in Chapter 3, these strategies are at best *ad hoc* and have therefore very little chance of promoting long-term social development, so important to sustain a democratic society. Although Schmidt's focus is Mexico and Central America, his arguments are generalizable to the South American region as well. The continued crisis of low savings and dependency on foreign capital, both public and private, is still critical all across Latin America. In addition, the urban-centered growth strategies pursued in most countries of the region have left millions cramming into metropolitan shantytowns, thus creating a politically volatile situation.

The most common state policy has been political exclusion of at least some segments of the popular sectors. Violent protests in provincial Mexico and Argentina as well as the gain in popularity of a few opposition parties, such as the Workers Party (PT) in Brazil, the Frente Grande in Argentina, and Movement towards Socialism and Convergencia in Venezuela, may be characterized as responses to the policies of political exclusion.[36] In several other countries the inadequacy of party politics and its inability to capture the support of the popular sectors in urban areas has had unpleasant political effects. Several states have at times attempted to crack down on the increasingly dissatisfied popular sector in the name of maintaining peace and order, whereas the moves are actually aimed at defending the austerity programs dictated by international agencies (e.g., IMF).[37] For example, in Peru, the national consensus against the Shining Path's disrupting tactics has helped President Fujimori to install an authoritarian rule during his first term.[38] Even during his second term, the Peruvian military judiciary has been consistently criticized for imposing arbitrary, severe sentences (without much legal representation) on the many accused of treason.[39] Insurgent movements are still active and thriving in Colombia and Mexico. In several Central and South American countries the role of the military remains largely undefined and could pose dangers to the future of a healthy civilian-military institutional arrangement. Schmidt warns that this potential crisis is a time-bomb and it encompasses the whole region unless private gains of elites are tempered by political and economic inclusion.

The welfare state's anti-poverty activities have been noticeably downsized in many countries, which have contributed to greater social inequity. Political liberalization, according to Schmidt, has not facilitated stronger intermediate level groups and organizations capable of linking the communities with the larger political structures. Compared to the work done in the Base Christian Communities and by other religious groups in the field of popular organization, the efforts of the secular groups, including political parties, leave much to be desired.[40] Under the climate of this void at the intermediate level, long-term democratic sustenance and stability in Latin America is imperiled.

Chapters 2 and 3 also highlight external factors that include the global economic restructuring as well as the role of the United States as major forces influencing much of Latin America's economic and political fate. But the influence of these forces is nowhere more evident than in Nicaragua. Recent events attest to the fact that external pressures can nullify domestic revolutionary programs of social development. Given the external pressures of global economic restructuring and continuing U.S. hostility, political reconciliation with the coffee-producing class would have been a smart strategy. However, as Jeffery Paige observes in Chapter 4, the reluctance of the Sandinista regime to subsidize private domestic investment in the coffee sector and its preference for greater state expenditures towards basic human needs alienated much of the domestic coffee-producing class. Politically, the Sandinista emphasis on popular participation, rather than political representation, did not curry much favor with the opposition. The fear of popular sectors organizing under an encouraging state crippled any chances Nicaragua might have had for political compromise, both internally and externally. The intransigence on both sides along with the pressure from the U.S-Supported anti-Sandinista forces contributed to the political demise of the Sandinistas.

Political coalition under crisis situations must include the most economically productive segment of a society. As Paige notes, in Nicaragua the Sandinista attempts to forge a political coalition to sustain its various social development programs did not include the coffee bourgeoisie. The coffee bourgeoisie could have generated the economic growth necessary to sustain the Sandinista programs of social development. Paige puts substantial weight on the lack of pragmatism on the part of the Sandinista leadership for the failure to consolidate the revolution by pursuing well-informed, pragmatic trade and investment policies.[41]

Although the Sandinista regime has fallen from power, the demands of the popular sectors it helped activate remain a thorny issue for the successor Chamorro government. Despite resource constraints, attempts must be made to forge a broad political coalition that includes the popular sectors as well as the coffee bourgeoisie. A failure to do so may very well jeopardize the survival chances of this fragile democracy.

The view that programs of economic growth must be complemented by a relatively egalitarian distribution of income and political inclusion in order to sustain political legitimacy on behalf of the regime is also echoed by H.B. Cavalcanti in Chapter 5. The scene in this case shifts to Brazil, the largest economy in Latin America. Economic globalization programs, first by the outgoing military and subsequently by the Collor Presidency, have prompted short-term economic gain in terms of GDP growth, but without a broad political coalition. Collor paid heavily politically for the predatory tactics pursued by his supporters in order to benefit from the policies of economic globalization and privatization of the public sector.[42]

Being politically responsive to external as well as internal forces of change is imperative if democracy is to persist in Latin America. As Cavalcanti notes, the Collor Administration put much weight on the economic restructuring programs in response to trends in the global economy. But domestic needs, especially the economic and political demands of the popular sectors, were ignored. An inclusive, politically conciliatory strategy is essential to ensure positive effects of economic growth on social development.

The Urban Process

There is no doubt that the problems of political exclusion, political illegitimacy, and social inequity highlighted in the earlier chapters have affected urban areas and set the tone for a certain brand of politics.[43] After World War II urban growth and popular sector politicization facilitated populist politics in several countries of Latin America, including Brazil, Argentina, Chile, and Peru. These populist coalitions attempted to mediate between the shocks in the international economy and the welfare of the popular sector through ambitious public sector expansion and subsidies.[44] But economically stagnant years of the 1970s contributed to the collapse of such populist politics. As the umbrella of state protection became increasingly smaller, the vagaries of the international economy created ripple effects on the living conditions of the poor in the shantytowns of not only the megacities of São Paulo, Mexico City, and Buenos Aires, but also in the smaller cities of Central America and the Caribbean.

As the urban way of life affected the vast majority of Latin Americans, understanding the urban processes became a chief concern for scholars.[45] Several studies noted that the bigger urban agglomerations in the larger Latin American countries have facilitated the development of a system guided by the principle of "urban primacy."[46] Briefly put, urban primacy refers to the absolute demographic, economic, and political dominance of a single city in the national urban system. These dominant urban centers house most major production, exchange, and distribution facilities that make lesser urban locations dependent on the primate city. Accordingly, lesser cities developed specialization in facilities that were geared towards either local or regional markets whereas the primate city was geared to the much larger national and global markets.

But with the new wave of production facilities mushrooming in areas other than the dominant city under the new economic globalization emphasis, urban systems are experiencing varying levels of change. As Pozos Ponce in Chapter 6 demonstrates, the Mexican urban system, previously dominated by Mexico City, is experiencing a noticeable shift in its degrees of specialization in the manufacturing of goods and services. Two other regional cities, namely, Guadalajara and Monterrey, have documented changes in specialization which are quite unique in their content and have important implications for overall social development. Pozos Ponce shows that the previously less important cities have gained in importance and have emerged as specialized producers of manufacturing and services. As cities form an important avenue of integration with the outside world, Pozos Ponce predicts that the emphasis on economic globalization will affect the larger economies of Latin America, particularly in stimulating the emergence of previously non-dominant urban centers.

This chapter has major implications for urban social development and the necessary state action to service basic human needs. It is possible that the present rural-urban migration stream flowing mainly towards one major city would disperse to these emerging urban centers. If persons, groups, and organizations proliferate away from the dominant city, this could have important consequences for the democratization process in Latin America. In that sense, the neoliberal strategy could potentially address some of the negative consequences of over-urbanization concentrated in a nationally primate city. But this is highly unlikely without state policies geared towards guaranteeing the basic needs of these emerging urban populations.

Mexico is a typical case of what is happening in the larger Latin American economies under the new climate of economic globalization. The formation of new and expansion of old export centers across Latin America has facilitated changes in national urban systems. The smaller urban systems of Central America and the Caribbean are being affected by this development as well. However, the nature of this impact has varied from one region to another.[47] Regardless of whether urban primacy has accelerated or declined, the problem of social development looms large. In the face of uncontrolled urban growth, effective state policies to promote employment, housing, and infrastructural facilities in the poorer urban areas become even more pressing.

The State Policy Dimension

Despite the recent neoliberal trend in Latin America, the importance of state policies to deal with the negative consequences of uncontrolled urban growth cannot be overstated. The resultant poverty from increasing globalization of the economy as well as the migration from rural to urban areas have been strongly correlated with much growth in the informal sector. Although it is rather simplistic to argue that the lack of employment in the formal urban economy has contributed to the growth of the informal (or popular) economy as a survival strategy, the evidence from much of Latin America shows that state policies have played a critical role in shaping the actual extent of the links between the formal and informal sectors.

Social scientists working on Third World development confront a major challenge in explaining the growth of the informal sector. Why and in what forms does it develop and sustain itself? Does it remain totally isolated from the formal sector or does it develop ties with it over time? A better understanding of the informal sector is imperative in order to promote social development in urban Latin America. Chapters 7 and 8 dissect the complexities of the ties between the formal and informal sectors. First, Alejandro Portes and Richard Schauffler in Chapter 7 put forward a new, structuralist approach to the study of the informal sector. They argue that, in many countries of Latin America, the informal sector sustains itself and grows by virtue of its multifaceted ties with the formal sector. The informal sector has already become very heterogeneous in its composition. Activities in the sector range from microenterprises that are dynamic and modern to the ones that are survival-oriented. Economic activities in the informal sector in many cases subsidize the lifestyles of the middle class and workers employed in the formal sector.[48] In other words, the informal sector is very closely tied to the dynamics of the modern capitalist system.

Although the state does not regulate the income generating activities in the informal sector, it can still alleviate less desirable working conditions through effective public policy. As Portes and Schauffler recommend, the state in Latin America must guarantee flexible labor codes and other active programs to support small entrepreneurial development. Decentralized state policies, sensitive to the peculiarities of the various communities, are advocated as most desirable by these authors. The importance of state policies with regard to the issues affecting the informal sector is taken up further by Mary Froehle in Chapter 8.

The informal sector, because of its current size and the future growth potential, is important for promoting social stability in Latin America. The size and the rate of growth of the informal sector has been impressive in many countries.[49] As the sector grows, employs more people, and wields greater political power, perhaps a mutual alliance between the state and informal sector enterprises is possible. Issues of social control in the informal sector also become a concern for the state leaders as they embrace the electoral system. In order for economic growth to facilitate social development, it is important to have effective public policy toward this sector. In that respect, the popular economy (as the informal sector is commonly known) has a major role to play in the democratization process.

Some Latin American states have already begun to make changes in existing policies toward this sector. For example, the Venezuelan state has embarked upon a policy of encouraging entrepreneurial activities in the informal sector through an alliance with *Fedeindustria* --- an institution created to support small entrepreneurial initiatives.[50] Furthermore, also in Venezuela a separate department recently created within the Ministry of Social Development concerns itself primarily with the informal sector problems.

The increasing inclination of states to pursue favorable policies toward the informal sector should be considered a good sign. But Froehle is particularly concerned with the role played by women in various enterprises that dominate the informal sector in Latin America. Informal sector activities are not conducive to the growth of popular organizations that would represent the interests of the affected parties. Women, in many instances, have been the particular victims of low wages, little protection from unscrupulous labor practices, and inadequate political representation. Unless state policies are geared towards ensuring some form of representation for the workers engaged in the various informal sector activities, the discontent might sow the seeds of less democratic political processes in the future.

Given the fact that politicians are beginning to show more interest in the informal sector and are willing to forge links with non-governmental agencies engaged in various social development programs in urban Latin America, effective state policies must recognize the structural locations of women and other disadvantaged sections of society. These locations constrain the extent of their participation in the informal sector. The trend toward feminization of the labor force in the informal sector must be complemented with safeguards in the form of state policy that guarantees some basic recourse for the socially most vulnerable segments of society.

The processes of economic globalization and the urban informal sector-growth in Latin America have made one point abundantly clear: judicious and effective use of the state to promote economic growth and social development. There is no doubt that the wasteful, rent-seeking activities of corrupt state bureaucrats must be curtailed to promote high economic growth. At the same time, basic legal safeguards guaranteed by the state is absolutely essential to protect the rights of the un- and under-represented in the informal sector. As the informal sector grows this will become increasingly obvious. As I address the changing nature of the state in Latin America in Chapter 9, I argue that initiating smart changes in state activities and policies is a pragmatic step forward. A blind ideological attack on the irrelevance of the state *per se* does not give us that. But that is where much of the neoliberal agenda concentrates.

Finally, in Chapter 10 I wrestle with the question of political legitimacy of the neoliberal agenda. I argue that the tenuous coexistence of economic globalization and political liberalization programs may soon be imperiled unless certain social safeguards are erected and sustained. Without these safeguards, an unilateral pursuit of high economic growth rates is unlikely to guarantee even a workable political democracy.

Notes

1. I thank Peter Knapp and Brian Jones for helpful comments on earlier drafts of this chapter.
2. Robert Bottome, *In the Shadow of Debt* (1992); Alma Guillermoprieto, *The Heart that Bleeds: Latin America Now* (1994); OECD, *Development and Democracy* (1992); Victor Urquidi, "Constraints to Growth in the Developing World: Current Experience in Latin America," *International Social Science Journal* 41 (1989): 203-10; Alejandro Foxley, "Latin American Development after the Debt Crisis *Journal of Development Economics* 27 (1987): 201-25;

Demetrius Joseph, et al., "A Brave New World: Debt, Default and Democracy in Latin America" *Inter-American Studies and World Affairs* 28 (1986): 17-38.

3. Statistical Abstract of Latin America (SALA), Vol 29, Part 1, Table 624, p.114.

4. Bela Balassa, *Toward Renewed Growth in Latin America (1992)*; Lowell Gustafson (ed.), *Economic Development under Democratic Regimes: Neoliberalism in Latin America* (1994).

5. Taken from Sebastian Edwards, *Crisis and Reform in Latin America: From Despair to Hope* (The World Bank, Washington D.C.: Oxford University Press, 1995), p. 7. The 22 Latin American countries are: Bolivia, Chile, Mexico, Costa Rica, Jamaica, Trinidad & Tobago, Uruguay, Argentina, Brazil, Colombia, El Salvador, Guatemala, Guyana, Honduras, Nicaragua, Panama, Paraguay, Peru, Venezuela, Dominican Republic, Ecuador, and Haiti.

6. See SALA, Vol 29, Part 2, Table 2471, p. 859.

7. The neoliberal agenda is much broader than economic globalization. Although it pays a lip service in many countries to genuinely involve all major segments of society in the political process, it does identify itself with the opening-up of the political system, especially to the electoral processes. In the economy it emphasizes an outward orientation, tax reform, overhaul in the interest and exchange rates, foreign capital involvement (in particular direct foreign investment), privatization, deregulation, less overall involvement of the state in the growth process, and withdrawal of selected social programs. See Lowell Gustafson, *Economic Development under Democratic Regimes* (Praeger, 1994), pp. 4-5.

8. SALA, Vol 29, Part 1, p. 404.

9. See SALA, Vol 29, Part 2, Table 3463, p. 1335.

10. SALA, Vol 29, Part 2, p. 859.

11. In Brazil data on household income show that the ratio between the richest 20% and the poorest 20% of households is 33 to 1 whereas in Mexico it is recorded at 20 to 1. See Gary Gereffi and Stephanie Fonda, "Regional Paths of Development," *Annual Review of Sociology* 18 (1992): 419-48. For more statistical information on income inequality, see Chapter 9 in this volume.

12. Read James Petras and Morris Morley, *Latin America in the Time of Cholera* (1992).

13. See in this regard, Amartya Sen, "Development: Which Way Now?," pp. 5-26 and Deepak Lal, "The Misconceptions of Development Economics," pp. 27-54 in Charles Wilber and Kenneth Jameson (eds.), *The Political Economy of Development and Underdevelopment* (1992). Also see Dependency literature, especially A.G. Frank, *Capitalism and Underdevelopment in Latin America* (1971) and Johan Galtung, *The True Worlds: A Transnational Perspective* (1980).

14. See Samuel Huntington, *The Third Wave: Democratization in the Late Twentieth Century* (1991).

15. Frances Rothstein and Michael Blim, *Anthropology and the Global Factory* (1992).

16. See Helen Shapiro and Lance Taylor, "The State and Industrial Strategy," (1992).

17. Robert Kaufman, *The Politics of Debt in Argentina, Brazil, and Mexico* (1988); Robert Bottome (1992).

18. See Jagdish Bhagwati, "Directly Unproductive Profit Seeking (DUP) Activities." *Journal of Political Economy* 90 (1982): 988-1002; James Buchanan, "Rent Seeking and Profit Seeking," (1980); Lance Taylor and Larry Westphal (1984); also see Deepak Lal, *The Poverty of "Development Economics"* (1983).

19. See John Williamson (eds.), *Latin American Adjustment: How Much has Happened* (1990).

20. P.T. Bauer, *Reality and Rhetoric: Studies in the Economics of Development.* London: Weidenfield and Nicolson, 1984; T.N. Srinivasan, "Neoclassical Political Economy: The State and Economic Development" Economic Growth Center, Yale University, 1985.

21. Samuel Bowles and John Eatwell, "Between Two Worlds: Interest Groups, Class Structure and Capitalist Growth," in Dennis C. Mueller (eds.), *The Political Economy of Growth* (1983); Brian Barry, "Some Questions about Explanations," *International Studies Quarterly* 27 (1983): 17-27; David Cameron, "Creating Theory in Comparative Political Economy" Paper presented at the 1983 APSA Meeting, Chicago.

22. William Cline, "Can East Asian Models of Development be Generalized?" *World Development* 10 (1982): 81-90; Albert Fishlow, "Trade, Development, and the State," (1986).

23. The East Asian success with export-oriented growth strategies has been facilitated by clever, effective state policies geared towards manipulating market forces in favor of growth in the external sector. See Gary Gereffi and Stephanie Fonda, "Regional Paths of Development" *Annual Review of Sociology* 18 (1992): 419-48; also see Hollis Chenery, Sherman Robinson, and Moshe Syrquin, *Industrialization and Growth* (1986).

24. Lance Taylor, "Gap Disequilibria: Inflation, Investment, Saving, and Foreign Exchange," Cambridge: MIT Department of Economics, 1989.

25. The evolution of the export and import price indexes for the region since 1928 has been biased against the exporting nations of the region. According to the SALA estimate, the export/import price ratio in 1987 was 311 to 488 in favor of imports. See SALA, Vol 29, Part 2, p. 914.

26. F.H. Cardoso and E. Faletto, *Dependencia y desarrollo en America Latina* (1978)

27. According to SALA reports (Vol 29, part 2, p. 1358) for the region as a whole, total external debt as percentage of GDP reached over 41 in 1987,

compared to 17 in 1970. Nicaragua was the most indebted nation at 400 percent and Guatemala was the least indebted at 29 percent.

28. See any recent issue of the Statistical Abstract of Latin America, in particular the section on "Foreign Trade."

29. Fernando Calderon, Alejandro Piscitelli, and Jose Luis Reyna, "Social Movements: Actors, Theories, Expectations" pp. 19-36 in Arturo Escobar and Sonia Alvarez (eds.), *The Making of Social Movements in Latin America* (1992).

30. Escobar and Alvarez, pp. 1-15.

31. Cathy Schneider, *Shantytown Protests in Pinochet's Chile* (Philadelphia: Temple University Press, 1995).

32. Arturo Escobar and Sonia Alvarez (eds.), *The Making of Social Movements in Latin America: Identity, Strategy and Democracy* (1992).

33. Ibid.

34. Albert Bergesen, "Crisis in the World System" pp. 9-17 in A. Bergesen (ed.), *Crisis in the World System* (1983).

35. Christopher Chase-Dunn, *Global Formation* (1992).

36. Abraham Lowenthal, "Charting a New Course," *Hemisfile* 5 (1994): 2-3

37. Ibid, 11.

38. See James Petras (Chapter 2) in this volume; also see Lowenthal (1994).

39. *The New York Times*, January 16 (1996).

40. See Satya Pattnayak (ed.), *Organized Religion in the Political Transformation of Latin America* (1995).

41. Jeffery Paige, "Revolution and the Agrarian Bourgeoisie in Nicaragua" in Terry Boswell (ed.), *Revolution in the World System* (1989).

42. Carlos Díaz-Alejandro, "Some Unintended Consequences of Laissez Faire," in A. Foxley et al., *Development, Democracy, and the Art of Trespassing* (1989).

43. Michael Todaro, *Economic Development in the Third World* (1981).

44. Guillermo O'Donnell, *Modernization and Bureaucratic-Authoritarianism* (1979).

45. Hernando De Soto, *The Other Path* (1989); Caroline Moser, "Informal Sector or Petty Commodity Production: Dualism or Dependence in Urban Development?" *World Development* 6 (1978): 1041-1064; Alejandro Portes and John Walton, *Urban Latin America: the Political Condition from Above and Below* (1976); Juan Pablo Pérez-Sáinz, *Informalidad urbana en America Latina: problematicas e interrogantes* (1992).

46. See Alejandro Portes, "Latin American Urbanization During the Years of the Crisis." *Latin American Research Review* 23 (1989): 7-44.

47. See Alejandro Portes, Jose Itzigsohn, and Carlos Dore-Cabral, "Caribbean Cities: Social Change and Adaptation During the Years of the Crisis" *Latin American Research Review* 29 (1993): 33-34.

48. Portes, Itzigsohn, Dore-Cabral (1993).

49. See Portes and Schauffler (Chapter 7, Table 7-3) in this volume.

50. See Guido Gimenez and Vladimir Monslave, "Microempresas y Comercialización" Caracas: Ministerio de la Familia, ILDIS and PNUD (1990).

2

The Transformation of Latin America: Free Markets, Democracy and Other Myths

James Petras

Over the past 20 years Latin America has been undergoing a major transformation of its socioeconomic, political, and ideological system. Among academics, government officials and bankers supporting the changes, Latin America has been experiencing the realization of political and economic freedom: liberal democracy in politics and free markets in the economy. Both, it is argued, are inseparably linked to a democratic revolution. Today, it is argued, Latin Americans are free to choose a new way to prosperity and freedom through the ballot box and the market.

These notions propagated among influential elites in North and South America have, however, failed to convince the vast majority of Latin Americans, despite the intense and extensive propaganda efforts carried out by the mass media. The question of why the twin doctrines of free markets and democracy have failed to gain the allegiance of the mass of Latin Americans requires us to analyze the nature of the transformations, beginning with an analysis of the origins and nature of the changes in the economic system, the strategies adopted by the foreign and democratic elites and the role of the United States. We will then examine the impact of "deregulated capitalism" on the economy as a whole over time as well as its impact on the class structure. Subsequently, we will critically analyze the key ideological concepts and the structures of political power associated with the ascendancy of deregulated capitalism to see whether they correspond to democratic or authoritarian politics. We will conclude by examining the political parabola of neoliberalism and the relationship between its rise and decline and the new sociopolitical forces shaping the post-free market political agenda.

Economic Change

The Latin American economies have experienced a series of basic changes over the past 20 years: a shift from national industrialization based on a mix of public and private capital and regulation at the national level to an export strategy linked to foreign and domestic private capital and regulated at the international level.

The origins and impetus for this strategy was not the result of any electoral mandate, nor was it the result of the free workings of the market. Rather, the new export strategy was the product of military dictatorship backed by the U.S. government, international lending agencies, private banks and a minority economic and technocratic elite within Latin America. Freeing markets was based on filling the jails. Deregulated economies grew out of the barrel of a gun: the authoritarian state increased its intervention in society, while it decreased certain types of activities in the economy. The proclaimed new doctrine promised to: (1) free the market, limiting state intervention; (2) deregulate the economy; (3) privatize and end public monopolies as harmful to competition; (4) promote supply side economies, provide incentives to investors, so as the rich get richer there will be a trickle down effect; (5) manage macroeconomic variables to avoid trade and budget deficits; and (6) promote export-oriented trade in specialized exports over industrial production for the domestic market.

Contrary to the stated principles of the free market advocates, the policies of the neoliberal regimes more often than not violated the doctrine.

State intervention did not lessen: what actually changed was the type and direction of state intervention. Instead of the state intervening to nationalize, it privatized. When private banks accumulated bad debts, the state intervened to "socialize" the debts, converting private to public debt. The state intervened to transfer economic resources from social services for wage and salaried groups to subsidies for exporters. The state intervened in capital-labor relations to restrain labor, to break unions, to arrest or assassinate strikers and labor organizers. The state intervened to lower tariffs, increase prices, lower salaries: it established new regulations and new institutions to enforce the new order. Free market was unfree for labor and made free for capital by state decrees. Nor was state action confined to an initial impulse: the state continued to intervene, defining the terms for private investments, foreign takeovers of local enterprises, etc.

Secondly, deregulation did not take place. A new "regulatory" regime came into being whose components and policies differed from the earlier versions. Regulations of the economy, in the sense of defining the relations between public and private property, budgetary expenditures and revenues, incentives and priorities for investments and loans, has shifted from the national to the international level. The new international regulatory regime is made up of international bankers, the IMF, the World Bank, top officials of the U.S. government and the export-oriented elites and technocrats in Latin America. The new regulatory regime imposes limits on local consumption of wage groups to promote the profits of export elites. The rhetoric of deregulation obscures the real shift in the nature of regulation.

Privatization has taken place, but it has not eliminated monopolies, rather it has shifted in kind. Privatization has changed public to private monopolies. The buyers of public enterprises have been the very wealthy, those who own and add to vast empires. Large-scale overseas multinationals have converted Latin American debt into equity in public firms throughout Latin America. The difference today is that the private monopolies are even less accountable than the formerly public owned firms.

Monopolies, regulation and state intervention continue under the aegis of the new neoliberal regimes as they did previously. The crucial difference is in the shift in power, control and benefits. Export and foreign conglomerates replace national industrialists, public sector employees and trade unions as beneficiaries and controllers: the international market replaces the national. Concentrated incomes replace more egalitarian ones. Private services replace public. Private affluence accompanies the impoverishment of public welfare. The "free market" is neither "free" for the many nor based exclusively on the market.

U.S. Hegemony and Free Market

With the advent of the military regimes, in some cases through direct involvement, U.S. policy makers gained strategic leverage and over time deep penetration.

The end of the Cold War has, if anything, *strengthened* the drive in Washington to *consolidate* its informal empire in Latin America. Moreover, the relative decline in the U.S. global position, particularly its displacement by Germany in Europe and Japan in Asia, has *intensified* Washington's efforts to hold onto its favored dominion of exploitation, profits and interest payments: Latin America.

Through trial and effort, improvisation and deliberate intervention, the U.S. has come to fashion a complex and coherent regional strategy that operates on three mutually reinforcing and interrelated levels: first, through the imposition of *economic policy* ("freeing markets") designed to dismantle a half century of state regulations, diminish the role of domestic producers and markets, privatize public enterprises, and lower the costs of labor. These policies facilitate the takeover by U.S. corporations of local productive and extractive enterprises, sustain the payment of foreign debts, and decrease U.S. corporate wage and tax payments. The doctrine of "free markets" is a euphemism for private foreign pillage through monopoly profits. The crucial theoretical point is that the U.S. strategy does not expand or create new sites of production, but takes over and drains the investable surplus to the imperial mainland. Unlike earlier periods when large-scale industrial expansion combined investments in new facilities, expansion of domestic markets and the appropriation of surplus, in the present context the political economy of financial pillage and debt-swap takeovers reigns supreme. Whereas the Alliance for Progress combined state, public and private investment for exploitation through the development of productive forces, the Bush administration's "Enterprise of the Americas Initiative" facilitates foreign takeovers of existing markets and firms. This fundamental shift in imperial relations is intimately linked to changes in the U.S. economy, the shift from industrial to finance capital, as well as to a dramatic transformation in the role and structural components of the U.S. imperial state: in the 1990s the military-ideological dimensions have clearly eclipsed the economic-political.

Second, the U.S. has designed a *military strategy* that is integrally related to the "free market" doctrine. Its overall goal is to install and sustain in power regimes promoting free market policies and to undermine national movements and governments advocating alternative development models. The military strategy operates on multiple levels, taking account of different political contexts, but all converge toward the same objective: (a) *narco-intervention*, basically covert counterinsurgency activities in order to establish a continuing military presence in South America (Bolivia, Peru, Colombia, etc.) so as to gain direct access to command structures and to promote a more repressive solution to the problems of guerrilla movements, peasant organizations, and other organized forces challenging the client regimes; (b) *low intensity warfare* in Central America, a euphemism for an expanded and intensified military offensive by the armed forces and their paramilitary death squad allied against the region's social and political movements -- funded by the White House with senior Pentagon officials directly controlling the military-political decisions regarding the prosecution of these wars; (c) *direct, large-scale military intervention*, involving U.S. armed forces (Grenada, Panama) or contra surrogates (Nicaragua) for the purpose of destroying the target regime, its state institutions and socioeconomic structures, and installing a compliant, puppet government; and (d) *routinized bureaucratic and ideological convergence* (the rest of Latin America) to prevent popular upheavals. Each of these military strategies is designed to strengthen regimes promoting free market policies (e.g., Peru, Bolivia), destroy indigenous movements challenging this model (e.g., El Salvador), or undermine regimes directly or indirectly in conflict with it (e.g., Nicaragua). The economic incapacity of the U.S. to compensate for the disastrous socioeconomic consequences accompanying the continent-wide "free market" pillage requires the elaboration of such a comprehensive military strategy.

Third, Washington has elaborated a *political strategy* which involves the promotion of electoral regimes in the interstices of its economic policy and military framework. The electoral regimes serve to provide pseudo-legitimacy to the authoritarian and exploitative system, while pursuing programs compatible with the imperial state's hegemonic interests. The pivotal cohabitation of civil regime and military power serves to facilitate domestic public support for imperial policies while retaining the armed forces as political insurance if the electoral regimes lose control or the disintegration of "free market" economies provoke popular uprisings. The existence of these tightly restricted civilian governments, and the parliaments, parties and political processes that accompany them, also serve (or attempt) to demobilize opposition social movements ("they endanger democracy"), coopt "progressive intellectuals" ("we have to ensure democratic 'governability'"), and restrict political agendas ("there are no alternatives to neoliberalism") in a way that U.S. policy makers could not accomplish directly. The new collaborator electoral regimes are a key ingredient in Washington's larger strategy, even as they are subject to continuing stresses and tensions in their relations with the military and the "free market." Therefore, the imperial state assumes the role of manager of such conflicts in order to ensure the continued success of its hemispheric policy.

Since the late 1970s and early 1980s the U.S. has employed its formidable military and ideological power to oust *hostile* Latin American governments and establish the groundwork for their replacement by civilian clients. Subsequently, it has endeavored to influence and shape the economic direction of these elected regimes. Products of U.S.-brokered "transitions," these regimes are highly receptive to the free market-trade liberalization doctrine promoted by Washington. But despite success in the short-run, a fundamental contradiction confronts White House and State Department officials: the imperial state has demonstrated increasing incapacity to provide sufficient infusions of capital, expertise, and technology to transform these political clients into viable capitalist associates. The decline in the U.S. global economic power (exacerbated by the dominance of parasitical-speculator over productive capitalist class forces through the 1980s) undermines efforts to construct and consolidate a cluster of dynamic electoral allies. The rhetoric of "growth through free trade and free markets" has provided an effective cover for a policy of pillage, not financial support and economic reciprocity. The appropriation of Latin America's dwindling economic resources (debt repayments, market takeovers, etc.) has substituted for long-term, large-scale productive investments. Paralleling this latter-day *sacking* of regional economies by U.S. public and private institutions, the Reagan-Bush administrations have systematically increased Washington's ties with the hemisphere's armed forces, an insurance policy in case the electoral experiments falter and collapse.

Washington Promotes the "Free Market" Doctrine

Since the early 1980s, Latin American governments have followed the economic directives of the United States, international banking institutions (multilateral and private) and local transnational capitalist interests by deregulating economies, privatizing state sectors, abolishing tariffs and permitting the *free flow* of capital profits. In return, the free market ideologues in Washington and elsewhere promised that the region would attract sufficient large-scale capital investments to sustain long-term development and growth, bring hyperinflation under control, and increase national income levels. To attract foreign investment, increase exports, and eliminate chronic trade deficits, Reagan-Bush policy makers and international bankers stressed the importance of Latin American economies making "adjustments" to lower government spending, wage levels, and the like.

The spread of free market export strategy programs across the continent has produced the exact opposite effect to that presumed by its advocates. Instead of large-scale inflows of foreign capital, the free market experiments have been accompanied by a net decline in new overseas investment, rising principal and debt interest payments abroad, and accelerated capital flight -- thus undermining any rational basis for creating stable economies and promoting long-term development and growth. The application and deepening of free market policies devastated Latin America's investment capacity which fell by 25 percent between 1980 and 1989. During the same period, aggregate figures on per capita Gross National Product (GNP) reveal a cumulative decline (of -9.6 percent), a trend which shows no signs of abating (-2.6 percent in 1990). Over the decade, the regions's terms of trade deteriorated by 21 percent, its foreign debt skyrocketed to $434 billion (end 1991), and it was transformed into a massive net exporter of capital (approximately $225 billion between 1982 and 1990). Finally, recent capital trends do not bode well for Latin America's future: new foreign commercial bank lending plunged from $5.5 billion in 1988 to $2.3 billion in 1989; and U.S. economic support funds declined from $545 million in 1988 to $350 million in 1990 (a fall of 36 percent). Not without justification was the 1980s termed a "lost [economic] decade" for the hemisphere.

The massive transfer of profits, interest and principal payments, and capital from Latin America to the United States and other advanced industrialized countries during the 1980s was the fundamental purpose (and overriding achievement) of the free market strategy. Washington's proposed solutions to the region's decapitalization problem were the "Baker Plan" (1985) and the "Brady Plan" (1989). The former involved the commercial and international banks providing $29 billion in new loans ($20 billion and $9 billion, respectively) to 17 (mostly Latin American) debtor countries between 1986 and 1988. But the failure of the scheme was virtually preordained given that the average annual negative transfers of financial resources from the proposed 17 recipients was $40 billion. Subsequently, the scheme was further undermined by the decision of the commercial banks to commit only slightly in excess of 50 percent of the amount requested by U.S. officials. The "Brady Plan" took a different track, announcing that it would seek to ease the transfer burden by promoting debt write-offs and other reduction programs such as debt swaps for local assets. This approach has been no more successful than its predecessor. Write-offs have been plagued by insufficient financial commitments from the commercial and international banks; debt reduction typically has done little more than shift the source of overseas transfers from interest payments to profits from newly acquired local productive enterprises. Ultimately, the failures of national development throughout the hemisphere were merely byproducts of the private successes of international and Latin American transnational capital, the real constituency of Washington policy makers.

The Reagan-Bush policies eschewed reciprocity (long-term, large-scale investments) in favor of short-term profit-taking (pillage). Calls for new economic adjustments in response to the failure of old economic adjustments were all directed toward the same interrelated goals: the seizure of regional resources, and the breaking down of barriers to U.S. commerce and investment expansion. During his

December 1990 tour of Latin America to sell Washington's economic prescription, President Bush spoke glowingly of the newly elected civilian leaders who were "stripping away state controls." For the great majority of the populations of these countries, however, the results have been disastrous: falling real wage levels; massive increases in unemployment; growing concentrations of wealth and income; and unprecedented declines in overall living standards.

Accompanying the deepening U.S. economic and military penetration of Latin America is the new Bush doctrine proclaiming the supremacy of U.S. law and sovereignty over Latin American law. First applied during the Noriega trial and subsequently with regard to the U.S. kidnapping and trial of a Mexican citizen, the U.S. is attempting to establish its juridical right to intervene throughout Latin America and in the world whenever its interests dictate ignoring the sovereignty of the targeted countries. This version on neo-Monroism captures U.S. imperial pretension. The very tepid opposition among the Latin American governing elites reflects their submission to the U.S. imperial order.

The U.S. strategy of promoting free markets, deepening and extending its military reach through drug, counterinsurgency, and bureaucratic stratagems, and consolidating client electoral regimes reached its high point of success at the end of the 1980s: Mexico was signed on for the free market, opening the door for unprecedented levels of pillage and exploitation; Panama was occupied and the contras were in power in Nicaragua; the continent was blanketed with electoral regimes pursuing free market policies, exonerating human rights violators, and increasing their role in policing society. Nonetheless, cracks and divisions were appearing at the top, and challenges were appearing from below. Most dramatically, the free market economic programs were killing the goose (industries) that laid the golden egg (interest and profits transferred abroad and imports purchased from U.S. exporters).

As the levels of pillage ravaged Latin America, as debt payments and capital transfers drove living standards lower, and as public services went bankrupt, nineteenth century diseases (cholera, malaria, yellow fever epidemics) returned: the adoption of the past century's economic doctrines reproduced that century's disastrous health conditions. Declining living standards and a decaying infrastructure, product of the "economic adjustments" promulgated by the free marketeers, drove out potential investors and attacked only short-term speculator capital. U.S.

politico-military domination in Central America was accompanied by its economic incapacity to revive these economies thus discrediting its ideological claims and delegitimizing its political clients even among the traditionally pro-U.S. "middle classes."

The strategy of projecting military-ideological power and pillaging the economy is delegitimating the loyal client electoral regimes: political abstentionism is growing, violent direct action (collective and individual) to redistribute wealth is increasing. In the 1990s, this process of disintegration will either revive the Marxist view of democratic collectivism or create a Hobbesian world of war of all against all.

Nowhere have the free market policies promoted economic recovery or growth; nowhere have the social polarization lessened; nowhere has unemployment diminished. The U.S. strategy has destroyed the status quo in a radical reactionary way. It has uprooted Indian communities with counter-revolutionary wars, undermined public-private relations through doctrinaire privatizations, increased the role of the state in civil society by increasing its military capability, and privatized long-standing social services at the expense of employees and consumers. Washington is hollowing out Latin American economy and society, returning the majority to a more backward, primitive form of individual existence. Paradoxically, the depth of the crisis has provoked its strongest defense: the systematic disaggregation and atomization of long-standing collectivities weakens the opposition and reduces the victims to strategies of absolute survival.

The fundamental weakness of Washington's strategy is the growing gap between its military-ideological power and its political-economic effects: the exhaustion of neoliberal ideology; the incapacity of the U.S. to finance and sustain its electoral or military clients. The most striking example is Panama where majority support for the December 1989 invasion has since turned against the U.S. and its imposed political client whose policies, or lack of them, have provoked rising large-scale opposition.

The U.S. is attempting to *intensify* its pillage of Latin America to counter-balance its trade deficits with dynamic imperial competitors, Japan and Germany, as well as its declining access to markets in their regional blocs. The heightened imperial presence in Latin America in the post-Cold war period belies the arguments that imperialism is a function of "superpower conflict:" imperial expansion is a product of the demands of U.S. domestic economic, political and military institutions.

In the 1990s, U.S.-Latin American relations revolve around conflicts engendered by the three levels of U.S. strategy: cleavages between proponents of free market pillage (the local neo-compradors and self-styled advocates of interdependency) and the neo-nationalists who seek to develop a national industrial policy grounded in the producer classes as a precondition for insertion in the international market; cleavages between the proponents of state militarization strategies and social movements and revolutionary formations in civil society; cleavages between coopted electoral political classes and their intellectuals and the institution of popular assemblies and their organic intellectuals.

The current decade will see sustained efforts by washington to follow the path of military influence, client regime and economic extraction. To counter this strategy requires a radical, rethinking of the prevailing notions about democracy and mixed economies: without dismantling the state, the electoral regimes and processes remain hostages to imperial military strategies; without uprooting the neo-comprador free market classes and technocrats, revitalization of the national market and producer classes is impossible; without replacing the elected class with direct representation of the popular movements, international political clientelism will continue.

The free market, neoliberal policies not only has its origins in undemocratic regimes but is largely supported and sustained by imperial policy makers. Externally based, authoritarian by origin, free markets have no linkages to national and democratic developments.

Impact of Free Markets on Social Structure

In a recent article, *Forbes* magazine took as a symbol of the successful application of "free market" economies in Latin America the growing number of billionaires. "On this list last year, eight Latin billionaires were visible. Now there are 21. Others crowd behind. When entrepreneurs flourish, so does an economy.... For too long it suffered under socialism and its first cousin, feudalism.... Having survived harsh economic and political conditions, these Latin billionaires are ready to become much larger players in the global economy. What began in the 1970s in Chile as radical heresy is now gospel in an entire continent."

While *Forbes* argues that "when entrepreneurs flourish so does an economy," there is a substantial body of evidence to the contrary, leaving aside the questionable characterization of the billionaires as "entrepreneurs."

In the last half of the 1980s, Latin America's poor increased by over 23 million. In 1986 there were 247.5 million poor, in 1990 that figure rose to 270.2 million-- 61.8 percent of the population. The most significant increase among the poor was those workers whose current income had declined below the poverty line. The "new poor" increased from 12 percent to 14 percent of the population during the latter third of the 1980s, precisely when the free market policies were in full swing and right after the IMF-World Bank "adjustment" policies were fully applied. Parallel to the growth in the number of impoverished workers and chronically poor were the three consecutive negative years of economic growth (1988-90).

The free market and adjustment policies had as a principal effect the creation of the conditions for the growth of billionaires based on increasing immiseration for 60 percent of the population and the continuing stagnation and regression of the economy.

The specific concentration in urban speculative activity and the transfer of state resources to the very rich generated a highly polarized economy in which the greater part of the growth of poverty was located in the urban areas. Poverty increased from 25 percent in 1980 to 30 percent of the urban population in 1986. With the exception of two countries benefitting from the drug trade (Colombia and Panama), the rest of the Latin American countries, following what *Forbes* describes as the free market gospel, experienced an increase in the level of poverty. In the case of Mexico, poverty declined during the expanding period of state capitalism and national industrialization from 77.5 percent in 1963 to 48.5 percent in 1981. Following the debt crisis induced with the advent of the speculative oil economy of the late 1970s and exacerbated by adjustment and free market policies that begun in the 1980s, poverty increased to 59 percent of the population.

In Argentina a similar process took hold. Under both military and subsequent civilian rule, the debt crisis adjustments and free market policies reduced national income by 11 percent between 1980-87. And the proportion of poor rose accordingly in the greater Buenos Aires region from 21 percent in 1980 to 35 percent in 1987. In large part, the new poor were the products of declining incomes provoked by economic policy: almost two-thirds of the poor in 1987 were casualties of the adjustment and free market policies reducing wages that had so successfully created the condition for the growth of billionaires.

Behind the technocratic rhetoric that describes policy decisions in terms of managing "macro-economics" is the new configuration of class power which shapes and benefits from the "management of macro-economic" variables.

The neoliberal policy results from the ascendancy of a new class of Latin American transnational capitalists who have large-scale investments and bank accounts in the U.S. and Europe and who own export oriented industries and banks linked to the international circuits. These groups control and define the outward looking strategy which the intellectuals and policy makers define as the "only alternative." This class emerged out of the protected, publicly funded mixed economy of the 1950s and 1960s. It benefitted enormously from external financing, military subsidies, depressed wage rates of the late 1970s and early 1980s, and became extremely wealthy and powerful with the debt write-offs, privatization and debts swaps of the 1980s and 1990s.

Local or national capital was either squeezed out by cheap imports or paid off by cheap labor (lowering wages and social legislation) or deregulation which allowed them to go "informal," employing labor without any social benefits. Others converted to importing overseas goods or became sub-contractors for the new foreign or domestic conglomerates.

The impact of free markets on salaried and wage labor was to polarize the labor force into a three tier system. Skilled, salaried technicians, professionals, researchers, managers, lawyers tied to the enterprises, multinational banks and overseas foundations became affluent. These segments of the labor force able to plug in to the upper end of the external financial and trade circuits have become the strongest supporters of the neoliberal regimes, particularly its civilian electoral variant.

Below is a range of stable employed public and private employees and workers, most of whom are downwardly mobile with declining living standards and deteriorating social services. Exploited at the workplace, they include the bulk of the poorly paid school teachers, public health workers, as well as those employed in large-scale industrial firms. This is a shrinking category as more and more of its members are transformed into temporary workers in rotating or seasonal employment. At the bottom is the most numerous and fastest growing sector of the labor force. It includes workers engaged in the informal economy, without steady employment or any social benefits, working at whatever work is available below the minimum wage or "self-employed:" a growing number of rotating workers in textiles and other consumer goods industries; home employed female workers doing "take home" work; a mass of seasonal farm, forestry and fishing workers; seasonal and temporary construction and low paid service workers, particularly in domestic services. Destruction of local industry, neoliberal policies cutting back on industrial and capital investments and social budgets and services, along with the concentration on raw materials specialization has contributed to the polarized social structure.

And at the bottom of the social structure is a growing army of lumpenproletariat who are engaged in illegal activities from drugs to contraband, to murder and assaults. Crime is spiralling out of control in many of the major Latin American cities with the advent of free market policies.

Within this polarized class structure, women and young people have been hit the hardest by the decline in employment and living standards. Family violence and family abandonment has increased. Unemployment rates for young people under 25 is three or four times the high national rates. Wage levels of women and young people are usually below the minimum wages, as they are most likely to be employed in the informal economy.

The free market has vastly increased inequalities between classes and undermined the basis for economic expansion based on mass domestic demand. The deepening class divisions have also undermined the basis for any democratically agreed social consensus to sustain democratic political institutions. Today in Venezuela a military figure involved in a coup attempt is more popular than the President. In most Latin American countries the parties and political leaders have lost credibility among the majority of the impoverished electorate. Free market policies, by subordinating the state to a narrow set of class interests, has eroded the basis for democratization.

Electoral Politics, Free Markets and Extra-Parliamentary Action: Unresolved Tensions

The assertions by politicians and media pundits that Latin America is experiencing a pairing of "free markets and democracy" is open to question on several counts. We will proceed by critically examining the ascendancy of electoral politics, then proceed to discuss the challenges to electoral politics, the implication of the right turn among former radical and reformist parties and the new political forces that define alternatives to the status quo.

To understand the meaning of the emergence of electoral politics and its relationship to free market economic policy, it is important to trace out the context and nature of political power. In Latin America free market policies were imposed by force through military regimes by "illegitimate" seizure of power. The economic policies were imposed by force and the basic institutions of the state (military, judiciary, civil bureaucracy) established by the military regimes remained intact during the transition to electoral politics. The subsequent emergence of electoral regimes was based on a particular contextual contingency: the deterioration of the military regime, the emergence of civilians ready to trade elections for the continuation of free market policies and state institutions and U.S. pressure on both to sacrifice regimes to save the state and the free market policies. Electoral politics were not the realization of the democratic ideal in association with "free markets." Rather, the practitioners of free market were able to transform the transition to electoral politics into power-sharing arrangements between the authoritarian state and the electoral regime. The case of Chile with President Aylwin and General Pinochet is emblematic.

Secondly, the new electoral regimes that emerged were able to perpetuate and deepen "free market" policies because of the non-democratic procedures and processes. The neoliberals did not campaign for office under the banner of "free markets," but rather on populist or social democratic programs. In Argentina, Menem campaigned as a traditional Peronist before converting to an ultra-free marketeer. Likewise, in Peru, Fujimori defeated his opponent Vargas Llosa on a specifically anti-free market platform before converting to the doctrine after the elections. Salinas in Mexico imposed his free market agenda through wholesale theft of elections. In sum, the electoral politicians associated with free markets engaged in massive fraud and manipulation and deceit to take power. The link between elections and free market is based on electoral deception.

Once in power, the electoral politicians, lacking a mandate, proceeded to implement policies through non-democratic procedures ---wholesale privatizations were decreed by fiat. Rule by executive decree was imposed upon recalcitrant congresses and unaccepting electorates.

In sum, the authoritarian political organs of free market policies, their continuation via power sharing between dictatorial and electoral forces and their implementation by neo-authoritarian procedures that free markets have a greater affinity for political exclusion than for democratic politics.

Challenges to Electoral Regimes

In Latin America, democratic politics, in terms of active citizen involvement in discussions of issues and organized participation, takes place among a wide range of grassroots sociopolitical movements. In some cases, guerrilla movements (Guatemala, Colombia, Peru) continue to secure popular support in the face of the failures of free market policies. Brazil, Colombia, El Salvador, Venezuela, Bolivia, Mexico, Chile, and Nicaragua have all experienced land invasions, Indian-led land recovery movements, barrio organizations, civic associations, street mobilizations of the hungry and unemployed, general strikes (in some cases) and large-scale confrontations with the military and police enforcing free market policies. These movements, with direct ties with the populace via popular assemblies at points of residence or work sites, reflect the direct debates and popular mandates so absent in the executive centered politics of the electoral regimes. The active massive opposition of these popular democratic forces to free market policies reflects the profound conflict between participatory democracy and free market policies.

The growing gap between an electoral elite pursuing free market policies and the majority of the electorate is not only manifest in public demonstrations, but also in growing abstention and alienation from the neoliberal dominated electoral arena. In Venezuela street demonstrations have been followed by majoritarian support to oust the neoliberal president Carlos Andres Perez. In Brazil a similar process of popular disaffection grew to the point where the President had to be impeached.

There is a growing sense among the populace that electoral politics controlled and financed by the free market elites through the mass media are not where change is likely to take place. Extra-parliamentary activity reflecting mass disenchantment is an effort to create democratic space independent of the closed venues of the neo-authoritarian electoral political regime. Electoral regimes face a growing problem of legitimacy in the face of mass disaffection. Equally important, they have squandered whatever initial political credibility they possessed through massive and all pervasive corruption scandals: Collor and family have been found guilty of accepting bribes and payments totalling tens of millions; Alan Garcia in Peru was said to have absconded with 50 million; the Perez regime and its predecessor in Venezuela are said to have taken tens of millions in oil revenues; in Chile the Pinochet regime "socialized" billions in private debt; a financial or drug scandal involving President Menem's family or Cabinet occurs almost every week --sometimes twice a week. Neoliberalism, with its policy of converting public resources into private, with its lax regulation of private activities and with its ethos of supply side policies, lends itself directly toward large-scale corruption. Moreover, with the overseas banks appropriating locally produced wealth on the one side and an elite of exporters squeezing wealth on the other, new upwardly mobile classes must rely on pillaging the state as a primary or initial source of capital and wealth. Free market policies by fostering corruption degrade democracy, turning electoral regimes into vehicles for personal enrichment, responsive to particular business or speculative clienteles willing and able to secure contracts, public property on special dispensation.

The presence of former leftist parties and leaders in government office does not change the general features of electoral policies. The presence of the ex-left parties does not testify to the flexibility and openness of the system as it does the accommodation and adaptation of these parties to the constraints imposed by free markets and the new authoritarianism. The right-wing shift of the ex-left is a continent-wide phenomenon: the Movement of the Revolutionary Left (MIR) in Bolivia shares the government with the right-wing former dictator, Banzer, both pursuing free market policies. The former guerrilla MR-19 in Colombia has joined the privatizing pro-free market Gaviria regime. The Sandinistas, at least the minority of its leadership, share power with the free market-oriented Chamorro regime. Peronism, the former nationalist-populist movement under Menem, is the principal free market force in Argentina. The Socialist Party in Chile, through the Minister of Economy Ominami, vigorously promoted ultra liberal policies. If free market policies corrupt and degrade democracy, the ex-leftist parties' assimilation to the electoral regime has severely compromised their capacity to articulate, represent or struggle for elementary needs of their historical constituencies. The ex-leftists, self-described pragmatists, have presided over declining living standards, growing unemployment and deteriorating social expenditures.

By embracing free market policies, they have become pragmatists who have failed. This is failure in the double sense: failure to renew the electoral system by providing broader democratic representation; failure in the basic sense of not being able or willing to link popular demands from below with the national political system. By becoming incorporated into the elite system and embracing free market policies, the ex-left has narrowed the political alternatives to the majoritarian public.

Democratic Alternatives to Free Markets

Four types of political responses to the neo-authoritarian free market regimes are present in Latin America: (1) new political formations; (2) residual groups from the past; (3) new social actors; and (4) guerrilla movements. The new political formation includes the Workers' party in Brazil (PT) and in Chile the Allendist Democratic Left Movement (MIDA). The PT is the most promising left-socialist mass political party, drawing its support from a broad array of forces, including rural and urban working class peasants, slum dwellers, Christian based communities, professionals and small businesses. It counterposes a welfare state based on national regulation of a mixed economy pursuing redistributive policies.

The second group, the "older left," includes the Broad Front (FA) in Uruguay and the Unified Mariatagui Party (PUM) in Peru. The FA is a coalition of electoral parties linking social democratic and left socialist parties around a program of national development and income redistribution through a mixed economy. With the election of the mayor of Montevideo, Tabare Vasquez, it stands a good chance of winning the next Presidential elections.

The third group, "the new social actors," responds to the growing presence of autonomous movements of working women in neighborhood organizations, the reemergence of a radicalized student movement (Venezuela) and the growing volatility and street protests of the unemployed youth. These groups have made the transition from opposition to military regime to confrontation with the free market, electoral regimes. The gap between the electoral promises of social welfare and the realities of elite concentration of wealth have broken the links between these groups and the electoral party-state apparatuses. Pointing to direct forms of action and participation, they lay the groundwork for a democracy with a popular participatory and social content.

Finally, the guerrilla group found in Colombia, the Colombian Armed Forces (FARC), the unified guerrilla groups in Guatemala and the Communist Party of Peru, Sendero Luminoso, attempt to occupy the political space left by the right turn of former left-wing forces.

While the electoral regimes continue to pursue free market policies that erode living standards, polarize society and nurture massive corruption, electoral and extra-parliamentary opposition groups will continue to confront the status quo: the unresolved tensions that exist between opposition movements and parties in civil society and the neo-authoritarian liberal regimes will continue to be exacerbated.

Conclusion

The ideology that links free markets and democracy is flawed in a double sense. First, the very terms of the discussion, "free market" and "democracy," fail to capture the powerful role of the state and the role of political intervention in determining the terms and actors in the market. Likewise, the simple association of electoral regimes with democracy fails to describe the powerful authoritarian state institutions and executive centered decision-making process.

If, indeed, "free markets" and "democracy" are not the appropriate categories to discuss the new political and economic systems --the violent origins and the powerful role of external powers in shaping neoliberal economic policies preclude any facile associations between the new economic system and political freedom.

The extension and deepening of neoliberal policies has polarized Latin america in a way that erodes the possibility of fashioning a social consensus. In its place, elite corruption, private concentration of wealth and declining living standards have eroded the legitimacy of electoral leaders. There is a direct relation between the expansion of neoliberal policies and increasing voter disenchantment. Increasingly, rule by decree, increasing use of force, co-optation of pliable former leftist politicians has emptied electoral politics of its popular, participating content.

Democratic politics in the form of popular social movements grow in direct opposition to neoliberal policies. At factory and community sites, in popular assemblies and in community movements, votes, and elections, responsive leaders have emerged as a democratic alternative to the combination of the neo-authoritarian electoral system and the state-directed neoliberal economy. The tension between democracy and neoliberalism is present at the bottom of the social system and expresses itself upwardly and outwardly against the reigning electoral politicians and their overseas backers in the banks and multinationals. By focusing on the close relationship between the neo-authoritarians in the regime and free marketeers in the economy, the deeper and unresolved tensions with the wider democratic movements emerging from civil society are obscured.

Notes

The following readings are recommended for the reader:

1. Carlos Díaz-Alejandro, "Some Unintended Consequences of Laissez Faire" In *Development, Democracy and the Art of Trespassing*, edited by Alejandro Foxley et al. South Bend: University of Notre Dame Press, 1989.

2. Keith Griffin, *Alternative Strategies for Economic Development*. London: Mcmillan, 1989.

3. Kay Cristobal, *Latin American Theories of Development and Underdevelopment*. London: Routledge, 1989.

4. Joseph Tulchin and Augusto Vargas, *From Dictatorship to Democracy*. Washington DC: Woodrow Wilson Center for Current Studies on Latin America, 1991.

5. James Petras and Morris Morley, *Latin America in the Time of Cholera*. London: Routledge, 1992.

6. "Democratization and Class Struggle," Special Issue, *Latin American Perspectives* 15 (3), 1988.

7. David Felix (ed.), *Debt and Transformation*. Armonk, NY: M.E. Sharpe, 1990.

8. *Forbes*, July 20, 1992, p. 150.

3

The Internationalization of the Economic Crisis in Mexico and Central America

Arthur Schmidt

With the demise of revolution in Central America and the ending of the Cold War, conventional wisdom in the United States now holds that an era of good feeling has emerged in US-Latin American relations. The post-1982 trends toward democratization and free-market economics in Latin America are said to have created an unprecedented unity of aspirations and interests with the United States as the foundation for a more amicable mutual future.[1] Moreover, it is held that this foundation can only be strengthened by time. "The longer the twin forces of economic and political liberalization are in place in Latin America, the more likely it is that they will reinforce one another over the mid and long term."[2]

While the new relationship may be disturbed from time to time by contemporary problems like drug trafficking and illegal migration or by legacies of the past such as political corruption and resistance to reform, it is argued that the configurations of the post-Cold War world basically oblige Latin America to identify its future with US goals and leadership.   By opening their economies to the world market, a new generation of Latin American leadership has abandoned the anachronistic and divisive "defensive nationalism" of the past. "Relations between the United States and Latin America and the Caribbean today are beginning to resemble the relations that prevail between the United States and Canada.   Security matters have been displaced from the top of the agenda by the search for positive outcomes and mutual gain in the economic sphere."[3]   Although the longstanding US "lack of interest" and "neglect" of Latin America remains a "great frustration" for new democratic leaders,[4] developments such as the North American Free Trade Agreement (NAFTA) and the Enterprise for the Americas Initiative are said to portend the emergence of a Western Hemisphere Free Trade Area that would ensure permanent and constructive US engagement with the rest of the continent.[5]

Like most conventional wisdoms, this one appears plausible by organizing certain aspects of a rapidly changing contemporary history into a coherent package.   Certainly it is true that parts of the formal apparatus of democracy have become more universally accepted as the instruments of rule in Latin America over the last decade just as there has developed a deeper and broader appreciation of the indispensability of market realism in making economic policy.   But neither of these healthy trends necessarily constitutes as yet the foundation of a stable future for Latin America and a guarantee of a harmony of interests with the United States.   The present conventional wisdom smacks too much of a premature post-Cold War ideology, one that would set Lenin on his head by making democracy "the highest form of capitalism" and that would too readily blanket all forms of Latin American nationalism as a negative historical force.   Since the history of the "New World Order" is still open to question,[6] it is worth exploring whether the events of contemporary Latin American history can be read differently.

A generation ago, Geoffrey Barraclough argued that contemporary history could only "justify its claim to be a serious intellectual discipline and more than a desultory and superficial review of the contemporary scene, if it [set] out to clarify the basic structural changes which have shaped the modern world."[7]   In structural terms, it is evident that political liberalization in Latin America has been accompanied by severe economic crisis, one pervasive and comprehensive enough to be legitimately termed a "crisis of development. "[8] Historically, two elements have formed the core of this development crisis: (1) the inability of Latin America to promote sustained economic growth with a reasonable degree of social equity; and (2) the region's low savings rate and its critical dependency upon external financing and technology.[9] It should not be assumed that the crisis of development has ended simply because economic growth and capital flows have now improved, providing a net transfer of capital into Latin America of almost $36 billion in 1991 and 1992, the first positive gain following a consistent and massive capital drain since 1981.[10] Continued low rates of domestic savings and a reliance upon capital inflows to cover a widening current-account deficit do not augur well for an economically stable future. Nor do the deteriorating living standards and growing social polarization that have accompanied Latin America's economic restructuring and reform since 1982.

Despite twenty years of aggregate economic growth (from 1960 to 1980), and a decade of democracy (1980 to 1990), Latin America today is not much better off than in the late fifties. In absolute terms, undeniable progress has been made in many fields; but the region has fallen further behind the industrialized world, its social and economic disparities are greater than before, and, at least in the short term, the hope for effective solutions to its problems is as dim as ever.[11]

It would be premature to declare an end to Latin America's crisis of development until the region's "neoliberal" economic reforms have demonstrated a capacity to improve social equity and to generate sustained internal savings in the near term, a measurement distinct from the presumption of their ability to do so in the long run.[12]

The durability of the Latin American development crisis calls into serious question the assumption of the conventional wisdom that economic liberalization *ipso facto* promotes democracy and amicable future relations with the United States. From the perspective of the recent history of Central America and Mexico, a region directly proximate to the United States and highly integrated into the US economy, communications industry, and labor markets, one might argue that economic liberalization is simply the most recent facet of a process of internationalizing a structure of crisis. The post World War II economic patterns and political systems of Central America and Mexico reached their apogee around 1960. A new historical period then began in which a prolonged regional crisis developed out of the conjuncture of four basic elements: (1) severe internal social inequality; (2) failures of political incorporation; (3) global economic restructuring; and (4) the reassertion of US hegemonic power in the area. The new historical period has unfolded in three chronological stages, each revealing the necessity of a wider sphere of action for the attempted solutions to the crisis: (1) 1960-72, in which domestic socioeconomic and political rigidities created a set of parallel but separate national crises in the region; (2) 1973-1982, in which global economic upheavals and internal political polarization transformed national crises into an increasingly unified regional crisis; and (3) 1983 to the present, in which elites have sought a comprehensive solution to the regional crisis through an internationalization of political life and through economic liberalization - the direct incorporation of the periphery into the productive forces of the core, particularly those of the United States.

The Onset of National Crises, 1960-1972

The first stage of the crisis emerged in the historical context of the Cuban Revolution, years that brought strong social and political conflict throughout Latin America as well as increased external intervention by the United States.[13] In Central America and Mexico, fundamental contradictions existed between the rapid growth achieved by postwar economic advance and patterns of increased internal social inequalities. In the words of Edelberto Torres-Rivas, "disorder began in the moment of progress."[14] Mexico's economy expanded at an average annual rate of over 6 percent between 1940 and 1970, a pace equalled only by a handful of other countries. In the process, Mexico became one of the most rapidly industrializing and urbanizing societies in the Third World.[15] Central America also produced one of the best economic growth rates of the postwar world; from 1950-1970, the region's economic output grew at an average annual rate of over 5.5 percent. Moreover, Central America diversified its economic bases, first adding cotton in the 1950s to the historic agroexports of coffee and bananas and subsequently venturing in the 1960s into cattle raising for the export of beef to institutional purchasers in the United States. The Central American Common Market, founded in 1960, became the basis for an expanding manufacturing capacity focused on serving the region's internal markets.[16]

In neither Central America nor Mexico did economic growth sufficiently alleviate underlying historical patterns of social inequality. Postwar growth in Central America promoted increased landlessness and failed to alter the established model of oligarchic socioeconomic domination, particularly in El Salvador, Guatemala, and Nicaragua.[17] Mexico's investment patterns emphasized urban areas and industry to the neglect of agriculture and rural areas, especially those dependent upon rainfed subsistence cultivation of basic foodstuffs.[18] Patterns of income distribution remained highly unequal and, for some sectors, were getting worse, with the bottom 40 percent of society in the 1960s earning a lower share of total income than it had in 1950.[19] By themselves, the social inequalities of economic growth were not enough to create a broad regional crisis. During the years 1960-1972, each nation state in the region had the ability to address socioeconomic issues individually. The character of those national responses was crucial to the buildup of a regional crisis. For example, through limited measures of agrarian reform and provisions for greater political access, Honduras and particularly Costa Rica attenuated some of the worst social aspects of postwar economic growth, preventing class and group conflict from building into revolt.[20]

Elsewhere, however, fearful elites pursued policies of political exclusion rather than incorporation, thus illustrating Héctor Pérez-Brignoli's[21] remark that "the failures of the ruling classes have always changed the course of history." (Guillermo O'Donnell[22] has defined an "incorporating political system" as one that "purposely seeks to activate the popular sector and to allow it some voice in national politics - or that, without deliberate efforts at either exclusion or incorporation, adapts itself to the existing levels of political activation and the given set of political actors.") Postwar development in Mexico and Central America generated the need for new state-society relationships that elites were unwilling to allow. By the 1960s, society had become more vigorous and more diversified, with more bases for internal organization than could be readily managed by the prevailing historical rules of national politics.[23] A host of new social elements had emerged, as urbanization expanded the middle and working classes as well as elements of the informal sector.[24] Postwar demographic growth had produced a younger population less rooted in the fixed systems of the past; by the 1960s, over 45 percent of all Mexicans and Central Americans were under sixteen years of age. New political creeds emerged as powerful motivations for organized dissent, whether they were of secular origin like the Fidelista mix of nationalist anti-imperialism with domestic radicalism, or of religious inspiration like the liberationist trends that developed in Latin America following the conference of Latin American Catholic bishops at Medellín in 1968.[25] Politics in El Salvador, Guatemala, and Nicaragua deteriorated from "facade democracies" in which military dominance hid behind constitutional appearances into regimes of outright repression. The military coup of 1963 in Guatemala initiated the total transformation of domestic politics into a regime of systematic terror.[26] "The counter-insurgency campaign of the late 1960s polarized political activity to such a degree that the negotiation of some space for even modest reform was viewed as a doomed venture by all except the most ardent advocates of constitutionalism."[27] The ascendancy of counter-insurgency commander Carlos Arana Osorio to the presidency in 1970 cemented the political overlordship of high military leaders determined to control society through repression and to make personal fortunes in concert with the domestic oligarchy and multinational investors.[28] Guatemala had become, in the words of Americas Watch,[29] "a nation of prisoners."

The year 1972 was a turning point for both El Salvador and Nicaragua. Under the combined pressures of social and political agitation and the forced return of 100,000 landless Salvadorans from Honduras as a result of the 1969 war, the regime lost its last major chance for liberalization by stealing the 1972 presidential election from the opposition coalition ticket of José Napoleón Duarte and Guillermo Ungo.[30] The catastrophic earthquake in Managua in 1972 precipitated an end to the tactical bargaining of President Anastasio (Tacho) Somoza with elements of the Conservative party. Thereafter, the entrenched Somoza bloc confronted more concerted opposition from economic elites tired of competing with the "greed and primitive patrimonialism"[31] of the Somozas and from the Frente Sandinista de Liberación Nacional (FSLN), a guerrilla movement that had formed in 1961.[32]

The Mexican political system had a far more complex and comprehensive set of relations between state and society than those of the "facade democracies" in Central America. Since its consolidation in the late 1930s,[33] the "inclusionary authoritarianism"[34] of the Mexican one-party system had artfully employed cooptation with a selective use of coercion to enforce stability. While there were signs of rural restiveness such as the movement of Rubén Jaramillo, the regime faced its principal difficulties in the cities where demands for public services and political democratization eluded the control of the official corporatist political structure and gained middle class support.[35] The attempts of party leader Carlos Madrazo to liberalize the PRI succumbed to the increasingly closed character of official politics. The violent suppression of the student movement of 1968,[36] highlighted by the massacre of Tlatelolco, generated the first of the *end-of-sexenio* political crises that have characterized Mexican politics ever since.[37]

Unlike El Salvador, Guatemala, and Nicaragua, the attempted solution to regime crisis in Mexico was not increased repression but rather the nationalist populism of new president Luis Echeverría Alvarez. Echeverría's program of *desarrollo compartido* alienated powerful elements in the private sector at that same time that it created a greater need for state revenue.[38] Postwar relationships between the state and the private sector in Mexico had established patterns of relatively low rates of taxation on upper-income groups.[39] Echeverría's failed bids to gain higher tax rates, the first of which came in 1972, forced the regime into a significant reliance upon external borrowing. Over the course of his government, Mexico's external debt nearly quintupled.[40]

The Formation of a Regional Crisis, 1973-1982

Echeverría's recourse to foreign borrowing illustrated the degree to which global economic forces were crucial elements in the transformation of national political crises into a broader regional crisis during the years 1973-1982. By the early 1970s, competition from Germany, Japan, and other countries had undermined the extraordinary postwar hegemony of the United States over the global economy. With the decline of US preeminence came a partial disintegration of the system of global economic regulation loosely known as Bretton Woods.[41] The rise of Eurodollar markets and chronic US balance of payments problems brought an informal end to the gold standard and system of fixed currency rates between 1971 and 1973. The OPEC oil price rise that began in 1973 further shook the global system. The high vulnerability of Central American countries to world market shifts meant that higher oil prices and floating currency rates were catastrophic events against which they had little protection. While overall economic growth rates in Central America by and large kept up with the standards set by the period of previous postwar development,[42] declines in the value of exports and substantial increases in the costs of imports meant that Central American growth could only be sustained through external subsidy.[43] By 1979, Central America paid almost seven times as much in debt service as it had in 1970.[44] Internally, the strong pressures to maximize exports to cover the deteriorating balance of payments produced more exploitation and repression, further increasing social and political tensions. Another major rise in oil prices and interest rates in 1979 made Central America's international economic position completely untenable.

For Mexico, the upheavals of the global economy at first were seen to have a liberating rather than a constraining impact. Echeverría used increased opportunities for foreign borrowing to avoid the restrictions of the international "aid regime"[45] as well as to buy freedom from the internal restraints of domestic finance. Mexico quickly became a major borrower from Western private banks engaged in recycling OPEC surplus revenues as well as their own expanding capital.[46] The new wave of private bank lending to governments, predicated upon the assurance that sovereign states could not go bankrupt, favored Third World societies like Mexico with ample natural resources and a significant industrial sector. While precarious finances and the alienation from the private sector produced another *fin-de-sexenio* crisis in 1976, Echeverría's successor, José López Portillo, was quickly able to renew the populist development strategy because of the much celebrated discovery of immense oil reserves. López Portillo embarked upon a highly ambitious program of international borrowing, state investment, and petroleum development that ultimately created tensions within the regime itself, especially when interests rates rose in 1979, raising questions about the sustainability of the country's economic course. Under conditions of private capital flight, Mexico inaugurated the "international debt crisis" in August, 1982 when it declared itself unable to service the foreign debt.[47]

The breakdown of the Mexican government's financial position under López Portillo signified more than just a question of reckless borrowing. It represented the end for Mexico's (and Latin America's) model of import substitution industrialization. Economic globalization had already begun to render that model an anachronism even before the onset of the "debt crisis." Latin America's share of world trade had been falling since around 1960, while the region's national economies could not generate either the markets, capital, or technology to sustain further industrial growth. Whether the result of foreign or domestic investment, Latin American industry was generally poorly positioned to generate industrial exports. Starting in the early 1960s, the textile and electronics industries had began transferring part of their production from First World to Third World sites,[48] opening up the possibility of export-oriented developing strategies for Third World countries bent upon industrialization. While East Asian countries like Taiwan and South Korea had moved from import substitution toward a substantial emphasis on export-oriented industrialization, Mexico had continued to rely much more on its domestic market even as it moved into heavier industrial production.[49] Without a strong industrial export sector, Mexico could obtain foreign exchange only through excessive dependence upon primary exports like petroleum and tourism, and upon external borrowing. Import substitution strategies made industry too dependent upon protected domestic markets and left the country highly vulnerable to the financial, technological, and industrial forces restructuring the world economy.[50] With the financial collapse of 1982, this vulnerability implied an increasing subordination of Mexican economic and foreign policies to external supervision and pressures.

In time, this fundamental change in Mexico's economic position would manifest powerful geopolitical consequences for the "historical rupture" represented by the Central American revolutionary process that emerged after 1972 in El Salvador, Guatemala, and Nicaragua. As "an autonomous irruption of the masses into the political arena,"[51] revolution in these three countries encompassed both armed insurgencies and the formation of broad popular movements committed to *reivindicaciones* of basic rights and needs. The autonomous character of these two elements and their patterns of cooperation constituted a major distinctive feature of the Central American revolutionary process,[52] one that made the increased regime coercion counterproductive as the social basis for insurgency broadened at a rapid pace.

The geopolitics of revolution created a difficult triangular relationship among Mexico, Central America, and the United States.[53] Central American revolution collided directly with a reassertion of US global hegemony that had been underway well before the 1980 election of Ronald Reagan. The highpoint in US-Soviet cooperation had come under Richard Nixon. Thereafter, an increasingly powerful right-wing mobilization over foreign policy developed in the United States in response to the US collapse in Vietnam, the loss of US economic dominance, Third World nationalism, fears of an enhanced Soviet military capacity, and Jimmy Carter's emphasis upon human rights and his conclusion of the Panama Canal treaties.[54] By the time of Reagan's challenge to Carter's re-election, aggressive analysts regarded revolution in Central America as a Soviet-sponsored "attack on the Americas"[55] and a prime example of Carter foreign policy failure.[56] Once the new administration was in office, Secretary of State Alexander Haig declared that El Salvador would be a "test case" of East-West relations.[57] Central America soon became a major US counter-insurgency theater as the Reagan administration established a program of covert aid to the Nicaraguan *contras* and built up the military forces of the government of El Salvador.[58] In 1981, US aid to El Salvador in the form of economic support funds and military assistance was five times greater than the year before.[59] US counter-insurgency efforts soon affected every country in the region[60] and became a significant source of controversy within the United States itself.

The Internationalization of Crisis, 1982-

The year 1982 can be seen as the start of another historical stage in the evolution of the regional crisis of Central America and Mexico, the starting point for the emergence of a solution based upon economic liberalization, an integration of economic elites, and the dominant presence of the United States. While subsequent events in the course of the Central American conflicts and the decline and eventual collapse of the Soviet bloc exercised powerful influence over events, the crucial turning point came in 1982 rather than the later 1980s. First of all, Mexico's financial crisis increasingly undercut its ability to act independently to protect Central American revolutionary change from the policies of the United States. Mexico's own revolutionary political traditions as well as its perceived geopolitical interests inclined the Mexican government to serve as a protector of the "young revolutions" in Central America,[61] at least those in countries other than neighboring Guatemala.[62] Ever since the Cuban Revolution, Mexico had resisted the most overt forms of US anti-Communist intervention in the Caribbean Basin.   Mexico's initiatives in Central America included diplomatic support for both the FSLN and the FMLN.   Mexico also provided economic assistance to Sandinista Nicaragua.   Through its September, 1981 joint communiqué with France and through López Portillo's February, 1982 Managua speech, Mexico made two high profile efforts to propose negotiation processes to end the conflicts and to assure Washington that "the national security interests of the United States would not be damaged by the coming era of revolutionary change in Central America."[63]

Despite López Portillo's nationalization of the Mexican banking industry in September, 1982, economic globalization soon showed itself more powerful than the Mexican state.   Unlike Lázaro Cárdenas' takeover of the petroleum industry in 1938, López Portillo's bank nationalization could not be sustained against the interests of investor classes, both foreign and domestic.[64]   The new Mexican government of Miguel de la Madrid Hurtado abandoned the economic populism of López Portillo and soon began a gradual process of devolving the expropriated properties to private ownership.   At the same time, economic stagnation over the next several years weakened the capacity of Mexico to provide economic support to Central America and created greater Mexican dependency upon the good will of foreign bank creditors and first world governments, especially that of the United States.   Under the first agreements with creditor banks and multilateral agencies like the IMF, Mexico suffered a significant level of external influence over its economic policymaking that, in turn, worked against its efforts at an independent diplomatic solution to the Central American conflict. Mexico's need to restructure its economy separated it from the struggling revolutionary movements of Central America and brought it into closer working relationships with first world economic and political hegemony.

The switch did not happen at once, but after 1982 the de la Madrid government found it increasingly difficult to mix independent international action with domestic economic restructuring.   The Contadora/Caraballeda process, initiated in 1982 as the centerpiece of Mexican foreign policy in the immediate region, sought a multilateral agreement that would reconcile legitimate US security interests with non-intervention and national self determination in the area.   Despite its lip service to Contadora, the United States remained consistently hostile to this initiative and ultimately rendered it an impotent diplomatic formula.[65] By 1985, weak petroleum prices, the Mexico City earthquakes, tense relationships with the United States, and electoral restiveness in the states of the north all suggested an increasingly untenable position for Mexico. In 1986, Mexico joined the GATT, began reducing tariffs and other trade barriers, and opted thoroughly for export-oriented development. Between 1986 and 1992, US-Mexican trade more than doubled as economic integration between the two countries proceeded at a rapid pace.[66] In 1989, Mexico became the first country to obtain a modest amount of debt relief under the Brady Plan. After his shaky position in the 1988 elections,[67] the new president Carlos Salinas de Gortari came to redefine Mexico's relationship with the United States as the fundamental pillar of his administration. The previous policy toward Central America was jettisoned as a gesture of good will to the US in Mexico's new quest to obtain a secure political and economic working relationship.[68] After watching the US-Canadian free-trade agreement get underway and recognizing the potential power of regional economic blocs in determining the world's future, Salinas decided to pursue a similar pact with the United States.[69] Canadian, Mexican, and US negotiators reached agreement on the North American Free Trade Agreement in August, 1992, followed by additional side agreements on some environmental and labor issues a year later.

The year 1982 was a crucial turning point in the triangular relationship among Central America, Mexico, and the United States, setting in motion a process whereby the internationalizing implications of economic restructuring blunted Mexico's geopolitical independence and undergirded the reassertion of US regional hegemony. The same year was also a key moment in the establishment of a political formula that would protect US counter-insurgency from its sizeable domestic opposition. The 1982 Salvadoran elections created the mechanism of elected civilian governments that would be able to obtain sizeable amounts of economic and military funding from the US Congress on the grounds that they represented "budding democracies" that deserved support, one that would be continued regardless of how subservient civilians remained to military power and regardless of how atrocious human rights abuses might still be.[70] Around the defense of "democratic" regimes, the United States after 1982 built up a complex web of "low intensity conflict" operations including constant military maneuvers, vast electronic and photographic intelligence gathering, support for proxy fighters (either the *contras* or local armed forces), economic assistance, and an intense campaign of political propaganda.[71] The vast superiority of US military and economic power in the Central American setting could be counted on to outlast local opposition, assuring that there would be at best a stalemate instead of a revolutionary victory. This did not prevent the new electoral mechanisms from becoming rooted enough to operate in ways that frustrated some aspects of US counter-insurgency policy, as was the case in El Salvador with the 1988 and 1989 electoral victories of Arena.[72] Nor did it prevent important reversals in US objectives such as the Iran-contra scandal, the development of the Esquipulas peace process independent of the wishes of the Reagan administration, or the FMLN offensive of November, 1989.[73]

Such setbacks did not derail the reassertion of US power, however, precisely because US hegemony depended upon more than a counter-insurgency strategy. Global economic restructuring undermined the viability not only of nationally-oriented industrial strategies like that of Mexico, but also of national liberationist revolution. The Central American struggles occurred precisely in the moment of history when global economic and political contexts denied the feasibility of revolution. So powerful has been this historical conjuncture of economic globalization and the end of the Cold War that ". . . the idea of revolution itself, central to Latin American radical thought for decades, has lost its meaning."[74] Social revolutionary regimes in small and poor countries faced a host of dilemmas that they could not solve on their own,[75] thus making the question of a revolutionary triumph a moot point in a world increasingly devoid of external patrons. The United States, as the most powerful capitalist nation in the world, could absorb the leap in its federal budget deficit in 1982 because it could attract global capital to underwrite its fiscal and trade deficits. Small and poor nations could not do the same nor could they expect the declining Soviet bloc to underwrite them. The Mexican debt crisis of 1982 signaled what succeeding years would confirm - that the rules of economics were establishing a transcendence of the nation state, obliging Third World nations to restructure their fundamental economic strategies and to abandon political policies disliked in the global centers of capital.

The cases of Nicaragua and El Salvador are illustrative. Armed popular movements could hold governments hostage or even take over the state, but the external factors in an age of globalization would nullify the use of revolutionary power. The Sandinistas, despite a deliberate policy of a mixed rather than a fully nationalized economy, could not maintain themselves against the combined pressures of US hostility and global economic restructuring. After 1982, the regime could not regain economic growth and generally lost the levels of Western aid it had previously obtained. While it continued to receive economic assistance from the Soviet bloc,[76] the disintegrating internal economy undermined the political foundations of the revolution.[77] In El Salvador, the revolutionaries demonstrated their capacity to maintain the country in political and military stalemate, despite the best efforts of US counter-insurgency to eradicate the FMLN. Yet, as the FMLN came to recognize, armed power and widespread popular organization would not produce the ability to govern on the basis of a revolutionary program at this historical juncture.[78] In both Nicaragua and El Salvador, war was brought to an end through internationally supervised processes of negotiation and demilitarization. The recognition of potential economic marginalization for Central America in a post Cold War era served as a strong incentive for negotiation for both elites and revolutionaries.

An Uncertain Future

While the unfolding of the crisis of Mexico and Central America has increasingly internationalized economic and political systems in the region, it has not solved the fundamental issues underlying the crisis. An atmosphere of uncertainty and worry remains. Clearly the internationalized context of economics and politics has been indispensable in establishing frameworks for political reconciliation in the cases of the Nicaraguan elections of 1990, the Salvadoran Peace Accords of 1992, and the Salvadoran elections of 1994. The record is somewhat checkered otherwise, however. Conditions ought to caution against triumphalist journalistic statements like that of Charles Krauthammer,[79] who praised the Salvadoran government ". . . which, thanks to American support, has now brought peace, without totalitarianism, to El Salvador." The regional crisis of Mexico and Central America still endures through incomplete political reform, an uncertain economic future, social instability, and a complex, potentially conflictive relationship with the United States.

In Central America and Mexico, the absence of military dictatorship and revolutionary insurgency does not mean a full-fledged transition to democracy. Instead of the notion of a mutually reinforcing process of democratization and economic liberalization, the crisis of Central America and Mexico has left three different types of state-society relationships: (1) Costa Rica, where the structures of Western bourgeois democracy antedate the crisis, but are now threatened by the decline of the welfare state; (2) Nicaragua, where the long *contra* war has destroyed the material foundations for any type of constructive democratic politics, raising the specter of endemic, futile violence; and (3) countries where "hybrid regimes" function through elections and limited party competition, under the shadow of "authoritarian enclaves" in the bureaucracy, military, and police, and in the presence of continued human rights abuses.[80] In varying ways, Guatemala, Honduras, and an ARENA-led El Salvador would fit this latter case. So would Mexico, where economic liberalization has deliberately taken precedence over political liberalization.[81] Economic liberalization has further strengthened *presidencialismo*, but its relationship to democracy remains more problematic.[82] Analysts have viewed new Mexican government initiatives such as the National Solidarity Program as an innovative presidential use of patronage and political manipulation rather than as a process of local empowerment.[83] While the August 21, 1994 elections were widely regarded as the most open in Mexican history, fairer elections alone do not create a full democracy. Serious challenges remain to separate the PRI from the apparatus of the state, to equalize the access of contending parties to the mass media and to sources of financing, and to rehabilitate the administration of justice.

Internationalization has not solved the political aspects of the Mexican and Central American crisis. At best, whether through United Nations supervised agreements, international election observation, or through the requirements for the ratification of NAFTA, internationalization has contributed only to a limited political liberalization. Popular struggles for a fuller political democratization and incorporation continue. Political democratization may be hard pressed to go beyond what Carlos Monsiváis has called "selective modernization" or "restrictive modernization"[84] if "adjusting to the new phase of capitalist development . . . requires a delicate balance between a strong state able to maintain law and order and a weak state willing to lend itself to privatization and budget cuts" as Fernando Rojas has argued.[85] This is a crucial issue in Mexico and Central America since the failure to institutionalize broad-based processes of democratization may frustrate successful social adjustment to rapid economic change and thus threaten stability.[86]

Global economic integration is likely to proceed very unevenly, both socially and geographically, and very rapidly. Can it promote genuine economic development rather than just the creation of new production zones in Mexico and Central America? Given its size and location, the experience of Mexico will be determining. Prior to 1994, Mexico was generally judged to be in a much better position to make the great leap forward into free trade than most other Latin American nations.[87] Nevertheless, since the collapse of the peso in December, 1994, its immediate future remains far from guaranteed. The policies of economic integration with the United States in recent years did succeed in substantially lowering inflation, reigniting economic growth, and bringing back flight capital. But they left Mexico with an unmanagable current account deficit and a precarious dependency upon speculative forms of foreign investment. When the devaluation of the peso undermined investor confidence in late 1994, Mexico plunged into a severe economic and political slump from which it has not yet recovered. It is not even clear how much increased manufacturing exports, Mexico's means of solving its international financial imbalances, can alleviate the country's high internal levels of unemployment and underemployment. Foreign manufacturing investment engaged in producing exports from Mexico still uses an extremely low ratio of domestic inputs, even in those sectors using the most modern technology,[88] an undesirable pattern for a country with a large relative labor surplus and substantial natural resources. Will free trade pacts simply mean a process of institutionalized economic integration dominated by elite criteria and investor interests[89] or will they represent the first step toward a more comprehensive form of integration in which genuine developmental needs are given institutional support?[90] Will wages and working conditions be harmonized upward or downward by more intense economic integration? Will there be further social unrest in have-not regions like Chiapas? Will Mexico's increased political and economic reliance on the United States prove unworkable for both countries?

Conventional wisdom in the United States has vastly underestimated the difficulties of making a smooth transition to the new era of globalized politics and economics. Daily life in the region reflects globalization at the level of popular consumption, the mass communications media, migration to US labor markets, the growth of the informal economy, narcotics trafficking, and in financial transactions as diverse as money laundering, migrant *remesas*, and transnational investment. The present period seems distinguished by a profile of widespread popular organization at the grassroots level[91] and significant international elite integration at the peak of society.[92] In between, economic and political systems appear weak and unable to articulate a viable relationship between the increased productivity of the globalized economic forces and the needs of social majorities. The nations of the region remain highly vulnerable to acute social conflict and to the disintegration of the institutional, cultural, and social relationships of national identity.[93] Whether there will be an adequate economic base for political stability is likely to remain an open question. In the meantime, the accumulated impact of increasing social inequality and restricted governmental expenditures deepens the problems of development.

Expectations of a simple harmonious future between the United States and Latin America recall the comments of T.D. Allman[94] about the dangerous role that fantasies of "shared ideals" have played in the history of the Americas. Cold War security issues may have evaporated, but economistic logic should not presume to erase politics and nationality as historical forces. "Pressures for systemic change [in Latin America], like those of the 1960s, are likely to reappear or to be strengthened in most countries as political failures multiply, restructuring fails to attract sufficient external resources, and economic performance remains well below that of the pre-1970 era."[95] Under these conditions, US relations with Mexico and Central America may be anything but harmonious and orderly. Economic integration should not be conceived as a laboratory exercise in which capital can move freely without creating new pressures for further social, cultural, and even political integration. International political alliances at the grassroots - already a feature of the Central American revolutions and the political struggles over NAFTA - will expand, encompassing labor, environmental, and other social issues previously considered domestic. Under the worst circumstances, internationalization in an era of instability could promote the renewal of direct US political and military intervention despite the end of the Cold War, especially in a proximate region such as Mexico and Central America. The thirty five-year old crisis of Mexico and Central America remains an unfinished historical process. It bequeaths to the next century its resilient forms of social struggle and its continual search for durable and authentic solutions to some of the most fundamental questions of contemporary world order.

Notes

1. See World Affairs Council, *Great Decisions Series* (Washington, 1991).
2. Baer (1993), p. 57.
3. Cohen (1993), p. 45.
4. Boeker, *Lost Illusions. Latin America's Struggle for Democracy, as Recounted by Its Leaders* (La Jolla: Institute of the Americas; New York: Marcus Wiener, 1990), p. 331.
5. Bailey and Perry (1993).
6. Woo-Cumings and Loriaux (1993).
7. Barraclough, *An Introduction to Contemporary History* (New York: Penguin Books, 1967), pp. 15-16.
8. Cardoso *et al.*, *Eight Essays on the Crisis of Development in Latin America* (Amsterdam: CEDLA, 1991).
9. Fajnzylber (1990), chapter 1.
10. CEPAL (Comisión Económica para América Latina y el Caribe), *Preliminary Overview of the Latin American and Caribbean Economy* (Santiago, 1992), p. 55.
11. Castañeda, *Utopia Unarmed. The Latin American Left After the Cold War* (New York: Knopf, 1993), p. 5.
12. Haggard, "Markets, Poverty Alleviation, and Income Distribution: An Assessment of Neoliberal Claims." *Ethics and International Affairs* 5 (1991): 175-196.
13. Wright, *Latin America in the Era of the Cuban Revolution* (New York: Praeger, 1991).
14. Torres-Rivas, *Centroamérica: la democracia posible* (San José: EDUCA/FLASCO, 1987), p. 26.
15. Levy and Székely, *Mexico, Paradoxes of Stability and Change* (Boulder: Westview Press, 1987).
16. Weeks, *The Economies of Central America* (New York: Holmes and Meier, 1985).

17. Weeks, "An Interpretation of the Central American Crisis," *Latin American Research Review* 21 (1986): 31-53.

18. Esteva, *The Struggle of Rural Mexico* (México: Universidad Autónoma Metropolitana, 1980).

19. Cypher, *State and Capital in Mexico: Development Policy Since 1940* (Boulder: Westview Press, 1990), p. 79.

20. See Booth (1991); Bulmer-Thomas (1991); and Torres-Rivas (1991).

21. Pérez-Brignoli, *A Brief History of Central America* (Berkeley: University of California Press, 1989), p. 179.

22. O'Donnell (1986), p. 240.

23. Aguilar Camín (1989) and Flora and Torres-Rivas (1989).

24. Portes, "Latin American Class Structures: Their Composition and Change During the Last Decades," *Latin American Research Review* 20 (1985): 7-39.

25. Lernoux, *Cry of the People* (Garden City: Doubleday, 1980).

26. Torres-Rivas (1987).

27. Dunkerley (1991), p. 142.

28. See Nairn (1983); Torres-Rivas (1991).

29. Americas Watch, *Guatemala: A Nation of Prisoners* (New York: Americas Watch Committee, 1984).

30. Duarte, *Duarte, My Story* (New York: Putnam's, 1986).

31. Loveman and Davies (eds.), *Che Guevara. Guerrilla Warfare* (Lincoln: University of Nebraska Press, 1985), p. 371.

32. Lozano, *De Sandino al triunfo de la revolución* (México: Siglo XXI, 1985).

33. Córdova, *La formación del poder político en México* (México: Era, 1972).

34. Knight (1992), p. 143.

35. Davis, "Social Movements and Mexico's Crisis," *Journal of International Affairs* (1990) 43: 343-367.

36. Zermeño, *México, una democracia utópica: el movimiento estudiantil del 68* (México: Siglo XXI, 1978).

37. Basáñez, *El pulso de los sexenios: 20 años de crisis en México* (México: Siglo XXI, 1990).

38. See Teichman (1988); Schmidt (1991).

39. Felix (1986).

40. Green, *Estado y banca transnacional en México* (México: Editorial Nueva Imagen, 1981), p. 60.

41. Gilpin, *The Political Economy of International Relations* (Princeton: Princeton University Press, 1987).

42. Weeks (1985), p. 62.

43. Rivera Urrutia, Sojo, and Roberto López, *Centroamérica, política económica y crisis* (San José: DEI, 1986), pp. 125-132.

44. Torres-Rivas (1983), p. 15.

45. Wood, *From Marshall Plan to Debt Crisis. Foreign Aid and Development Choices in the World Economy* (Berkeley: University of California Press, 1986).

46. Stallings, *Banker to the Third World. US Portfolio Investment in Latin America, 1900-1986* (Berkeley: University of California Press, 1987).

47. Canak, *Lost Promises. Debt, Austerity, and Development in Latin America* (Boulder: Westview Press, 1989).

48. Henderson, *The Globalisation of High Technology Production. Society, Space, and Semiconductors in the Restructuring of the Modern World* (London and New York: Routledge, 1989).

49. Gereffi (1990).

50. Castells and Laserna, "The New Dependency: Technological Change and Socioeconomic Restructuring in Latin America," *Sociological Forum* 4 (1989): 535-560.

51. Torres-Rivas (1989), pp 73-74.

52. Berryman, *The Religious Roots of Rebellion. Christians in Central American Revolutions* (Maryknoll: Orbis, 1984).

53. Jauberth et al. (eds.), *The Difficult Triangle: Mexico, Central America, and the United States* (Boulder: Westview Press, 1992).

54. Wills (1988); also see Moffett (1985).

55. American Security Council Foundation, *Attack on the Americas!* (Boston, Va.: Coalition for Peace Through Strength, 1981).

56. Kirkpatrick (1981).

57. LaFeber, *Inevitable Revolutions. The United States in Central America* (New York: Norton, 1993).

58. Arnson, *Cross-Roads: Congress, the Reagan Administration, and Central America* (New York: Pantheon, 1989).

59. *Envío*, "Trends in US Aid to the Region." Dec. (1990): 18-19.

60. Vergara Meneses et al., *Centroamérica, la guerra de bajaintensidad* (San José: DEI, 1987).

61. Fuentes, *Latin America at War with the Past* (Toronto: CBC Enterprises, 1985).

62. Programa de Estudios Relaciones México-Estados Unidos, "México en la encrucijada de Guatemala," *Informe Relaciones México-Estados Unidos*, Juldic (1982): 10-71.

63. Aguilar Zinzer (1988), p. 100.

64. Maxfield, "The International Political Economy of Bank Nationalization: Mexico in Comparative Perspective," *Latin American Research Review* 27 (1992): 75-103.

65. See Aguilar Zinzer (1988).

66. Council of the Americas, *Washington Report* (Fall, 1992).

67. Butler and Bustamante (eds.), *Sucesión Presidencial. The 1988 Mexican Presidential Election* (Boulder: Westview Press, 1991).

68. Castañeda, "Salinas' International Relations Gamble," *Journal of International Affairs* 43 (1990): 407-422.

69. Gentleman and Zubek, "International Integration and Democratic Development: The Cases of Poland and Mexico," *Journal of Interamerican Studies and World Affairs* 34 (1992): 59-109.

70. Brown (ed.), *With Friends Like These: The Americas Watch Report on Human Rights and US Policy in Latin America* (New York: Pantheon, 1985); also see Epstein, "The Reagan Doctrine and Right-Wing Democracy," *Socialist Review* 19 (1989): 9-38.

71. Klare and Kornbluh (eds.), *Low Intensity Warfare. Counterinsurgency, Proinsurgency, and Antiterrorism in the Eighties* (New York: Pantheon, 1988).

72. Lungo, *El Salvador en los 80: contrainsurgencia y revolución* (San José: EDUCA/FLASCO, 1990).

73. Coleman and Herring (1991).

74. Castañeda 91993), p. 241.

75. Colburn, *Post-Revolutionary Nicaragua: State, Class, and the Dilemmas of Agrarian Policy* (Berkeley: University of California Press, 1986).

76. Philip (1988).

77. Martinez Cuenca (1990).

78. Lungo (1990).

79. Krauthammer, "The Neoconservatives Hope Clinton Will Deal Them at Least One Key Foreign Post," *Philadelphia Inquirer* 19 January (1993): A10.

80. Karl, "Commentary on the Future of Democracy in Latin America," Conference on Alternatives in Latin America: A Panel of 1993-94 Presidential Candidates. Princeton University, April 16, 1993.

81. Rubio, "El talón de Aquiles de la reforma económica," *Vuelta*, Julio (1993): 36-39; also see Salinas de Gortari, "North American Free Trade: Mexico's Route to Upward Mobility," *New Perspectives Quarterly*, Winter (1991): 4-9.

82. Smith, "The Political Impact of Free Trade on Mexico," *Journal of Interamerican Studies and World Affairs* 34 (1992): 1-25.

83. Dresser, *Neopopulist Solutions to Neoliberal Problems: Mexico's National Solidarity Program* (San Diego: Center for US-Mexican Studies, 1991); also see Ward (1994).

84. Ortiz Pinchetti, *La democracia que viene, ejercicios de imaginación política* (México: Grijalbo, 1990), p. 139.

85. Carodso et al. (1991), p. 116.

86. Gilly, "The Mexican Regime in Its Dilemma," *Journal of International Affairs* 43 (1990): 273-290.

87. Sanderson, *The Politics of Trade in Latin American Development* (Stanford: Stanford University Press, 1992).

88. Wilson, *Exports and Local Development. Mexico's New Maquiladoras* (Austin: University of Texas Press, 1992).

89. Development Gap, *US Citizens' Analysis of NAFTA* (Washington, 1992).

90. Castañeda and Heredia, "Another NAFTA: What a Good Agreement Should Offer," *World Policy Journal* 9 (1992): 673-685.

91. Escobar and Alvarez (eds.), *The Making of Social Movements in Latin America: Identity, Strategy, and Democracy* (Boulder: Westview Press, 1992).

92. Sklair (1991).

93. Guillermoprieto, "Report from Mexico: Serenading the Future," *New Yorker* 9 Nov (1992): 96-104.

94. T.D. Allman (1984).

95. Coatsworth (1993), p. 170.

4

Agrarian Policy and the Agrarian Bourgeoisie in Sandinista Nicaragua

Jeffery M. Paige

The Sandinista party came to power in 1979 through a national unity alliance with progressive sectors of the Nicaraguan bourgeoisie, including a significant sector of the agrarian elite, based on the principles of a mixed economy, political pluralism, and non-alignment.[1] By the time the party lost power eleven years later, the mixed economy was in chaos, political pluralism had led to electoral defeat and the national unity alliance had dissolved into civil war polarized by great power rivalry. The fall of the Sandinistas, like their rise, was decisively affected by their complex relationship with the Nicaraguan bourgeoisie, rural and urban. But in a small export economy dependent since the nineteenth century on coffee, later supplemented by cotton and sugar in the 1960s and 1970s, relations between the party and the agrarian bourgeoisie, especially the coffee producers, were critical to the economic as well as the political survival of the revolution.

Although coffee growers in Nicaragua never succeeded in achieving the political and economic prominence that they did elsewhere in

Central America, many were members of leading elite families, and both before and after the revolution exerted decisive influence over the country's principal export commodity. Even after the revolution the agrarian bourgeoisie controlled a substantial share of the three quarters of agro-export production, not only in coffee, but in cotton, cattle and sugar as well.[2] Furthermore, the fortunes of the elite were tied to the much larger number of small and medium producers who looked to them for political and economic leadership. The elite's international political connections, particularly in the United States, also made them a force to be reckoned with. The economic and political power of the agrarian elite had been a significant factor in the success of the revolutionary coalition. It would also exert a decisive influence on the failure of the Sandinista experiment.

Although many members of the Nicaraguan bourgeoisie were tied to the Somoza dynasty through a complex web of corruption, cooptation and privilege, a significant fraction (perhaps as much as 40%) of the agrarian elite, usually termed "the middle bourgeoisie," had been excluded from the spoils of the Somoza economy and initially backed the revolution.[3] Many coffee and cotton producers gave money to the Sandinistas while others allowed their farms to be used by Sandinista combatants. Some did much more, including sheltering Sandinista leaders in their homes or even taking up arms themselves. Many had sons, daughters or other close relatives with the Sandinista combatants and most were exposed to the arbitrary searches and martial law terror of the closing days of the Somoza dynasty.[4] Seven years after the revolution, when many of them were interviewed by the author, they still expressed implacable opposition to the Somozas and all their works.

Nevertheless the formal alliance itself scarcely survived the first anniversary of the revolution. For many coffee growers the turning point in relations with the Sandinistas was the death of Jorge Salazar, a prominent coffee grower and founder of the Coffee Growers' Association of Matagalpa, in a shoot out with Sandinista police on November 17, 1980. Salazar had also been a founder and the first president of the Agricultural Producers Association of Nicaragua (UPANIC), an organization that brought together representatives of large producers in all Nicaragua's principal commercial crops, and Vice President of the principal voice of the Nicaraguan business community COSEP, The Higher Council on Private Enterprise, in which UPANIC was a core member. Years after Jorge Salazar's death officers of both UPANIC and the Matagalpa Association had his black bordered picture on the wall of their offices. All regarded him as a martyr to Sandinista duplicity despite his apparent involvement in armed conspiracy against the government.[5]

By the second anniversary of the revolution many of the most prominent coffee growers and other members of the agrarian elite associated with UPANIC and COSEP were in increasingly vigorous opposition to Sandinista rule. By 1982 interviews by Dennis Gilbert found "deep, often passionate disaffection" in all sectors of the bourgeoisie.[6] Nevertheless a surprising number of coffee producers and other members of the agrarian elite remained in Nicaragua and continued trying to work in a system that many of them had initially supported but now distrusted.[7] Even when bourgeois alienation was at its height those members of the agrarian elite who remained in Nicaragua continued their economic relations with the revolutionary government and never entirely abandoned efforts at negotiation and accommodation. These efforts continued even after the Sandinistas' 1990 electoral defeat.[8]

In fact, relations between the Sandinistas and the agrarian elite waxed and waned during more than a decade of Sandinista rule. Rose Spaulding divides the Sandinista relations with the bourgeoisie into three periods---the first two years of attempts at accommodation and cooperation, the period from 1982 to 1987 when relations reached rock bottom, and a third period, from 1988 to the Sandinista defeat in 1990, when increasing but inconsistent efforts were made to revive the national unity alliance.[9] The author had an opportunity to interview many prominent members of the Nicaraguan coffee elite and some leading cotton producers in July and August of 1986 when relations between the Sandinistas and the bourgeoisie were at their nadir and the contra war was at its height.[10] By this time most members of the coffee elite had given up entirely on the Sandinistas and many were privately hoping for a contra victory or even a United States invasion.

Although in 1986 opposition to the Sandinistas was nearly universal among those interviewed differences in both tone and content make it possible to divide the growers into three groups: "politicals," "technicals," and "patriotic producers." The politicals were in general associated with the leadership of the Coffee Growers' Association of Matagalpa or UPANIC and its other affiliates actively opposed to Sandinista rule. They were more interested in politics than economics or technology, rejected any possibility of accommodation, and denounced the Sandinistas in the language of cold war anti-Communism. The technicals were often just as opposed to Sandinista policy, frequently belonged to the same private associations, but were more interested in the technical and economic aspects of production than in politics, were considerably more willing to compromise and were less given to cold war rhetoric. They eschewed the outspoken opposition and high political profile of the Association leadership.

"Patriotic producer" was a term used by the Sandinistas to refer to private farmers believed to be loyal to the revolution, particularly those associated with the Sandinista dominated National Association of Farmers and Ranchers (UNAG). Although the overwhelming majority of large producers remained loyal to the private sector associations, a small number actually joined the Sandinista farmers' organization. Interviews revealed that some of these producers were scarcely more enthusiastic about the revolution or the Sandinistas than those associated with the private associations, but their willingness to risk public identification with the Sandinistas set them apart from other growers. "Patriotic producer" will be used here to refer to all associates of UNAG, whatever their views, and to those members of other associations who were generally sympathetic to the Sandinistas even if they opposed specific government policies. But patriotic producers themselves, as well as other growers, acknowledged that they were a small and unrepresentative minority of large producers.

Despite their disagreements over tone and tactics there was considerable agreement among all three groups on both the specific failings of the Sandinistas and the reasons for the breakdown of the national unity alliance. The alliance had been based on a commitment by both the Sandinistas and the bourgeoisie to the three basic principles--a mixed economy, political pluralism, and non-alignment. It is clear, however, that the Sandinistas and the bourgeois had different understandings of these principles and the policies they implied.[11] Furthermore, it is unclear to what extent the principles were generally accepted within the party, even among the dominant national unity fraction that first proposed them, and government policy shifted continually during a decade of Sandinista rule.[12] By 1986 most members of the bourgeois were convinced that the Sandinistas had abandoned all three principles, if they had ever supported them in the first place. "The Sandinistas promised political pluralism, a mixed economy and non-alignment, and have done none of them," was a typical view. Nevertheless, the principles provide a useful framework for examining both government policy and elite alienation during the Sandinista period.

The "Mixed Economy" and the State as the Center of Accumulation

Although a mixed economy usually implies a mixture of state and private enterprise operating in a free-market economy it is clear that the Sandinistas had an entirely different interpretation and that initially the policies pursued ". . . came down on the side of a fairly orthodox principle of state centralization and the creation of a planned economy...[with] strong indirect controls over the remaining private sector."[13] In practice this meant that the state would be privileged as the "center of accumulation" and that government controls would effectively eliminate product, labor, capital, producer and most consumer good markets in the nominally private sector.[14] The Nicaraguan economy bore no relation to the "mixed economies" of Western Europe despite the Sandinistas' warm relations with Western European social democratic parties. Despite orthodox economic adjustment policies introduced in 1986 and, with a vengeance, in 1988-89 state control remained the economic model until the Sandinista electoral defeat in 1990.[15]

The state centered model also influenced Sandinista agrarian policy. After a wave of confiscations of properties of the Somozas and their close allies immediately after the revolution, agrarian reform was deemphasized and direct action by the landless to seize land was discouraged by persuasion or, when necessary, direct state action. The confiscated Somoza properties were converted to state farms and cooperatives; relatively little land was distributed to the landless. An agrarian reform law was not announced until the second anniversary of the revolution and even then it was extremely conservative by Latin American standards.[16]

In 1985 landless peasants encouraged by Sandinista agricultural organizations invaded both state and private farms in Masaya and precipitated a confrontation between the influential Bolaños clan, leaders of the agro-export "middle" bourgeoisie and the government. The confiscation of the Bolaños properties was another turning point in the deteriorating relations between the government and the agrarian bourgeoisie.[17] In January 1986 a new law extended the agrarian reform and greatly accelerated the pace of confiscation. 1986 was the peak year for confiscations, with over 400, and the low point in bourgeois-Sandinista relations. By 1988, however, concerns about declining production and the failed national unity alliance led Agrarian Reform Minister Wheelock to declare the reform over. Only 3 properties were confiscated in that year.[18] The damage to bourgeois confidence in stable property relations, however, had already been done.

The Sandinista state-centered model of agro-industrial development directly attacked the political, proprietary and economic base of private accumulation in the agro-export sectors, despite continual public affirmation of a commitment to the mixed economy. The result was a marked decline in the incentives for private capital accumulation, a subsequent decline in investment and production, an increasingly acrimonious debate over economic policy, and near total collapse of business confidence. At the time of the interviews large growers required surprisingly little prompting to provide a detailed critique of the Sandinista policy. Although the tone varied there was surprisingly little variation among "politicals," "technicals" and "patriotic producers" on the specific problems of Sandinista agrarian policy.

Producers Against the State: Free Markets and Free Men

If a single theme animated the bourgeoisie's political and economic opposition to the Sandinistas as expressed in the interviews it would be the idea of freedom. In the words of an officer of the Association of Coffee Growers of Matagalpa, member of one of Nicaragua's most socially prominent families and leading candidate for the agricultural ministry under both the Sandinista and the Chamorro regimes, when asked what he would tell the Sandinistas if he were their advisor, "Liberty, in one word liberty. . . freedom of everything, economic freedom, political freedom. That we be allowed to buy and sell freely without government control and restrictions." Another grower, a thoughtful political neutral who was one of Nicaragua's two or three most productive coffee growers, said ruefully, "you know it's paradoxical. We had complete [economic] freedom in the midst of a dictatorship. And now we have no freedom at all."

Few growers had any doubts that the Sandinista economic model was state-centered accumulation with only a temporary or transitional role for private producers. And almost all of those interviewed, including politically moderate technicals and even some Sandinista sympathizers, believed that the eventual goal was a Soviet style command economy. For most of those interviewed the mixed economy was as one of them said, "a myth," sustained largely for the benefit of opinion abroad. "They tell that to foreigners," said a prominent cotton grower of the mixed economy, "but everything is directed." Even a technically oriented, politically moderate coffee producer, when asked about the Sandinistas' commitment to a mixed economy, replied, "Lies, they're all lies. Everything they say is a lie."

None of those interviewed argued that a Soviet style command economy had yet arrived and many were aware of the internal debates within the Sandinista directorate itself over the pace and nature of socialist reform. But they regarded the debates as tactical only and the future direction set, no matter what the present policies implied. "Look," said one grower in English, "you come here and you don't see Soviet style collective farms. You don't see an East German style security system and you think it isn't Communism. But even the Communists know that state farms can't work . . . It's just a new version of the Communist system." A moderate cotton grower, who said he would stay in Nicaragua and continue producing if the government moderated its position, nonetheless referred to what he called "this Communist system." "It's just a dispute about the pace of change," said another cotton grower of the opposition of the official Nicaraguan Communist Party to Sandinista policy. "The Communist Party wants an immediate change, but it's not convenient for them [the Sandinistas] now."

With the exception, once again, of a very small number of UNAG officers and allies, none of the producers saw any future for themselves, other large producers or, many said, even for small and medium producers in the Sandinista model of state-centered accumulation. Almost all expected to be confiscated in the long run and many expected the end to come sooner. One coffee grower, when asked if he thought there would be a future for private growers in five years, replied, "no, not in one year. The pressure is increasing all the time." Another, asked the same question, replied that the future of the large growers was "uncertain in the long run, possibly the short run." "I think this is my last year of planting cotton," said another moderate, technically oriented grower. "When the war [i.e., the contra war] is over we are all going to be gone," said a dissident UNAG member.

As might be expected of producers with such profound pessimism concerning their own immediate future, substantive questions on specific Sandinista agricultural policy were frequently met with skepticism and impatience. When asked what the Sandinistas could do to improve the economic situation of large producers one coffee grower close to the Matagalpa Association replied derisively, "Get out of the country!" Another noted that economic questions were beside the point--the real questions were political--and a third interrupted the interviewer to tell him that economic questions were a waste of time. Although such comments were common, they were not universal, and even among such profound skeptics it was usually possible to pursue specific economic issues. In fact a detailed economic critique emerges from the interviews even though the producers' fundamental belief in the ultimate triumph of a Soviet command economy made the discussion academic for many of those interviewed.

Confiscations and Insecurity

Growers complained bitterly and almost universally about the Sandinistas' policy of continued confiscations and it is clear that this more than any other single factor was responsible for their profound pessimism concerning their own future and the Sandinistas ultimate intentions. Confiscations, occurring on almost a daily basis at their peak in 1986 when the interviews were conducted, were conclusive evidence for most producers that they were expendable and a command economy the ultimate goal. "It's like a sword swaying over our heads all the time," said the secretary of the Matagalpa Association of the confiscation policy." "One day the bell tolls for my neighbor, the next day for me," said another, "There isn't any future for private producers in Nicaragua. We are just subsisting." "There is no private economy," said a third, "when you can take everything away." For most of the growers an end to confiscations was a prerequisite for any successful economic policy and their continuation, fatal to the national unity alliance.

Given the prevailing insecurity, investment beyond what was necessary to maintain production was irrational and with one or two exceptions growers simply shelved expansion and indefinitely postponed replantings. "There is no point in investing in coffee if it's going to be taken away," was one typical view of a Matagalpa association activist. ". . . They [the Sandinistas] are more interested in politics than in economics. So they continue the confiscations for political reasons even though they know it will affect production," said a technically oriented and highly productive grower. The threat of confiscation served both to maintain minimal levels of production in the short run in order to forestall confiscation based on abandonment or "decapitalization," and to discourage investment that would make possible increases or forestall declines in production in the long run.

The confiscation policy affected, directly or indirectly, almost all of those interviewed. Many of them had lost some or, in two cases, all of their lands to confiscations, many had experienced land invasions or other forms of political pressure against their lands, almost all knew close friends who had lost their lands and with one or two exceptions (both members of UNAG) all expected to lose their lands eventually. Many had shelved expansion plans in anticipation of eventual confiscation and maintained minimal production levels to avoid immediate confiscation. The government's policy of continual piecemeal confiscation had destroyed its economic credibility and squandered its political support among these large producers. It had also significantly reduced the production potential of the private agro-export sector. According to those interviewed, other Sandinista private sector economic policies simply exacerbated this effect.

The Nominal Market Economy

Although both the Sandinistas and their bourgeois opponents thought that state-centered accumulation would eventually prevail, most agro-export production during the Sandinista period remained under private ownership. Strong indirect government controls, however, eliminated most market forces in this nominally private sector. Foreign trade in agro-export commodities was a state monopoly and export products were sold to government trading boards at fixed prices. Credit was made available at negative real interest rates and relatively little consideration was given to the credit worthiness of the recipients. An acute foreign exchange crisis made it difficult if not impossible to obtain imported inputs even at exorbitant black market prices and both foreign exchange and inputs were allocated by government agencies and producer organizations. Rates of pay for each agricultural task were set by the government and fell increasingly behind inflation, seriously eroding rural living standards and undermining the rural labor market. Seriously depressed estate prices froze most land sales, other than distress sales, and confiscations undermined the market that did exist. As a result, no effective markets existed in land, labor, capital, producer goods or product markets.[19] The results of these indirect controls were price distortions, production disincentives, declining production and increasing bourgeois alienation.

Product Prices, Profits and Incentives

Growers complained bitterly about administered prices for export crops, particularly coffee, which, they argued, were too low to provide an investable surplus. Prices were paid in local currency at levels which in real terms were a small percentage of the hard currency prices prevailing in international markets. The government retained the foreign exchange difference between external and internal prices in effect imposing a substantial export tax amounting at times to more than 90 percent of the external price. The more politically outspoken growers denounced such price levels as little better than theft and even growers more sympathetic to the revolution acknowledged that at such prices it was difficult to make an operating profit let alone accumulate sufficient funds to reinvest in standing crops or equipment. In fact, the effective export tax levels realized through the internal-external price differential would have eliminated any incentive to produce if they had not been offset by price controls and subsidies on other factors of production.

Although prices were set at levels which theoretically permitted an operating profit to be realized at the artificial prices prevailing in the land, labor, producer good and capital markets, little or no investable surplus was realized by any of the growers. In fact, government policy paid little attention to the distinction between operating profits and profitability, i.e., sufficient return on investment to encourage reinvestment in equipment or standing crops. As one cotton grower noted when asked if production were profitable, "Yes, in terms of this Communist system . . . the government calculates costs and allows a certain profit. So it is profitable in a limited sense."

The situation for coffee growers was even worse. "The price structure is completely crazy," said a coffee grower, "you can't calculate costs." Most coffee growers said that they had barely been able to pay their operating expenses or make a minimal operating profit during the revolutionary period. Even a politically neutral grower who favored negotiation with the government complained that "they paid us ridiculous prices in cordobas and it was impossible to make any money." "The coffee grower has no choice," said another grower, "[because he] has a huge investment tied up in the trees and he can't leave them. . . . And the government has treated him the worst of all." "They really abused us," concluded another leading coffee producer.

With minimal or non-existent operating profits and no investable surplus there was, as might be expected, little or no reinvestment among coffee growers. One producer noted that "nobody has planted any new coffee trees since the revolution," and interviews with other growers, for the most part, confirmed his observation. "We are replacing trees, but no, we are not expanding--just trying to maintain ourselves," was a typical view. "You need a surplus to invest," said another grower, "but at these prices you aren't getting any . . . I keep going with bank credit--all the money I am investing comes from the bank. Without it I wouldn't be investing at all."

Producer Goods: Shortages and Political Allocation

The acute foreign exchange crisis and efforts to resolve it through administrative allocation of imports and foreign exchange effectively eliminated the market in agricultural inputs, created scarcities of critical items, drove up black market prices, and required further government efforts to supply these items. Almost all growers complained of shortages of critical items like chain saws (for pruning coffee trees) and agro-chemicals (critical in cotton cultivation). One of Nicaragua's leading producers had one full time employee who devoted his time to searching for spare parts. The wife of another grower said she and her husband "went nuts" trying to find spare parts and inputs.

When inputs were available they could usually only be obtained through the Sandinista farmers organization, UNAG, providing, as one UNAG officer conceded, a substantial incentive to join the organization. A private association officer agreed, "If you are a member of UNAG you get everything, credit, inputs, fertilizers. But we [i.e.. association members] have to buy it on the black market at 200 times the official price." Many private growers nonetheless refused to join UNAG as a matter of principle. "It's a government organization, . . .you have to submit to the line of the Front [FSLN] and I am not going to do it." But even many UNAG members reported that they were unable to get critical inputs.

Labor Markets

Growers reported that labor was in short supply, although many attributed it to the demands of the contra war rather than the absence of a rural labor market. But they also argued that many workers had found more remunerative ways to make a living under prevailing economic conditions and that agricultural wages were inadequate to attract labor or to support workers. "The shortage of field hands," said one grower asked to name his principal problem, "as a result of the militia and military service which, in turn, are a result of the war." Another grower complained of both the shortage and poor quality of labor. "All the workers have become vagabonds and live by robbing people. . . They can make more money stealing things than they can by working." "A good many rural people have moved to the city to take advantage of low food prices and government support," said a UNAG member, "and others have moved to escape the war so there are many fewer peasant producers around to supply labor."

Most growers compared rural living standards and wage levels unfavorably with the pre-revolutionary period although they admitted that they could not afford to pay more given internal coffee prices even if the government would permit them to pay more, which it would not. "And who are the real exploiters of the poor?" asked one politically oriented producer. "They [the government] only allow my workers four ounces of rice a day. I want to give them more so who is exploiting the workers?" Another grower claimed that his workers had actually come to him and asked why he didn't pay them as much as he did in 1979. "At what we pay them they can't even buy clothes. And if I paid them any more, which I can't afford to do anyway, then I am a bad administrator." Another grower cheerfully admitted that he had been unable to give his workers a negotiated wage increase because the government had disallowed it.

Credit Markets

One factor of production not in short supply, however, was credit.

Many growers said that they kept producing largely because of the easy availability of credit and the fear of confiscation. "Basically it's the credit," said one coffee grower when asked why he continued producing. "As long as they're willing to advance it you can keep producing. "All the money I am investing comes from the bank. Without it I wouldn't be investing at all," said another coffee grower. "They [the Sandinistas] are extremely liberal with credit and it is easy to get," said another grower, "there is no real problem." When asked if credit was difficult for him to obtain a leading cotton grower conceded that "really it isn't. There is an adequate supply of credit." None of the private growers interviewed complained of any difficulty obtaining credit.

Despite the easy availability of credit, shortages of labor and agricultural inputs as well as low real crop prices created an unfavorable environment for increased or even constant production. Those interviewed did not hesitate to attribute the substantial decline in production from pre-revolutionary levels (more than 50% by the time of the interviews[20]) to Sandinista policy. Indeed some of the most outspoken politicals denied that the Sandinistas were interested in producing anything at all. "They're interested in politics not economics," said an officer of the Matagalpa Association. "The economy is a basket case," said another outspoken political, "the only thing they're interested in is expansion. The only export of this country is revolution. That's the business they're in. They export revolution and the Russians send them wheat, oil, arms. That's the way the economy really runs." Even a sympathetic "patriotic producer," however, conceded that "they [the Sandinistas] weren't very concerned about coffee."

By the time of the interviews almost all of the growers, with the exception of one or two "patriotic producers," had given up on Sandinista agricultural policy and viewed any effort to change it as a waste of time. When asked whether he saw any possibility for flexibility on the part of the government one technically oriented grower replied, "no, none. They are taking their orders, following orders from outside [i.e. the Soviet Union]." "If you try to explain to them about prices they just say . . . you are part of the exploiting bourgeoisie," said an officer of the Matagalpa association. When asked about a change in policy a technically oriented producer said, "They are not going to change their line. . . the only solution is a total change, a total change in government." Although several of the patriotic producers and political neutrals said there actually had been a change in government policy for the better in the previous year (1985-86) with more financial incentives and more interest in production, by 1986 Sandinista economic policy had lost whatever credibility it once had with most growers.

Sandinista policies of state-centered accumulation, piecemeal confiscations, and indirect market controls led to nearly unanimous rejection of the Sandinistas on the part of those interviewed. The "mixed economy" became an area of conflict rather than consensus between the Sandinistas and the agrarian bourgeoisie. Indeed, it is likely that Sandinista economic policy alone would have driven the large producers into political opposition. But economic disagreements were exacerbated by conflicts over the theory and practice of democratic pluralism and by deteriorating political relations between the large producers and the government. The promise of democratic pluralism, like the promise of a mixed economy, became a major source of bourgeois discontent.

Democratic Pluralism and Participatory Democracy

It was clear from the outset that the bourgeoisie and the Sandinistas had dramatically different views of democracy. For the bourgeoisie democracy meant representative parliamentary democracy with contested elections and opposition political rights. The Sandinista view was more complicated. Initially, the Sandinistas rejected representative democracy as "democratism" and "liberal bourgeois ideology" and emphasized "popular hegemony" expressed by mass organizations and the party vanguard. Nonetheless the party accepted national representative elections in 1984 and 1990 and its own electoral defeat in the latter year. The Sandinistas, however, never resolved this contradiction between their support for a representative democracy that included the bourgeoisie and their commitment to hegemony by the popular classes that, most assuredly, did not include the bourgeoisie.[21] The agrarian bourgeoisie, on the other hand, became convinced that there was no possibility of either freedom or representative democracy in Sandinista Nicaragua despite national elections and the continued debate among the Sandinistas themselves on the issue.

Sandinista Democracy: The View of the Agrarian Bourgeoisie

Those interviewed thought democracy, as they understood it, did not exist in Nicaragua. The more politically oriented argued that in politics, as well as in economics, the goal was a Soviet- or Cuban-style party dictatorship. "Elections are a fraud," said one politically oriented producer, "only one party was permitted to run an effective campaign [i.e., in the 1984 elections]. . . You can't organize politically." When asked to compare the political situation under the Sandinistas with that under Somoza, an officer of the National Coffee Association said, "Elections are no different now. They are predetermined. How can you have an election when there is no freedom to get involved before the election--we have all the worst aspects of the Somoza system." "They think democracy in the style of the East, not the West," said another politically oriented grower.

Only UNAG officers defended representative democracy in Nicaragua while technically rather than politically oriented growers expressed disappointment rather than rage that their early hopes for democracy had not been realized. "We basically believed the Charter of Punta Arenas when they [the Sandinistas] supported democracy. The period of the revolution, the first government of Violetta Chamorro and Alfonso Robelo, but after that they changed and we found out it was all lies," said one technically oriented coffee grower. Although most of the technicals were disappointed in the Sandinistas' political philosophy they, unlike the politicals, were at least open to a more moderate policy. When asked if he would stay in Nicaragua and continue producing if the Sandinistas moderated their policies a technically oriented cotton producer readily agreed. But as the interviewer was leaving he called after him, "see you in Miami." Many of the technicals appeared receptive to Sandinista efforts at representative democracy, but, as this parting comment indicates, in 1986 they had little hope that such efforts were serious.

Democratic Rights and Civil Liberties

The Sandinistas had made respect for human rights one of the fundamental principles of the revolution and there were none of the summary executions or arbitrary vengeance against members of the old regime that characterized the Cuban revolution. Independent human rights groups reported that there were relatively few violations of human rights in Sandinista Nicaragua and those that did occur were usually punished.[22] Nevertheless, under a state of emergency declared in 1982, most democratic rights were suspended, prior censorship was imposed on the press, and the activities of bourgeois political parties were restricted. Even at the nadir of Sandinista bourgeois relations, however, in 1986 members of the bourgeoisie were willing, as the material reported here indicates, to attack the government in no uncertain terms in private conversation, although most indicated they would be reluctant to do so in public. Not even the most outspoken politicals contended that a Soviet-style police state existed in Nicaragua although a number argued that there would be one in the future.

Nevertheless, many of those interviewed felt that their political rights and liberties were in jeopardy in Sandinista Nicaragua. Politically prominent growers feared confiscation of their estates for their political views. "If you speak out politically they will confiscate your estate," said one grower active in the Matagalpa association. Most of those interviewed reported being under immense pressure from Sandinista police, militants and mass organizations. "There is tremendous pressure on us all the time," said one UNAG member who nonetheless opposed the government, "from the government, the ATC, the Front. They have threatened me personally . . .they point a gun at me--the ATC--pressure and more pressure." Visits by security forces were one of a number of forms of pressure on growers that included arrest, violence, land invasions and mob action or the threat of the same.

Only one of those interviewed reported that he himself had been arrested and he turned out to be one of the revolution's most loyal supporters among those interviewed. "... [T]hey arrested me, stripped me naked, completely naked and interrogated me," he said. "There was no physical violence but there was considerable psychological abuse." Another grower who reported that a friend of his had been arrested, held for two weeks and then expelled from the country, said, "they don't break your jaw or tear off your lips. They put you in a chair, in a closed room--hot--and question you for hours." None of those interviewed reported anything other than detention and prolonged, psychologically abusive interrogation by the police.

Among those interviewed only some, but not all, UNAG members seem to have been largely exempt from such pressures. When asked if he had any problems with land invasions a UNAG member replied, "No, nothing like that . . . I haven't had any problems. I obey the laws. If you do, you don't have any problems." Another grower and UNAG officer argued that it was possible for them to criticize the government but the same criticisms coming from the Association could create problems. "The difference is the Association is making the criticisms basically to undermine the government, to support the counter-revolution. If the government thinks you are supporting the contra then you would have problems." But even technically oriented growers who were not active in the association reported pressures from the police and mass organizations. Although only active UNAG members seem to have achieved any immunity to political pressures, a technically oriented association member argued that "most of the large producers who join, join because they are frightened."

There is no denying that many if not most of those interviewed seemed frightened, although this did not prevent many of them from attacking both the government's economic policies and its civil rights record in private. But many insisted that they not be quoted by name and almost all said they believed they could not make the same criticisms in public without risking arrest. One grower when asked how we could be talking critically of the government when he claimed there were no political rights in Nicaragua said, "Sure, but that's because we're speaking privately. If I were to go out on the street and say what we are saying here, I would be arrested." Even a political neutral sympathetic to the government acknowledged, "If you go out in the street and demand higher prices--no that isn't possible," but argued that it was possible to negotiate in private. "You can't say one word of criticism of the government," said one of the most outspoken politicals, "you will be arrested, thrown in jail. Look what happened to Jorge Salazar."

Despite the government's commitment to human rights and, after 1984, electoral democracy the agrarian bourgeoisie in 1986 felt itself to be a threatened and persecuted minority. The limits on political rights imposed in the state of emergency contributed to this feeling as did their vulnerability to pressures from mass organizations and the security forces. By 1986 the contra war was at its height and government security forces suspected, not without reason as the interviews indicate, that many large producers sympathized with the contra. Even though they were not faced with a police state the bourgeoisie found itself without either governmental representation or guaranteed security of its person or property. Their official position in Sandinista society was well described by Sandinista Vice President

Sergio Ramírez--"survivors of the shipwreck. "

Governmental Access and Personal Relations

Despite an absence of both electoral democracy and civil liberties during the Somoza period, the elite nevertheless had some access to the regime. But after the government reorganizations of 1979 and 1980 the bourgeois ceased to have its own representatives in influential positions and experienced increasing difficulties in influencing policy. This was not so much because the Sandinistas were unwilling to meet with prominent coffee and cotton growers; many growers in fact reported such meetings. But the meetings were often contentious and counterproductive leading to more not less bourgeois alienation. As an officer of the Matagalpa Association put it, "Yes, we get together and have meetings. And we tell them what we want. But they do nothing. It is just propaganda. "

Particularly at the beginning of the Sandinista period the anti-bourgeois rhetoric of the Sandinistas further alienated the growers. "For a long time the government abused the coffee growers, " said one sympathetic grower. "We would go and try to say something to the ministry and they would not believe us. . . . We were the bourgeois exploiters. " And an official of the Matagalpa Association described his own frustration with meetings with government officials. "If you try to explain to them about prices they just say you know why you think that--it's because you are part of the exploiting bourgeoisie. " Although some of the more sympathetic growers saw a substantial change in attitude in government ministries in the year preceding the interviews the earlier attitudes had alienated many growers.

In the final analysis, however, responsibility for the political alienation of the bourgeoisie did not rest solely with the Sandinistas. Early Sandinista emphasis on participatory democracy, popular hegemony and rule by the vanguard did not give much weight to bourgeois notions of electoral process or civil liberties. But most observers think that the 1984 elections were reasonably fair and yet bourgeois representatives, supported by the private sector agrarian organizations, refused to participate. United States pressure was certainly a major factor in the decision not to participate,[23] and by 1984 the contra, backed by the United States, offered a non-democratic alternative route to power. The contra war itself placed immense pressures on the Sandinistas to increase surveillance and curtail civil liberties which, as the interviews indicate, further alienated the agrarian bourgeoisie. Sandinista policy deserves a major share of the blame for both the political and the economic collapse of the mixed economy. The blame for the failure of the second principle of the revolutionary coalition, political pluralism, is more widely shared.

Non-Alignment and the Contra War

The third major principle of the national unity alliance, non-alignment, was a casualty of the contra war. Initially the United States and been the revolution's principal aid donor and initially most Sandinista foreign aid came from sympathetic Western European governments and other Third World governments rather than from the then Eastern bloc.[24] Although relations with the United States deteriorated the revolutionary government continued to maintain its relations with Western European Social Democratic parties. In 1988 a report by the Swedish government on the state of the economy had a major impact in moving the Sandinistas to embrace an orthodox economic stabilization program.[25]

The election of Ronald Reagan on a platform which strongly implied efforts to overthrow the FSLN, a renewal of cold war rhetoric in the United States, and the beginning of United States support for the contras quickly ended whatever possibilities there might have been for continued ties with the United States. By the time of the interviews in 1986 the politicals among those interviewed saw their relations with the Sandinista government in terms of the same cold war rhetoric used by the Reagan administration and increasingly identified their interests with those of that administration. Support for the contra was universal among those classified as politicals and widespread even among technically oriented producers and some nominally patriotic producers. Only a few UNAG members and one or perhaps two technically oriented producers expressed any reservations about the contras. Contra supporters among the politicals were surpassingly outspoken about their views and even cautious technicals let it clearly be known where their sympathies lay. By 1986 not only had the national unity alliance with the bourgeoisie ended, most members of the agrarian bourgeoisie were giving tacit, although probably not active, support to an armed movement dedicated to the overthrow of the Sandinista government. Differences among those interviewed on this issue were largely questions of political rhetoric.

Despite the risks associated with support for the contra in Sandinista Nicaragua several of the politicals not only did so, but also backed United States military intervention. Some appeared to view the interview as an opportunity to lobby for military intervention. "Everyone would be down on the beach waving American flags," said a Matagalpa association officer when asked about the possibility of United States intervention. At least two growers tried to convince the interviewer that if the United States didn't intervene the United States would itself be faced with invasion and Communist insurgency across the Rio Grande. "When the Senate voted the 100 million (aid for the contra) 90% of the population were secretly happy," said a dissident UNAG member who also backed direct United States intervention.

Although such outspoken opinions are the defining characteristic of the group here called "politicals," even cautious technically oriented growers obliquely signalled their support for the U.S.-backed contra effort or, possibly, for invasion. When asked how Sandinista policy could be changed one efficient technically oriented moderate replied, "Only through total change. And this will not come from within. There will have to be aid, pressure from the outside." Another technically oriented producer introduced the interviewer to a friend as a "cub of Reagan," making a politically daring play on the Sandinista slogan "cubs of Sandino" used for members of the Sandinista Popular Army (EPS).

There was clear opposition to the contra and United States intervention only among a few UNAG members, one Association member, and the one political and organizational neutral among those interviewed. For members of the agrarian elite such opposition could be costly. Members of the immediate family of two UNAG members had been murdered by the contra, another member narrowly escaped a contra ambush himself and still another worried about contra mines on the road to his estate. The one political neutral among those interviewed lost several hundred head of cattle to a contra raid. "There is a lot of pressure, pressure from both sides," said an Association member sympathetic to the government, "there is pressure from the government. But also pressure from the contra to take up their position." The only UNAG member among those interviewed who did not face direct threats from the contra was in fact an outspoken contra supporter.

Among the three types, the politicals had clearly taken a position of open disloyalty to the government. The technicals while supporting the contras and possibly United States intervention seemed most concerned about a real change in policy and might have supported the government under other circumstances. The small minority of patriotic producers had paid substantial personal costs for their loyalty to the government and disloyalty to their class. "They are interested in opposing the government," said a UNAG official of the Matagalpa Association. "Basically they simply want to find things to complain about. They think everything is bad." The government sympathizer among the Association members, who had resigned from the Association board because he disagreed with their political intransigence said that "maybe 50 percent" of the Association members think politically and follow the Association line. "The rest think the way I do--it's better to stick to production."

The extreme anti-Communist and anti-Sandinista sentiment among the private association officials and their followers combined with their enthusiastic support for the violent overthrow of the Sandinista government would seem to make any renewal of the national unity alliance difficult if not impossible. In fact COSEP and UPANIC have in general opposed the de facto coalition between the Chamorro government and the Sandinista dominated armed forces that emerged after the Sandinistas' electoral defeat. The loyalty of the technically oriented producers, however, while lost at the time of the interviews, might have been maintained or even regained with different economic policies and an unequivocal support for parliamentary democracy from the outset.

There is little doubt, however, that the polarization introduced by the unremitting hostility of the Reagan administration to any form of Sandinismo encouraged the more intransigent anti-Communist faction and that the contra war strained political tolerance on both sides and undermined the electoral democracy that it was supposed to establish. The extreme pressure that both supporters and opponents were subject to, evident in the interviews, is a dramatic indication of the practical political effect of the contra war. In the end collapse of the national unity alliance depended, in part, on events outside Nicaragua's borders and outside Sandinista control.

Conclusions

Some tentative conclusions concerning both Sandinista policy and bourgeois ideology can be drawn from the experience of the agrarian bourgeoisie in revolutionary Nicaragua as revealed in the interviews. First, it is clear that the peculiar Sandinista combination of state-centered accumulation and nominal private enterprise was both a political and economic failure. It undermined the agricultural export sector on which the economy rested and alienated the large growers that were initial supporters of the national unity alliance.

Second, the initial Sandinista emphasis on participatory rather than representative notions of democracy and popular hegemony rather than opposition political rights contributed substantially to the alienation of the agrarian bourgeoisie. Even a subsequent commitment to representative democracy was not sufficient to reduce alienation especially once bourgeois opposition had been solidified by a hostile United States government and the contra war. The war and unremitting United States official hostility to the revolution were, however, significant factors in undermining both parliamentary democracy and the national unity alliance.

At the heart of the collapse of the national unity alliance were two opposed definitions of its basic principles, each of which was undermined by its own contradictions. For the Sandinistas the ideas of state-centered accumulation and participatory democracy contradicted the economic and political existence of the agrarian bourgeoisie as a class. Nevertheless, the Sandinistas never fully renounced their commitment to the continued existence of this class in Nicaragua and indeed their economic and political survival to a large extent depended upon it. It was precisely this commitment that made the Sandinista revolution such an anomaly among modern socialist revolutions.

For the bourgeoisie their notion of freedom did not necessarily include the popular classes represented, whether they liked it or not, by the Sandinistas. They told the interviewer many times that the solution to Nicaragua's problems was to get rid of the Sandinistas. Few seemed troubled by the fact that the popular support that the party might command (over 40 percent of the vote even in the 1990 election) might be left without representation. If the central contradiction of Sandinista policy was building socialism while including the bourgeoisie, the central contradiction of the agrarian bourgeoisie was building parliamentary democracy while excluding the Sandinistas. Neither of these contradictions was resolved in the Sandinista period. Both remain on the agenda in the futures of both the Sandinista party and the Nicaraguan nation.

Notes

1. On the origins of the alliance see George Black, *Triumph of the People* (London: Zed, 1981), pp. 101-106; Shirley Christian, *Revolution in the Family* (New York: Vintage, 1986), pp. 43-45; Donald C. Hodges, *Intellectual Foundations of the Nicaraguan Revolution* (Austin, Texas, 1986), pp. 239-241.

2. George Irwin, "Nicaragua: Establishing the State as the Center of Accumulation," *Cambridge Journal of Economics* 7 (1983):128; David E. Ruccio, "The State and Planning in Nicaragua," pp. 64-65 in *The Political Economy of Revolutionary Nicaragua*, edited by Rose J. Spaulding (Boston: Allen & Unwin, 1987).

3. Dennis Gilbert, *Sandinistas* (New York: Basil Blackwell, 1988), pp. 105-108; Jeffery M. Paige, "Revolution and the Agrarian Bourgeoisie in Nicaragua," p. 115 in *Revolution in the World System*, edited by Terry Boswell (New York: Greenwood, 1989).

4. Gilbert, *Sandinistas*, p. 108; Paige, "Agrarian Bourgeoisie," p.116.

5. The most detailed account of the Salazar affair is contained in Christian, *Revolution in the Family*, "Jorge Salazar and the Elections," pp. 197-215. Christian, a conservative critic of the Sandinistas, nonetheless concludes that Salazar was deeply implicated in an attempted coup. The exact circumstances of Salazar's death, however, remain in dispute. Information on the Association of Coffee Growers of Matagalpa was provided by interviews with Association officials.

6. Gilbert, *Sandinistas*, p. 119.

7. Calculations by the author based on Nicaraguan government statistics indicate that by 1986 somewhat less than half of the prerevolutionary large producers were still in control of their estates. These were overwhelmingly from the "middle bourgeoisie." (Paige, "Agrarian Bourgeoisie," p. 113).

8. The process of accommodation was called "concertación" in Nicaragua and began in the last two years of Sandinista rule. See Mark Everingham, "From Insurrection to Concertación in Nicaragua: Alliances, Businessmen, and Elite Consensus," paper presented at the Latin American Studies Association Meetings, Los Angeles, September 24-27, 1992.

9. Rose Spaulding, "Capitalists and Revolution: State-Private Relations in Revolutionary Nicaragua (1979-80)," paper presented at the Latin American Studies Association Meetings, Washington D.C., April 4-6, 1991.

10. For details on the sampling procedures used to select those to be interviewed see Paige, "Agrarian Bourgeoisie," pp. 125-126.

11. This was particularly true in regard to the mixed economy and political pluralism. See the discussion in Gilbert, *Sandinistas*, pp. 114-117 and Spaulding, "Capitalists and Revolution."

12. Gilbert commenting on Sandinista agrarian policy notes that "an astrologer might have as good a chance as anyone else of divining the long-term direction of Sandinista agrarian policy," *Sandinistas*, p. 104. In his prologue to Alejandro Martinez Cuenca's memoirs (*Sandinista Economics in Practice* [Boston: South End Press, 1992], p.1), Vice President Sergio Ramirez went so far as to deny that any Sandinista model existed as such.

13. Malia Chamorro Z. and Richard A. Della Buono, "Political Economy of the Sandinista Electoral Defeat," *Critical Sociology* 17 (Summer 1990): 96.

14. Irwin, "The State as the Center of Accumulation;" Ruccio, "The State and Planning in Nicaragua;" David Kaimowitz, "Nicaragua's Experience with Agricultural Planning: From State Centered Accumulation to the Strategic Alliance with the Peasantry," *Journal of Developing Societies* 4 (July 1988): 115-135; Michael Zalkin, "Food Policy and Class Transformation in Revolutionary Nicaragua, 1979-1986," *World Development* 15 (July 1987): 961-984; Bill Gibson, "The Nicaraguan Economy in the Medium Run," *Interamerican Studies and World Affairs* 33 (Summer 1991): 28-29; Richard Stahler Sholk, "Stabilization, Destabilization, and the Popular Classes in Nicaragua, 1979-1989," *Latin American Research Review* 25 (1990): 55-88.

15. On the 1986 adjustment see Robert Pizarro, "The New Economic Policy: A Necessary Readjustment," pp. 217-232 in *The Political Economy of Revolutionary Nicaragua*, edited by Rose Spaulding (Boston: Allen & Unwin, 1987). On 1988-89 see Swedish International Development Authority, *Nicaragua: The Transition from Economic Chaos toward Sustainable Growth* (Stockholm, 1989).

16. On the agrarian reform see Ilja A. Luciak, "Popular Hegemony and National Unity: The Dialectics of Sandinista Agrarian Reform Policies, 1979-1986," *LASA Forum* (Winter 1987): 15-19 and *The Political Economy of Transition*, unpublished manuscript, Department of Political Science, Virginia Polytechnic Institute and State University, and Spaulding, "Capitalists and Revolution," pp. 12-18.

17. Luciak, 'Popular Hegemony," p. 17.

18. Spaulding, "Capitalists and Revolution," p. 34.

19. For overviews of Sandinista economic policies in the agrarian sector see Pizarro, "New Economic Policy;" Zalkin, "Food Policy;" and Sholk, "Stabilization."

20. The contrast with neighboring Costa Rica is particularly dramatic. While Nicaraguan production had by 1989 reached a low point of a little more than 50 percent of its 1978-79 average, Costa Rica had increased its production in

the same period by more than 50 percent (United Nations Food and Agricultural Organization, *FAO Yearbook: Trade of the United Nations*, FAO Statistics Series No. 91, Vol. 33 (1979): 77-79 and Vol. 44 (1990): 88-90.

21. Gilbert, *Sandinistas*, p. 34. For an insightful discussion of the Sandinista view of democracy see Luciak, *Political Economy of Transition*, pp. 21-29.

22. See Americas Watch Committee, *Human Rights in Nicaragua* (New York, 1984, 1985, 1986, 1987); Amnesty International, *Nicaragua: The Human Rights Record* (London, 1986).

23. On this point there seems little doubt. See Robert A. Pastor, *Condemned to Repetition* (Princeton: Princeton University Press, 1987), p. 249.

24. Barbara Stallings, "External Finance and the Transition to Socialism in Small Peripheral Societies," pp. 54-78 in *Transition and Development: Problems of Third World Socialism*, edited by Richard R. Fagen, Carmen D. Deere and José Luis Conaggio (New York: Monthly Review, 1986).

25. Swedish International Development Authority, *The Transition*.

5

Brazil at the End of the Century: Presidential Impeachment and Economic Integration in First World Markets[1]

H.B. Cavalcanti

During the 1960s and 1970s, under military rule Brazil built an industrial park that made it the 10th economy in the world, with a GNP equal to Canada's. The military's economic miracle was built at the cost of political repression and unilateral developmental guidelines. After the 1973 oil crisis Brazil's economic "miracle" came to a halt, when the oil-based economy led the country deep into debt. More importantly, the import-substitution military strategy imposed perverse levels of inequality on the Brazilian population. The slow return to civilian rule in the 1980s did not change the growth strategy (heavily state-owned, capital-intensive economy, sustained by high trade protectionism and geared to priority trade with Third World nations). Protectionism meant that Brazil lost an opportunity for integration into First World markets to Asian nations. With the first free presidential election Brazilian hope was renewed; the president ran on a platform of domestic prosperity, economic privatization, and free trade with the

First World. However, graft and corruption led the new president to impeachment. This chapter looks at the direction of the Brazilian political economy in recent years and what the impeachment means to Brazil's integration in First World markets.

Latin American countries are struggling at the turn of the century to become fully integrated into a new world order. The worldwide political and economic changes of the last ten years have made it a hard task. A changing world requires from Latin American nations also a changing model of political economy.

The end of the Cold War and the collapse of the Communist block has led to a reorganization of First World nations. Economies based on an escalating arms race now have to readjust to peace time production. Political systems based on a previous antagonistic climate now have to operate within a single ideological frame.

If the end of the Cold War brought political consequences for First World nations, it also brought serious repercussions for the rest of the world. Entire regions lost their geopolitical importance. Countries once kept at artificial levels of economic prosperity now have to struggle and develop the economic muscle to survive. Less Developed (LDCs) as well as the Newly Industrialized Countries (NICs) can no longer use the Cold War to extract favors from the superpowers. Furthermore, the political opportunities and investment possibilities in Eastern Bloc nations leave less resources for LDCs and NICs--whether in the form of development funds or financial investments.

The heated trade wars of the 1980s only increased the domestic and foreign problems of Latin American countries. Competition for markets is bound to continue beyond the end of the century. And while many countries have efficient industrial capabilities, not many have the internal markets to absorb production.

As a consequence, there are more nations fighting for limited shares of First World markets today than there have ever been since World War II. Renewed levels of productivity in Western nations (especially the European countries) and the Pacific Rim boom only intensified the competition. Countries not fully equipped to deal with the highly competitive international trade are left at the margins of First World markets, losing ground quickly.

At the end of the century, Latin American nations face that kind of scenario. Their industrialization was based on a centralized, statist economic model (in most cases under authoritarian military regimes, and they struggle with inefficient, heavily subsidized, or state-owned industrial parks that cannot perform well domestically nor internationally (with a few rare exceptions) that might not be responsive to either external markets or internal demands. Furthermore, centralized, state-controlled development created as a by-product segmented workforces that are unable to compete with their international counterparts.

Where development followed political priorities rather than market incentives, one ends up with perversely segmented economies: pockets of industrialization and skilled workers in industries and geographic areas that governments consider important. In those pockets development works relatively well (see the case with the oil industries in Mexico and Venezuela or steel production in Brazil). And those inserted in the pockets are generally better off than the rest of the population in their countries.

But segmented development imposes a heavy social cost. The weight of the less developed areas saps Latin American countries' competitiveness in the world market. While Japan, Korea, and Taiwan have literate, healthy, and fully integrated populations, most Latin American countries struggle with illiteracy and high mortality rates amidst starving and unskilled masses.

If anything, the worldwide political and economic changes of the end of the century forced many Latin American nations to undertake deep structural changes. During the 1980s most of them turned to democratic governments and economic liberalization. There were ambitious economic programs such as privatization of State industries, revamping of stock markets, and development of sound, modern financial institutions (efforts witnessed in Mexico, Brazil, Argentina, Chile, or Peru). There was also talk of continental and regional trade areas (MERCOSUR) that might foster further economic development in the region.

But a decade later the Latin American continent still seems incapable of reinventing itself. Some countries have gone back to semi-dictatorial regimes (like Peru) or suffered threats of military coups (as is the case of Venezuela). The ones that transitioned to stable democratic models are still embroiled in political corruption and unable to create lasting political coalitions to solidify insurgent democratic institutions (as are the cases of Argentina, Brazil, and Bolivia).

Economically, ten years later Latin American countries are not faring any better. The Venezuelan coup attempt, for instance, stemmed as much from political corruption as it did from the economic problems facing that nation. Peru had precious foodstuff imports held at bay for lack of payments.   In many Latin American countries foreign investment is still scarce, state companies still control domestic markets, and local economies are still plagued with inflation, unemployment, and low productivity.

To these nations' economic difficulties are added the social problems of poverty, hunger, and homelessness.   Since development was based on intentional pockets of industrial strength, social inequality reached unbearable levels in the 1980s, draining insurgent democratic regimes of popular legitimacy.   In many Latin American cities such as Rio de Janeiro, São Paulo, or Buenos Aires raids on supermarkets and grocery stores were so frequent that many were forced to use security forces to stay open.

Why is it so hard for Latin American countries to achieve economic and political progress?   Part of the answer is political, part is economic.   Unstable governments or hierarchical, centralized authoritarian regimes do not provide the necessary conditions to foster broad, inclusive development.   Eventually, political participation becomes a necessity to build a national agenda.   Countries built on authoritarian government usually fail to listen to their most hard-pressed constituencies. Since most Latin American countries' economies were built on weak political institutions, they represent a skewed, exclusive vision of development that does not take into account the surrounding misery.   And as economies built under artificial conditions (heavy governmental subsidies, harsh tariffs, state interventionism, etc.) they lack the muscle to withstand world level competition. Brazil is a good example of that--after 16 years of heavy military boosting of manufactured exports, the nation's exports still accounted for less than two percent of the world market in 1980.[2]

Unequipped to compete in the new world order and hard-pressed to survive domestic crises, Latin American nations keep adopting short-term policies that sustain self-defeating patterns.   Brazil, again, is a good example.   As the largest nation and economy in South America the country is still struggling to find its niche in First World markets and sustain a higher level of domestic prosperity.   By examining some of the challenges to Brazil's development model this chapter seeks to illustrate and explain the difficulties that hold development at bay in most nations of the continent.

The Brazilian Miracle

Under military rule during the 1960s and 1970s Brazil built an industrial park that pushed its economy from the 30th to the 10th place in the world. In the early 1980s Brazil's GNP was equal to Canada's (US$ 250 million). The fast economic growth based on a strong import-substitution strategy led many to proclaim the "Brazilian miracle" as the model to change a less developed nation into a world power.

Heavy state intervention throughout the period created over twenty million new jobs and a share of manufacturing only exceeded by five and equaled by two of seventy-six developing countries.[3] In two decades Brazil achieved one of the fastest growth rates in the world-- nearly a nine percent annual growth rate from 1968 to 1980. Industrial output boomed from a 10% annual growth rate in the late 1960s to nearly 15% at the peak of the military regime (early 1970s) to 8% in the late 1970s. By 1980 57% of Brazil's exports were industrial goods compared to 20% only 12 years early.[4]

In Brazil, economic growth did not preclude concern with social problems. Despite the unevenness of resource distribution caused by the fast development, the Brazilian government created an array of social welfare programs: public housing and literacy programs were instituted, utility rates restructured to cost less to low income people, labor had access to profit-sharing in companies (PIS/PASEP), social security was extended to all Brazilians age 70 or older, and health care reached rural populations.[5] Adult literacy rose from 60% in 1960 to 76% in 1978; elementary education rose from 57% of the school age population in 1960 to 94% at the end of the same period.[6] No other country in Latin America experienced similar rates of economic growth and welfare expansion during the period.

However, the 1973 oil crisis drastically changed the direction of the Brazilian "miracle." The oil-based economy built by the military led the country deeper into debt. And since the economy was built on political repression, the regime had no popular support for plans the Brazilians had not asked for. More importantly, the import-substitution strategy that created pockets of development in the nation continued to impose perverse levels of inequality on the rest of the Brazilian population.

Thus by the early 1980s when civilians returned to power, 58% of all Brazilians (almost 90 million) lived below the poverty level, with average family incomes of US$ 58 a month for the poor and US$ 28 a month for the indigent. Some 1,000 children under the age of four died daily from mostly preventable diseases. 15 million children lived in the streets of Brazil's largest cities. While the per capita GDP steadily grew, the relative income share declined: the poorest 50% of the population saw its share drop from 17% in 1960 to 15% in 1970 to 13% in 1980, while for the top 10% the share increased from 40% in 1960 to 47% in 1970 to 51% in 1980.[7]

The 1980s return to civilian rule did not change the country's development strategy. Despite the writing on the wall, the state maintained for as long as it could a heavily state-owned, capital-intensive economy, sustained by import-substitution and high trade protectionism (along with priority trade with Third World nations). The opportunity for real integration into competitive First World markets was lost to Asian nations.

The first freely conducted presidential election brought renewed hope for Brazilians. Fernando Collor de Mello, the young president, ran on a platform of domestic prosperity based on economic privatization and free trade with the First World. After a number of reforms to stabilize the economy and reverse a staunch recession, the president's plans came to a halt with his process of impeachment. Evidence of graft and corruption led to his resignation in the last week of December 1992.

What does Collor's impeachment process mean to the Brazilian integration in First World markets? What lessons does it bring to other Latin American nations? The answer is explored here through a review of the country's political economy and of the policies that led to the current economic and political standstill.

Building State-led Development

During the last agricultural boom of the Brazilian economy (last half of the 19th century) the means for industrialization became available in large scale. The expansion in the world coffee trade created the surplus that was reinvested by Brazilian elites in the acquisition of industrial technology. State intervention in industrialization dates back to that period.

The Brazilian government saw in the insurgent industrialization process the means to better manage the country's balance of payments, and the opportunity to keep economic growth under a "nationalistic" agenda. Thus, for the first half of this century, despite international market conditions, the state closely supervised foreign capital investment especially in strategic industries (steel and energy are two good examples), and subsidized native industrial elites with further means to develop local industrial strength.[8]

The import-substitution strategy was a negative response to the changes in the world market. While the North American industrialization followed from internal expansion needs,[9] Brazilian industrialization responded to both external pressures (interruption of foreign trade during the two world wars, crises and booms in the international agricultural market) and internal demands.[10] To keep the country independent of world market fluctuations, the State adopted a strategy of import-substitution that lasted throughout the century, up to the late 1980s.

Import substitution meant the State created companies to supply subsidized capital input to private industrial growth, maintained high protective tariffs, and supported an unequal inter-industrial (low governmental support for raw material production, higher support for capital goods, and the highest support for finished consumer goods), inter-regional development.[11]

As the military took power in 1964 the only change in the old formula was to attract more foreign capital in an effort to contain high inflation and unemployment. Import-substitution remained, but the early protective mechanisms controlling profit-remittance for multinational corporations were dismantled as the military granted tax-exemption to investments in selected industrial sectors. The State kept investing heavily in capital input,[12] in a "division of tasks where the State took up the heavier responsibility of supplying at low costs the domestic market with basic inputs and external economies which were used by the multinationals for their own expansion both domestically and in export markets."[13]

Boosted by State and foreign capital the country achieved an annual industrial output growth of nine percent during the military period, led by modern, capital-intensive sectors of the economy (chemicals, steel, transport and electrical equipment). But State ownership of companies in privileged industries jumped from 15% in 1948 to 21% in 1962.[14] By 1974 the State dominated the industries of steel, mining, petrochemicals, power generation, all maritime and rail transportation, iron, and the exchange market.[15] Of the total 440 State companies created until 1983, 63% were established after 1964, with 38% between 1964 and 1973 and 25% between 1974 and 1983.[16]

State companies had access to earmarked taxes, compulsory loans, and general government funds. It is no wonder that at the end of the period the State owned 22 of the top 25 and 44 of the top 100 largest corporations in the country[17] and controlled 74% of combined assets and 63% of the profits of the top 100 corporations. State control also involved 56% of total financial deposits and 65% of the loans to private industries held by the 50 largest financial institutions in the country.[18]

The figures did not change much throughout the military regime. By 1981 the State owned 78% of the capital, 47% of the sales, and 67% of the profits of the top 200 corporations. Some 48% of these corporations' workforce was employed by the government. State banks controlled 70% of all investment loans and 60% of all financial business then. Capital ownership of the largest 6,945 firms were shared in the following proportion: 51% by the State, 38% by domestic capital and 11% by foreign capital.[19]

With the boost from State ownership, the Brazilian economy, especially its manufacturing sector, grew steadily throughout the military period. In the pre-oil crisis period (between 1970 and 1973) agriculture grew 9% a year, mining 14%, construction 19%, utilities (electricity, gas, water) 20%, transport/commerce 24%, trade and finance 10% and manufacturing 21%. The gross domestic product increased at an average annual rate of 18%. After the first oil crisis (between 1973 and 1980) the economy experienced lower rates-- agriculture grew 6% a year, mining 6%, construction 10%, utilities (electricity, gas, water) 15%, transport/commerce 12%, trade and finance 7% and manufacturing 8%. The GDP annual growth rate fell to 9%.[20]

Brazil's integration into the modern world market, then, is divided into two periods: a period of initial growth under the military regime, and its eventual decline after the first oil crisis. During the initial period the Brazilian growth rate in manufactured exports outpaced the growth rates for the world and comparable developing countries. Between 1970 and 1973 Brazil had a nominal annual export growth rate of 27% compared to 20% for the world, 23% for developing economies, 18% for LAFTA (Latin American Free Trade Association), and 26% for Asian nations. After the first oil crisis, in the 1973-80

period, the Brazilian manufactured exports growth rate lost ground--
17% for the period compared to 18% for the world, 23% for
developing economies, 18% for LAFTA, and 22% for Asian nations.[21]

The Unraveling of the Miracle

The military's economic miracle came at a heavy political and social
cost. Politically, the miracle demanded a repressive apparatus that
eventually drained the regime of all legitimacy. Socially, it meant the
further escalation of an inequitable distribution of resources that led to
the 1980s social unrest.

The political repression started in the Presidency of general
Humberto Castelo Branco (1964-67), peaked during the Presidencies of
the generals Artur da Costa e Silva (1967-69) and Emílio Garrastazu
Medici (1969-74), and phased out during the Presidencies of the
generals Ernesto Geisel (1974-79) and João Figueiredo (1979-84) when
the military regime transitioned into civilian rule.

Less than two weeks after taking power the military issued an
Institutional Act (April 9, 1964) to amend the Constitution and give the
military president powers to decree state of siege, to rule by executive
orders and to suspend any citizen from political office, canceling
his/her political rights for 10 years. The first military President made
full use of his powers: he revoked the political rights of two former
presidents, removed 62 Congressmen from office, dismissed 4,500 state
officials, and retired 122 military officers.

Popular organizations (Catholic lay groups, professional associations,
student organizations and peasant leagues) were banned, taken over or
censored. For instance, the national labor confederation (CGT) was
outlawed and the Ministry of Labor took direct control of over 409
unions and 43 federations. Quickly, all forms of political input were
blocked.[22]

On October 27, 1965, after the opposition won five out of eleven
state governorships, the President issued the Second Institutional Act
reorganizing the existing plural party-system into a two-party model,
decreeing indirect presidential elections, and giving the president
additional powers to intervene in the administration of the 22 states.
The IA-3 soon followed (February 1966) establishing indirect elections
for state governors and direct appointment for mayoral offices.[23]

On December 31, 1968, after a year of heavy civilian unrest, the regime issued its harshest Institutional Act. The IA-5 gave the military Presidency full dictatorial powers--powers to shut down Congress, state General Assemblies and City Councils; to further intervene in the management of states and cities; and to revoke the political rights of any citizen without consulting Congress. The repression escalated--33 Congressmen lost office and political rights then and 37 went through similar process a month later. By February even state assemblies were in recess. On February 26 the regime issued the IA-7 canceling all elections. The cycle of political repression was complete.[24]

Despite the repression, it became increasingly hard for the military to control the population because of the social costs of the economic boom. Workers' wages fell 15 to 30% in 1968 alone. Between 1973 and 1977 they fell another 34%. College-educated workers who earned four times more than minimum-wage workers and 10 times more than unskilled workers in 1960 earned respectively nine times and 15 times more in 1970. By 1980 the ratio between the average income of the top decile of the economically active population (Cr$ 57,183) and the lowest decile (Cr$ 1,404) was almost 41 to 1.[25]

Brazil reached one of the highest economic growth rates in the world in 1970 as ECLA listed the country as the third worse in Latin America in terms of absolute poverty--Honduras had 65% of families living below the poverty line, Peru had 50%, Brazil had 49%.[26] The country became the world's third largest agricultural exporter, while a population of 131 million Brazilians lived on the threshold of malnutrition.[27] If the share of the national income for the lower 40% of the population decreased from 11% to 9% between 1960 and 1970, the top 5% of the population had its share increased from 27% to 36%.[28]

To contain unrest the regime used armed forces against popular demonstrations and workers' mobilizations. Civilian demonstrations continued throughout the 1960s in all major Brazilian cities, but phased out after the IA-5 when the military repression reached its peak. During the period the regime arrested, tortured, and tried 7,367 Brazilians for "subversive" activities (ranging from belonging to an underground organization to being a playwright, or a journalist, or a college professor). To those numbers were added other 10,034 individuals investigated by the security police, 6,385 of whom went through preliminary interrogation and trial.[29]

To the domestic pressure of the early 1970s was added the international challenges. The price of oil quadrupled in 1973 bringing the military model of oil-based industrial development to a halt. The government had to borrow heavily to continue financing its major investments *and* meet the fuel bill. Rather than slowing down the economy, the regime opted for further growth combining promotion of nontraditional exports with a new phase of import substitution in capital goods and basic inputs.[30]

The strategy worked for a while because during the early 1970s international financial markets were quite open (petrodollars were easily available at rather low rates). The country managed the balance of payments, kept manufactured exports heavily subsidized, and maintained the real exchange rate relatively stable at the cost of heavy borrowing. The results were still positive--some industries (steel, chemicals) achieved international competitiveness and the country maintained its growth pattern but at lower and artificial rates.[31]

Eventually, the escalating oil prices led to the 1979 shock, when the whole system began to unravel. Then, Brazil was borrowing foreign capital simply to keep up with debt payments. The foreign debt rose from US$ 5.5 million in 1970 to US$ 22.2 million in 1975 to US$ 60.8 million in 1980. Further heavy borrowing added to the principal, spiraling the debt to US$ 103.1 million by 1985. While in 1970 Brazil used 9% of its exports in 1970 to pay net interest on the debt, that number grew to 17% in 1975, to 31% in 1980, and 38% in 1985.[32]

Internally, foreign debt pressure translated into further wage loss and higher inflationary measures. The Brazilian inflation rate grew from 19% in 1970 to 29% in 1975 to 110% in 1980 to 235% in 1985. By 1989 Brazil reached hyperinflation with an annual rate of 1,783%.[33]

With wage compression, the pressure for political participation grew. Between 1973 and 1974 there were 34 major strikes in the most developed industrial sectors (automobile production, electronics, chemicals, construction, utilities, and consumer goods). In 1978 alone 300 companies were affected by strikes that lasted up to 10 months and involved 539,000 workers (in industries such as steel production, textiles, oil, banking, and maritime facilities). In 1979, 180,000 metalworkers went into national strike. When the armed forces intervened other unions joined in and raised the number of striking workers to three million. The 1979 general strike broke the animus of the military, restoring the workers' power to limited collective bargain and higher wage adjustments.[34]

With an economic model plagued by hyperinflation and negative growth and a regime that lacked political support, the military slowly began the transition to civilian rule. The "abertura" process (the opening to democratic rule) started with President Geisel, who eased censorship of printed and electronic media and reinstated elections for November of 1974. Brazilians flooded the polls. With an 80% voting turnout they gave the opposition 16 of 22 seats in the Senate and 86 of 160 seats in the House (44% of its members). By the end of Geisel's presidency the military was losing ground even with their closest allies--the business community--when international loans dried up and economic hardship increased. On the way out of office Geisel revoked IA-5.

General Figueiredo's was the last military presidency. Political liberalization was rampant--the National Student Union was reorganized along with two national labor confederations; there was the 1979 amnesty for more than 7,000 political exiles, the end of censorship, and the end of the two-party system. The November 1982 elections replaced 22 governors, 25 Senators, 479 House deputies, 3,840 mayors, and 50,920 councilmen. 59 million Brazilians turned out--30 million of whom had never voted before--to give the opposition the 10 most important state governorships, a majority in the House and a minority of the Senate. The military cycle was coming to a close.[35]

The Political Economy of the New Republic

The transition to civilian rule, as planned by the military, was slow (1974-1984) and smooth. The pro-military party (PDS--Social Democratic Party), which commanded a majority in the House until 1982 (and a plurality until 1985) and in the Senate until 1985 was the centerpiece of the military transition.[36] After the November 1982 elections, the next step was the November 1985 presidential election. The military hoped to control the process but economic problems derailed their plan. The foreign debt that had been evenly shared in the mid-1970s (50% private and 50% public) had now become 90% public. To maintain its course the government even had to borrow heavily domestically.

The regime adopted a last-minute strong stabilization program (between 1981 and 1983) to reduce the budget deficit, but the high interest rates paid by the State and the increase in both foreign and domestic debt defeated the effort. By 1983, the devaluation of local currency led to a 15% drop in real wages during a three-year period, and unemployment rates led to food riots in major cities. That was followed by a perverse wage-price spiral that kept the annual inflation rate at 200%.[37]

By then, significant political allies began to leave the military camp. In January of 1984 the opposition launched a national campaign for direct presidential election ("Diretas Já"). In April, representatives of the PDS barely defeated an amendment in Congress to hold it that year. Tancredo Neves, governor of Minas Gerais and a politician who predated the military regime, renewed efforts to round up PDS defections. He offered PDS members the opportunity to form a broad national front to rebuild the civilian government into a "New Republic." By June, key PDS leaders left the party to join Neves' newly formed PFL (Party of the Liberal Front).

With their support, Neves was elected president by an overwhelming margin on January 15, 1985. However, Neves took ill the day before his inauguration and died later, leaving his Vice-President--José Sarney at the helm of the State. Sarney was a former pro-military politician. With him in power the transition simply stayed the course planned by the military. Sarney filled his government with pro-military officials. His February 1986 cabinet had eight former PDS members (six of whom had been governors during the military regime) and six active-duty military officers. He also filled a significant number of high-ranking positions and thousands of second and third level positions in State companies, federal government agencies and State governing organs with pro-military loyalists.[38]

To shore up the economy Sarney introduced two economic packages during his presidency--the Cruzado plan and the Summer plan. The plans drastically re-structured the local currency, indexed prices and wages, and reorganized some of the government's debt. To invite further foreign capital, Sarney approached the International Monetary Fund (IMF), using his plans as the basis for renewed help.

By early 1984, with the IMF's help and the renegotiation of the foreign debt, the economy showed some signs of recovery. In 1985 the gross national product grew 8.3% and the country produced an export surplus of US$ 12.8 billion (the third largest in the world).

Nevertheless, the inflation rate remained high (235%) and the overvalued Cruzado currency created by Sarney led industrial production to shift from the export to the domestic market. By the end of 1986, the trade surplus had shrunk from an average US$ 1 billion a month in 1985 to US$ 100 million. Again, Brazil would lose an important opportunity to carve its niche in First World markets.[39]

The problem with Sarney's Cruzado plan was that its wage and price freeze to fight inflation would only work if the government had cut its own spending, while keeping interest rates high. Instead, Sarney kept government spending at the level and lowered interest rates arguing that in real terms the rates were high because inflation would fall. Faced with greater government spending and low interest rates, Brazilians responded to the uncertainty of further inflation by cashing their savings and spending them.[40]

To counter the problem, Sarney issued the Summer Plan, setting real interest rates high. As interest rates climbed, the cashing in decreased but the government had to spend more to service its domestic debt. Debt payment took 10% of the Brazilian's treasury spending in 1987, two-fifths in 1989, and three-fifths in the first two months of 1990. The government was caught between setting interest rates low enough to balance its budget and high enough to keep the public from cashing its savings.[41]

As President Collor took office on March 15, 1990 Brazil was still fighting the recession. Inflation had reached hyper levels--81% for the month of March, 1,795% for the year,[42] the deficit in the public sector had risen from 4% of the GNP in 1985 to 12% in 1989,[43] and the military model was still unraveling. The 1980s return to civilian rule did not change the country's import-substitution growth strategy. Development continued to be equated with a heavily state-owned, capital-intensive economy, sustained by high trade protectionism.

That is why Collor's Presidency is so important for Brazil. It signaled the first effort to replace a protectionist, subsidized import-substitution strategy with one of technological upgrading, increased export productivity, and strong competitiveness in First World markets.[44] It is Collor who let go of an 90-year old import-substitution strategy.

As the first freely elected civilian to take presidential office in 30 years, Collor carried with him the renewed hopes of the Brazilian people. Holding degrees in Economics and Journalism, he came to office with impressive credentials and a meteoric political career--

mayor of his state's capital city at the age of 28, he followed that up with a term as a Brazilian congressman and as governor of his home state.

As state governor he acquired a reputation for running a modern and professional political system. While in office he fired powerful civil servants for abusing the system by holding multiple offices; abolished retirement benefits for former governors and officials with short term government careers; refused the political perks of his office (house, paid expenses, etc.); closed state organs that duplicated services; cut in half government officials' spending with trips, public cars, and per diem; and created an array of social services--literacy programs, a unified health care system for the entire state, a fair criterion for allocation of public housing, and a fee-free public school system.[45]

He ran his presidential campaign on a platform of political accountability, economic reform and insertion into the modern world. He wished to clean the national government from corruption, welcomed foreign and private domestic capital over State ownership as the means to promote national economic growth, favored the creation of stable economic guidelines to give the business class the means to make rational investments, and asserted science and technology in higher education as the way to Brazil's greatness in the world markets.[46]

In the social arena, Collor's platform favored: the establishment of agricultural cooperatives to strengthen the small farmer, the shoring up of urban workers' wages, the pegging of economic growth to sound ecological practices, the deepest and broadest overhaul of the national health care system, and the end of discrimination toward all minority groups in Brazil.[47]

Running on a newly created political party (PRN--Party of National Reconstruction), Collor bypassed the old party establishment and all other intermediaries (business groups, unions, civic organizations) to reach the masses (the "descamisados") with a moralizing campaign based on domestic prosperity, economic privatization, and free trade with the First World.[48]

The new president began to deliver on his promises the day after inauguration. He launched an economic plan that included a drastic monetary reform, the blockage of some 70% of the private sector's financial assets, a fiscal adjustment, income policies based on a new price freeze, and a floating exchange rate. To pursue his medium term policies--the liberalization of foreign trade and the privatization of State companies--Collor abolished an old import ban on more than 1,000 sorts of imports and in the first week in office closed 11 of Brazil's 24 ministries, as well as 13 other state organs, selling off all nonministerial government cars and 10,000 government apartments.[49] The plan brought mixed results. Politically, it gave Collor public support but at the cost of enmity with Brazil's clientelist party establishment. Rather than negotiating his economic reforms with Congress, Collor chose (much like the military presidents before him) to conduct the country's business through Presidential decrees. In doing so, he lost his first chance to change the military-inherited unequal relationship between the Executive and the Legislative powers in Brazil.

His first plan was implemented without giving all the interested parties (business class, labor unions, civic organizations, political parties) the chance to have any input. In that sense, while reforming the military economic model, Collor left its political way of doing business--interventionist and authoritarian--untouched.[50] Even the business community greeted the plan as debilitating and unconstitutional.[51]

Economically, his policies seemed to turn the tide for a while. The inflation rate fell from 81% in March to 11% in April to 9% in May. With a large portion of the domestic debt frozen together with private financial assets, Collor managed to cut domestic debt by half in real terms.[52] Furthermore, the plan brought in new taxes (especially a capital gains tax on equity, bonds, foreign currency holdings and gold deposits), cut off tax loopholes, and capitalized the government by allowing individuals and companies to use some of their frozen financial assets to pay taxes, debts and fines to the federal, state, and city governments.[53]

But the blockage of financial assets disorganized industrial production and led to a gross domestic product growth of -2.4% for the first quarter of the year. São Paulo's factories output dropped 17% in April 1990, while economic activity in Brazil fell 24% during the same month and 300,000 factory workers were put on paid leave.[54] Between January and August of 1990 real wages fell drastically in all major Brazilian cities (from 2.16 to 1.54 in Recife, 2.85 to 1.97 in Salvador, 2.94 to 2.19 in Belo Horizonte, 3.26 to 2.27 in Rio de Janeiro, 4.21 to 3.15 in São Paulo and 3.56 to 2.62 in Porto Alegre). Unemployment rose from 7% in December 1989 to 11% in April to 12% in June and 10% in September of 1990.[55]

When the first plan did not bring all the expected results, Collor issued the second (January 31, 1991) de-indexing the formal economy, freezing wages and prices, and creating a new instrument for the monthly adjustment of interest rates (taxa referencial de juros). He also kept pushing for the privatization of State companies. By the time he resigned from office, the country's privatization program had held its 18th auction, with the sale of the Acesita steel mill (a company with 13,600 workers that produced 650,000 tons of steel annually for more than 50 countries). Acesita's sale alone brought in US$ 451 million to the country's coffers.[56]

Throughout his three years in office the President kept an agenda of conservative modernization. His efforts did not indicate an interest in changing the basic property or power relations in the country; but showed instead his desire to redistribute power from the old to a modern elite through administrative reform, deregulation and debureaucratization. For instance, by the end of his first year Collor eliminated 107,000 State employee positions including some 32,000 filled by political appointment. He also re-opened the Brazilian market and economy to foreign capital breaking the military protectionist scheme.[57]

The key problem in Collor's presidency was his inability to sustain Neves' broad coalition as the base of his political power. Throughout his term in office he alienated more political allies than he could afford. His support in the elections had come from less developed areas of the country, the rural and small-town Brazil while his policies affected deeply those in major cities and the industrialized South and Southeast. Coming from a small, less developed state in the Northeast he also lacked Neves' important territorial power base.[58]

Collor's reluctance to build congressional loyalty also cost him in the long run. With a less than two year old party, he had to rely on the support of the old party establishment to get things through Congress. He did very little to gain that support. For instance, to eliminate 107,000 State positions he ordered all government agencies to cut 30% of personnel. The decision affected the best and the worst agencies, which cost in terms of loyalty to the President. When he eliminated some 32,000 political jobs he cut off the conservative, clientelist party establishment's means to distribute political favors. With an authoritarian style, impatience with Congress and distaste for political parties Collor made it hard on others to work with him. As he ignored the Legislative, Congress became more assertive to defend its constitutional gains.[59]

Despite all political problems, the economy under Collor slowly began to respond to the new guidelines. Exports to Argentina in June 1992 finally boosted Brazil's trade surplus up 66% from a year earlier. The surplus was the biggest since the President took office. June exports totaled US$ 3.3 billion (15% higher than the previous year) against US$ 1.6 billion of imports (12% lower than the year before). The accumulated trade surplus for the first six months reached a high of US$ 7.5 billion, 5% higher than the figure for the same period in the previous year.[60]

While Argentina was Brazil's second largest importer, the reach for First World markets was clear--Brazil's number one importer during the period was the United States (US$ 3.4 billion between January and June), followed by the European Community (US$ 1.1 billion) in third place. Exports of manufactured goods rose 32% during the period giving Brazil the third largest trade surplus in the world, behind Japan and Germany.[61]   From all the evidence, the country seemed to be finally moving toward a competitive, high tech, private-led economy, fully integrated in First World markets.

Brazil's First Impeachment Process

Unfortunately, Collor's public agenda had a parallel personal agenda based on graft and corruption, a darker by-product of his own policies. Taking advantage of the President's efforts to privatize State companies, Collor's campaign treasurer (Paulo Cesar Farias) used front companies, rigged accounts, and government money to build a personal empire--bribing in the process key officials in the Brazilian government, all appointed by the President himself. According to the Brazilian Internal Revenue Service, Farias' assets increased 70 times since Collor assumed the Presidency, jumping from US$ 72,500 to US$ 5 million. Using the President's influence Farias set up a complex web of illegal transactions that handled nearly one million dollars a day for the period of 1990 and 1991. Among other things, he used the money to pay for the President's household bills, expenses and investments. Altogether, the Collor family received US$ 230 million.[62]

Farias' bribing extended beyond the President's household to reach key officials in Federal Ministries. Through them, he obtained illegal financing and highly marked up contracts for his companies. He also profited from the President's privatization of State companies, using government money to bid on their acquisition.

The trail of corruption extends over at least six ministries and two State organs. At the Ministry of Infra-Structure he was involved in at least three scandals--the SOS Highways, the Petrobras (the Brazilian oil corporation) and in his aid in the acquisition of VASP (the São Paulo State Airline). At the Ministry of Education he sold marked up meals for the public school system at a cost of US$ 1.5 billion a year. At the Ministry of Health, his brother (appointed by Collor as the Executive Director) managed purchases that left the ministry US$ 4 million in red. At the Ministry of Social Welfare (Ação Social), Farias had rigged utilities and housing projects worth US$ 5 billion a year. At the Ministry of Labor, he "invested" US$ 2.3 billion from the general pension fund money and reached control over the pension funds of the State companies' employees.[63]

When unable to take over, Farias would use ministries as extensions of his own personal power. Through the Ministry of the Economy he obtained access to State companies being privatized and the support of the country's highest financial institutions (the Caixa Economica Federal and the Bank of Brazil). At the Ministry of Agriculture Farias obtained access to development funds (such as a subsidy of US$ 1 billion a year for sugar-cane growers in the Northeast).[64]

When the depth and breadth of the corruption became known, Congress suspended the President from office, and eventually initiated an impeachment process. In the last week of 1992, to avoid the impeachment, the President resigned in disgrace. The resignation left a legacy of malfeasance that further eroded the confidence of the Brazilian public in the government. It also affected the level of trust of the business community, sending shockwaves through the country's stock exchange market.

Following Constitutional provisions, Collor was replaced by his Vice-President, Itamar Franco. Mr. Franco, like Mr. Neves--a politician from Minas Gerais who predates the military regime, has two years to rebuild the administration. Although he has a reputation for honesty and hard work, his vision of economic development is entirely different from Collor's.

As a member of the opposition party he had rallied against the military regime and was deeply involved in the efforts to bring direct presidential elections. But unlike Collor, Mr. Franco has strong nationalistic views and a distaste for free trade with First World markets. As a member of the Assembly to reform the Constitution in 1986 he was opposed to concessions to foreign business and criticized President Sarney for approaching the IMF. He does not believe in exporting at all costs either--in the assembly he sought to impose controls on arms and nuclear exports.[65]

What happens to Brazil next? Some of the early steps of the Franco Presidency indicate that he is committed to a different kind of economic development. Although keeping the former President's schedule of privatization of State companies, for instance, his economic team seem guided by another vision. The first company he privatized (the Goiasfertil) had its controlling interest acquired in the Rio de Janeiro stock exchange.[66]

On the political side, Franco has tried to recreate Neves' broad coalition. His eclectic cabinet has four members of the former opposition party (PMDB--Party of the Brazilian Democratic Movement), four from the former pro-military party, three from Neves' PFL, two from the PSB (the Brazilian Socialist Party), and two (one each) from the two labor parties (PDT--Labor Democratic Party and PT--Labor Party).[67] The political issue for the next two years will be how to outline new guidelines for the country's needs in broad enough strokes to satisfy all parties involved. How long the coalition will last remains to be seen.

On the economic side, Franco dealt with the crisis by proposing a new package of reforms. On the fiscal front, he has introduced three new taxes to raise US$ 15 billion for the cash-strapped government, allowing State companies to declare bankruptcies and forbidding states and cities to issue new bonds until 1999. On the financial front, he has reformulated the banking system, giving the Central Bank greater autonomy over the local currency. On the labor front, he wants to direct bargaining between employers and employees while at the same time the strengthening of the wage power of the workforce's poorer segments. Finally, at the structural level, he is expected to continue Collor's deregulation of the economy.[68] Whether the country is ready for another economic shock also remains to be seen.

Political Instability and Economic Progress

The presidential impeachment in Brazil and the hasty efforts by the new president to keep the Brazilian economy afloat seems to send a clear message to other Latin American countries. It says that economic growth based on political instability (whether of the authoritarian or corrupt kind) does not lend itself to lasting effects. Although other impeachments are not foreseen for Latin American countries, the notion that economic growth has to be sustained by a broad, accountable and inclusive political base has become clearer.

In Venezuela, for instance, President Carlos Andréz Pérez is still dealing with the aftermath of a failed military coup that was staged to stop government corruption. The social unrest ranges from housewives banging pots and pans in the streets of main cities to armed vigilante groups. The "Bolivarian Forces of Liberation" shot labor leader Antonio Ríos, sent a grenade through the home of former President Jaime Lusinchi (charged with allowing massive fraud during his 1984-89 administration), and have a list of 127 alleged Venezuelan leaders to hunt next.[69]

In Peru, under popular pressure, President Alberto Fujimori reopened the court case against former President Alan García for allegedly embezzling public funds. The President has even vowed to extradite García from Colombia if he refuses to stand trial. In Mexico, President Carlos Salinas de Gortari launched an anti-corruption campaign that led to the arrest and conviction of Joaquin Hernandez Galicia, the leader of the powerful petroleum workers' union. Recent polls in Mexico list corruption as the third most important issue in the country, behind only the economy and environmental protection.[70]

If Latin American countries wish to be integrated in the new world order they may have to engage in a more thorough overhaul of their development strategies; and their political elites may have to back it up with broader, sounder and more stable political institutions. This is no longer the time for centralized, statist economic models, nor authoritarian regimes. The external pressures from the end-of-the century worldwide changes and the internal pressures from unruly local societies may eventually deliver the message with full force.

If Brazil teaches us anything, it shows that no government can afford to remain irresponsive to *both* changes in the international environment and growing dissatisfaction at home. The military and later the Sarney government paid dearly for holding on to an import-substitution strategy at a time when the world was gearing up for tough competition in First World markets. Since the strategy was doggedly pursued at the exclusion of most sectors of the Brazilian society, when it floundered there was no domestic support. Artificially boosted economic growth had come at the cost of political repression and great social inequality. If the Collor government was responsive to the international environment, it failed to do so domestically. Collor changed the import-substitution strategy to respond to changes in the international environment, but he failed domestically by not sustaining Neves' broad coalition and worse yet, for not being democratically accountable to the Brazilian citizens who put him in power in the first place.

At the threshold of a new century, Latin American development is being pushed by internal and external conditions to abandon its old colonial Hispanic/Iberian vision of the patrimonial State (be it military or civilian)--the ever-sovereign ruler, granting favors to its closest loyal followers at the expense of the larger society. To become fully part of a new world order, Latin American countries need to adopt a more *entrepreneurial* and *democratic* vision of the State. Entrepreneurial, because the State is quite aware of its interconnectedness with the modern world, because it responds to the competitiveness and the demands of world markets. Democratic, because the State's authority must stem from a broader, legitimate and popular base of support; and be accountable to its citizens--both in responding to their most pressing needs and in sustaining a clean house. That is the challenge for the Latin American continent in the post Cold-War era, when it seeks to become fully integrated in a new world order.

Notes

1. I am grateful to Marshall Eakin for extremely helpful comments on an earlier draft of this paper.
2. Paus, "The Political Economy of Manufacture Export Growth: Argentina and Brazil in the 1970s," *The Journal of Developing Areas* 23 (1989): 173-200.
3. Morley, *Labor Markets and Inequitable Growth* (Cambridge: Cambridge University Press, 1982).
4. Serra (1983).
5. Costa (1981, 146).

6. Knight, "Brazilian Socioeconomic Development: Issues for the Eighties," *World Development* 9 (1981): 1063-1082.

7. See Brazilian labor Information (1984); Hagopian and Mainwaring, "Democracy in Brazil," *World Policy Journal* 4 (1987): 485-514; Schneider, Brazil Under Collor: Anatomy of a Crisis," *World Policy Journal* 8 (1991): 321-347; Serra (1983).

8. Evans, *Dependent Development* (Princeton: Princeton University Press, 1979); Fox, "Has Brazil Moved Toward State Capitalism?" *Latin American Perspectives* 24 (1980): 64-88.

9. Chandler, *Strategy and Structure* (Cambridge: MIT Press, 1962).

10. W. Dean, *The Industrialization of São Paulo 1880-1945* (Austin: University of Texas Press, 1966); Frank, *Capitalism and Underdevelopment in Latin America* (Hamondsworth: Penguin, 1971); and Miller, "Latin American Manufacturing and the First World War," *World Development* 9 (1981): 12-25.

11. Bergsman, *Brazil: Industrialization and Trade Policies* (London: Oxford University Press, 1970); Morley (1982); Suzigan, "Industrialization and Economic Policy in Historical Perspective," *Brazilian Economic Studies* (Monograph Series) 2 (1976).

12. Flynn, *Brazil: A Political Analysis* (Boulder: Westview Press, 1979); Syvrud, *Foundations of Brazilian Economic Growth* (Stanford: Hoover Institute, 1974).

13. Bacha, "Issues and Evidence on Recent Brazilian Economic Growth," *World Development* 5 (1977): 58.

14. Morley and Smith, "Import Substitution and Foreign Investment in Brazil," *Oxford Economic Papers* 23 (1971): 120-136.

15. Baer (1976).

16. Diniz and Boschi (1989).

17. Fox (1980).

18. Bacha (1980); Suzigan et al. (1974).

19. Wesson and Fleischer, *Brazil in Transition* (New York: Praeger, 1983).

20. World Bank, *World Tables* (Washington D.C, 1984).

21. Paus (1989).

22. Erikson, *The Brazilian Corporate State and Working Class Politics* (Berkeley: University of California Press, 1977); Pang, "Brazil's New Democracy," *Current History* 82 (1983): 54-89; Roett, *Brazil: Politics in a Patrimonial Society* (New York: Praeger, 1984); Wesson and Fleischer (1983).

23. Flynn (1979); Roett (1984); Wesson and Fleischer (1983).

24. Ibid:

25. Denslow and Tyler, *Perspectives on Poverty and Income Inequality in Brazil* (Washington DC: World Bank, 1983); Morel, *Lula, O Metalúrgico* (Rio de Janeiro: Nova Fronteira, 1981); Morley (1982).

26. Baer (1976); Erikson (1977).

27. *The New York Times*, "Brazil's Bishops and Priests Hold a Fast on Plight of the Poor," (12 October, 1984)

28. Baer (1976).

29. *Brasil Nunca Mais* (1985): 85-88.

30. Paus (1989).

31. Evans (1979); Paus (1989).

32. Hagopian and Mainwaring (1987).

33. Pereira and Nakano (1991).

34. Brazilian Labor Information (1984); Dunkerley, *Unity is Strength: Trade Unions in Latin America* (London: Latin American Bureau, 1983); Morel (1981).

35. Wesson and Fleischer (1982).

36. Hagopian and Mainwaring (1987).

37. Ibid; Pereira and Nakano (1991).

38. Hagopian and Mainwaring (1987).

39. Ibid; Pereira and Nakano (1991).

40. *The Economist*, "The Right Stuff," 9 June (1990): 75-77.

41. Ibid.

42. Pereira and Nakano (1991).

43. *The Economist*, "The Right Stuff," 9 June (1990): 75-77.

44. *The Brasilians*, "The Brazilian Privatization Program," August (1992): 16.

45. Claret, *O Fenomeno Collor* (São Paulo: Martin Claret Editores, 1989).

46. Ibid.

47. Ibid.

48. Pereira and Nakano (1991); Schneider (1991).

49. *The Economist*, "The Right Stuff," 9 June (1990); Pereira, "Collor, Zélia, Marcílio e os Planos Econômicos," *The Brasilians*, October (1992, 18); Pereira and Nakano (1991); Schneider (1991, 1992).

50. Diniz and Boschi (1989); Schneider (1992); Vianna, *De Um Plano Collor a Outro* (Rio de Janeiro: Editora Revan, 1991).

51. Crabtree, "The Collor Plan: Shooting the Tiger?" *Bulletin of Latin American Research* 10 (1991): 119-132.

52. Pereira and Nakano (1991).

53. Crabtree (1991).

54. *The Economist*, "Sleight of Hand," 21 April (1990): 46-47.

55. Crabtree (1991).

56. *The Brasilians*, "State Steel Mill Sold," November (1992): 4.

57. Schneider (1991).

58. Crabtree (1991); Schneider (1992).

59. Schneider (1991).

60. *The Brasilians*, "Brazil's Trade Surplus Rises to $1.62 billion," August (1992): 7.

61. Ibid.

62. *The Brasilians*, "Corruption and Scandals Plus Illegal Transactions," August (1992): 7; *The Brasilians*, "German Experts Say Brazil Needs to Modernize State," September (1992): 4; *Veja*, "O Ministerio do Itamar," 14 October (1992): 32.

63. *Veja*, "Trama Ligadíssima," 29 July (1992): 20-26.

64. Ibid.

65. *The Brasilians*, "Focus: Hopes and Challenges: New Brazilian President," October (1992): 4.

66. *The Brasilians*, "Privatization Continues," October (1992): 1.

67. *Veja*, 14 October (1992): 32.

68. *Isto É*, "Bússola Calibrada," 3 December (1992): 16-20.

69. *The Brasilians*, "Collor Impeachment: A Light at the End of the Tunnel for Latin America?" October (1992): 2.

70. Ibid.

6

Economic Restructuring and Change in Urban Specialization in Mexico*

Fernando Pozos Ponce

Many previous studies on the relationship between global economic restructuring and urban specialization have generally focused on the core cities.[1] However, few have studied cities of the semi-periphery and periphery. This chapter identifies the major effects of economic restructuring on the cities of Latin American countries. Specifically, this study examines the effects of Mexico's economic restructuring on the urban economies of Guadalajara and Monterrey and, in particular, their urban specialization.

---

* A portion of this chapter has been previously published in Spanish under the title "Reestructuración económica y cambios en la especialización urbana: los casos de Guadalajara y Monterrey (1980-1988)" in *Anuario de Estudios Urbanos* No 1, 1994 (Mexico). The permission to reprint has been obtained from the Editor.

Data for the study are obtained from the *Industrial, Commerce and Service Census* for 1975 and 1980 as well as the *Resultados Oportunos de los Censos Económicos* for 1986 and 1989.

Urban Specialization

According to human ecology theory urban specialization is a natural outcome of the process of competition and interdependence among cities or regions linked by a web of communication and transportation routes.[2] Additionally, urban specialization is explained as a relationship of domination between cities that develop the metropolitan function in a region and those that are subordinated to the former.[3] Subsequently, the city with the metropolitan function exerts control and coordination through its higher order administrative and distributive activities over the productive activities of other cities in the region. In this approach, cities become instruments through which specialized regions are integrated and articulated in a wider national economy.[4] However, this approach does not consider ties between the national and global economies and their implications for urban specialization. This is significant because nations are interdependent and they engage in permanent economic and political relations with each other that often are asymmetric.

In seeking to overcome this limitation, the world-system approach explains urban specialization as a function of the global mode of capital accumulation, one which involves cities to different degrees of intensity according to their population size, geographical location, urban infrastructure and type of economic activity.[5] There are different types of cities: world or global and national or regional. This categorization of cities is based on their relationship with other nations, regions and cities in the capitalist world system.[6] The urban specialization of cities is explained within the whole process of capital accumulation, where structural factors, such as the three circuits of capital, the international division of labor, and spatial organization are emphasized. Additionally, national and local factors are incorporated in this approach, because core cities, as well as cities of the semi-periphery and periphery, specialize in different economic activities. Thus, global, national and local factors influence the cities' urban specialization.[7]

Specialization occurs when a productive activity is concentrated in an urban area.[8] This urban specialization is related to the three spheres of capital accumulation: 1) the transformation of money into capital, 2) the circulation of merchandise, and 3) the production of commodities.[9] There are cities which become principal financial and service centers such as New York, or main distribution centers such as Dallas, or key manufacturing centers such as Detroit.[10]

In non-core countries there are a few large urban centers and a greater number of smaller cities subordinated to the large urban centers.[11] The smaller cities transfer local material resources and labor force through migration flows to the largest metropolitan centers. In turn, these resources are transferred to foreign urban centers through trade and financial transactions.[12] These large metropolises are heterogeneous in terms of urban specialization as they develop in different national urban systems. To a great extent, the direction of the urban specialization depends on the kind of regional, national and international markets that these cities cater to.[13] In Latin America, there are cities that have developed an industrial specialization and have followed a model of economic development based on the national and international markets, such as São Paulo and Monterrey. There are other cities, such as Guadalajara, that have developed an industrial specialization based on the regional and national markets.

In a study of 140 largest U.S. SMSAs in 1976, Stanback and Noyelle[14] have found that economic restructuring generates two fundamental forces. On the one hand, the largest cities (more than 2 million inhabitants) tend to specialize as producers and exporters of producer and distributive services while declining as manufacturing centers. On the other hand, smaller SMSAs (less than one million inhabitants) tend to intensify their specialization as producers of manufactured goods. Services are also important in smaller cities, reflective of a general trend for this sector to increase its importance in the economy as a whole.

Others have noted that the largest SMSAs tend to show a disproportionate concentration of producer and distributive services, an above average concentration of retailing and social services, and a below average concentration of manufacturing and government.[15] Furthermore, a correlation between size and type of service exported has been noted.[16] In other words, the larger the SMSA the greater the weight of producer services when compared with distributive services.

Manufacturing and distributive, producer, social and personal services are highly relevant in shaping the urban specialization of a city. Many previous studies have considered manufacturing sector as homogeneous.[17] However, I believe that it should be considered heterogeneous given the types of goods produced, the technology requirements for the production process, and the proportion and level of skill of the labor force employed. Therefore, I disaggregate manufacturing into three subsectors, according to the type of goods produced: 1) basic goods, 2) intermediate goods, and 3) capital and durable goods.[18] Furthermore, because of the heterogeneity in the service sector I disaggregate it into distributive services, producer services, and social and personal services.[19] In analyzing the effects of economic restructuring in these urban economies I use the following indicators: employment, value added, number of establishments and level of productivity.[20] In the service sector I do not use level of productivity because of the measurement difficulties.

To identify the economic performance of the manufacturing and services subsectors I classify them in the following three categories: expanding, moderate growth, and stagnant. Expanding subsectors are those that have a positive average annual growth rate in three indicators, such as employment, value added, and number of establishments. Moderate growth subsectors have only a positive average annual growth rate in two of these indicators. Finally, stagnant subsectors are those that experience a positive average annual growth rate in one or none of the three indicators.

Economic Restructuring in Mexico

Economic restructuring in the Mexican economy is part of the restructuring of the world economy, a process which has brought about basic changes in the mode of capital accumulation. A new international division of labor has emerged in which countries of the semi-periphery and periphery have become not only exporters of raw materials and mineral goods, but also outlets for foreign industrial investment and markets for foreign merchandise.[21]

In Mexico, the general outcome of economic restructuring has been a switch from an import-substitution model of development to export-oriented industrialization. The role played by the internal market, state intervention in the economy, and local entrepreneurs in economic development has declined. Instead, direct foreign investment and international markets are considered critical to promoting economic growth.

For the purposes of analysis, I divide the period of economic restructuring into the following two sub-periods: 1) Mexico's economic crisis (1980-1985); and 2) the "opening" of the Mexican economy (1985-present).[22]

The economic crisis unfolded when the deficit in the balance of payments and high inflation rates could not be overcome as revenues from oil exports and external loans supporting the economic prosperity of the second half of the 1970s began to collapse. International oil prices started to decline in 1981; in 1982, oil represented approximately 77.6 percent of the total exports of goods and services.[23] Additionally, there was a reduction in foreign loans and an increase in interest rates as core countries themselves became outlets for capital investment after several years of recession.[24] In order to overcome this economic crisis, the Mexican government applied "stabilization and adjustment" policies.[25] Recession along with devaluation of the peso, reduction in real wages, high inflation rates, and lack of foreign exchange were the most important economic events during this period.

The "opening" began in 1986 when unfavorable conditions led the Mexican government to modify the model of economic development. The "structural change" policies emphasized economic growth based on participation in the international market and on stimulation of direct foreign investment.[26] Under this policy, the import barriers for manufactured goods and direct foreign investment were reduced substantially and Mexico became a member of the GATT.[27] Inflation was controlled and reduced through the *Pacto de Solidaridad Económica*, a trilateral agreement between the Mexican government, private entrepreneurs, and organized labor. Mexico gradually gained the confidence of the international business community, attracted foreign capital, and rescheduled its external debt, all of which stimulated national economic growth. By 1990, the changes in the economic structure were sufficient to identify export-oriented industrialization as the official development strategy.

The Case Studies: Guadalajara and Monterrey

For the period of economic restructuring in Mexico, it is important to compare Guadalajara with Monterrey since they are Mexico's second and third largest metropolitan centers (approximately 3 million inhabitants each).[28] Guadalajara and Monterrey became the most important population and manufacturing centers outside of Mexico City during the import-substitution phase (1940-1980), when internal market was the motor of the national economy.[29] Moreover, these two cities developed a different productive structure and based their economic development in different markets. Guadalajara became an administrative, commercial, and services city with a traditional, small and medium-scale manufacturing, all of which encouraged a large informal sector articulated to formal enterprises. This city's manufacturing production as well as its diverse services were oriented toward the local, regional and, to a lesser degree, the national market.[30] In contrast, Monterrey was characterized by its modern, medium and large-scale industrial base whose manufacturing production was oriented primarily toward the national and international markets. A regional market had not been important for Monterrey as most of the city's and region's population had easy access to diverse goods and services in the Texan market between 1940 and 1975.[31]

The nature of capitalist entrepreneurs in each city is also different. Guadalajara's capitalists are very conservative in terms of investment in large-scale and dynamic industries. They are also very heterogeneous. For example, there are 16 industrial chambers in Guadalajara while in Monterrey there is only one. Monterrey's capitalists are a small homogeneous group, aggressive in terms of investing in modern and large manufacturing projects in their own as well as in other Mexican cities, including Guadalajara and Mexico City.[32]

Guadalajara and Monterrey specialized differently during the import-substitution phase, despite the fact that they were similar in population size. Guadalajara developed a dual urban specialization centered on distributive services and basic goods production. In contrast, Monterrey developed a unitary urban specialization in which manufacturing production was concentrated in intermediate goods production. Monterrey specialized in a productive subsector that required a more skilled and formal labor force than the two productive subsectors in which Guadalajara specialized during the import-substitution phase of development.

Finally, both urban areas are located in strategic geographical points to meet the requirements of the new export oriented model of industrialization. Guadalajara's location in the western region is the natural door for trade and capital flows between the Pacific Rim and Mexico. Monterrey is located in the northeast region, where trade and exchange flows between the United States and Mexico are expected to increase because of the NAFTA.

Figure 6.1.
Manufacturing Subsectors by Economic Performance
in Guadalajara

	75-80	80-85	85-88
Expansion	Intermediate Capital/Durable Total Manufacturing	Intermediate	
Moderate Growth	Basic	Basic Capital/Durable Total Manufacturing	
Stagnant			Basic Intermediate Capital/Durable Total Manufacturing

Source: Industrial, Commerce and Service Census, 1980; Resultados Oportunos de los Censos Económicos de 1986 and 1989.

Economic Restructuring and Urban Change

a) Economic Crisis Period (1980-1985) - Guadalajara:

Figure 6.1 depicts manufacturing trends in the Guadalajara region. The manufacturing sector as well as basic, capital and durable goods had a moderate growth during 1980-1985 in contrast to the previous period of 1975-1980. Additionally, all manufacturing subsectors declined in their level of productivity.[33] This is consistent with the process of deindustrialization that Mexico suffered during this period. But this process was not so dramatic in Guadalajara as it was in the Mexican economy as a whole. Figure 6.2 illustrates the trends in the Mexican economy.

Figure 6.2.
Manufacturing Subsectors by Economic Performance
in Mexico

	75-80	80-85	85-88
Expansion	Intermediate Capital/Durable Total Manufacturing		Basic Intermediate Total Manufacturing
Moderate Growth	Basic	Intermediate Capital/Durable Total Manufacturing	Capital/Durable
Stagnant		Basic	

Source: See under Fig 6.1.

Guadalajara's capitalists experienced serious problems during this period, because of the constraints of the internal market, the tightening of credit, and difficult access to foreign industrial inputs. Because of the heterogeneity of this group of entrepreneurs, divided by several industrial chambers and enterprises of a wide range of sizes, they were unable to develop a cohesive strategy to deal with the effects of the economic crisis.[34] They adopted several strategies, one of which was capital investment in real estate in the city. This is a traditional response to economic uncertainty in Guadalajara.[35] As a result, production of intermediate goods such as construction materials and accessories expanded during this period.

Micro and small-scale enterprises were the most affected by the economic crisis, largely due to the lack of easy access to credit and a decline in the local and regional demand for their manufactured goods. Many micro and small-scale enterprises closed and others moved from Guadalajara, looking for better productive conditions elsewhere. For example, 530 out of 921 small-scale enterprises were no longer registered at the end of the 1981-1985 period.[36] Most of these enterprises were concentrated in the basic goods subsector.

In general, Guadalajara's manufacturing sector was not as dramatically affected as Monterrey due to the following factors: First, direct foreign investment continued to arrive in Guadalajara, taking advantage of the devaluation of the peso and of the transformations of the Mexican economy undertaken during this period. Many foreign-owned industries, such as IBM, were established in the "Parque Industrial de El Salto," located on the outskirts of Guadalajara. The number of industries located in this industrial park increased from seven in 1980 to 61 in 1984; it became the most dense industrial area in the state of Jalisco.[37] Second, the traditional nature of Guadalajara's manufacturing sector, mostly devoted to basic goods, did not require a large proportion of foreign investment. Third, there was little horizontal integration within this sector, meaning one branch not depending substantially on other branches for industrial production. And finally, the flexibility of small-scale enterprises and the diversification of the manufacturing sector ameliorated the negative effects of the economic crisis on Guadalajara.[38]

As in manufacturing, the services sector in general, distributive and personal services in particular, also had a modest growth during the economic crisis. Figure 6.3 illustrates that quite well. This is in contrast to the earlier period in which all services subsectors had expanded. Additionally, social services expanded and producer services stagnated. It is likely that the labor force displaced from manufacturing looked, to a large extent, for employment in the service sector. For example, during this period there was a proliferation of "tianguises," street markets selling basic goods that move every day from one neighborhood of the city to another. The prices of these goods vary depending on the income status of the neighborhood. These types of activities supplied employment to a large number of individuals in the distributive services.

Figure 6.3.
Service Subsectors by Economic Performance
in Guadalajara

	75-80	80-85	85-88
Expansion	Distributive Producer Social Personal Total Service	Social	Producer Personal
Moderate Growth		Distributive Personal Total Service	Distributive Social Total Service
Stagnant		Producer	

Source: See Under Fig. 6.1.

Monterrey:

In Monterrey, manufacturing experienced a sharper decline than in Guadalajara as well as in the country as a whole during the economic crisis period. This sector along with the intermediate goods sub-sector stagnated in Monterrey, while in the earlier period all subsectors of manufacturing had experienced substantial expansion. Figure 6.4 depicts these developments. The production of intermediate goods stagnated during this period in contrast to the period of import-substitution, when this city developed its urban specialization as a producer of intermediate goods. In contrast, capital and durable goods became a moderate growth subsector and basic goods experienced a significant expansion. Basic goods became more important in this city as regional demand rose. The population from the border and as well as the northeastern region could no longer rely on the Texan market to obtain diverse goods. This occurred due to the lack of foreign exchange and the disparity between the dollar and the peso. Basic goods was also the only subsector that increased its level of productivity, which suggests that manufacturing production in this subsector was in modern establishments.

Figure 6.4.
Manufacturing Subsectors by Economic Performance
in Monterrey

	75-80	80-85	85-88
Expansion	Basic Intermediate Capital/Durable Total Manufacturing	Basic	
Moderate Growth		Capital/Durable	Basic Capital/Durable
Stagnant		Intermediate Total Manufacturing	Intermediate Total Manufacturing

Source: See Under Fig. 6.1.

The Monterrey industrial base was highly affected by the economic crisis as the manufacturing sector was dependent on foreign technology and foreign capital. Monterrey's capitalists accumulated a large debt in dollars, when loans were easy to obtain and interests rates were low.[39] Additionally, manufacturing in Monterrey was highly integrated vertically with interdependent industries. For example, the VITRO group that produced beer also produced the bottles and the boxes to pack the beer. With the economic crisis the internal market, the main outlet for Monterrey's beer, had less demand for this product. As a consequence, not only did the beer factory have serious problems, but the factories that supplied the inputs for the bottling and packing of the beverage also suffered.

ALFA, VITRO, CYDSA, and VISA were the entrepreneurial groups most affected by the economic crisis as the income from industrial sales was not sufficient to cover their financial commitments, mostly with foreign banks.[40] In contrast, IMSA and CEMEX did not suffer serious problems largely due to the fact that in the previous period they had not become as indebted as the other groups. The most affected entrepreneurial groups developed the strategy of reducing labor in their enterprises. Additionally, they sold or closed industries created or acquired during the second half of the 1970s. For example, the ALFA and VITRO groups fired 17,000 and 11,000 employees respectively during the 1980-1983 period.[41]

Figure 6.5.
Service Subsectors by Economic Performance
in Monterrey

	75-80	80-85	85-88
Expansion	Distributive Producer Personal Total Service	Personal	Distribution Social Personal Total Service
Moderate Growth	Social	Distributive Producer Social Total Service	Producer
Stagnant			

Source: See Under Fig. 6.1.

Figure 6.5 illustrates the subsectoral performance in Monterrey. During the period of economic crisis, the service sector became a moderate growth sector in both Monterrey and Guadalajara. However, employment and the number of establishments grew faster in Monterrey. Additionally, distributive, producer and social services became moderate growth subsectors, while personal services expanded in Monterrey. This growth in the employed labor force and in the number of establishments was encouraged by employment constraints in the manufacturing sector during this period. Displaced employees from manufacturing started small businesses in the service sector, ranging from small corner stores to restaurants and professional service offices. During the economic crisis period, the major entrepreneurial groups reduced their labor force as part of their restructuring strategy. The firms changed from the constant expense of permanent employees, to variable expenses, hiring services only when needed. These entrepreneurial groups fired professional and clerical employees from the headquarters offices, but they still needed their services. Therefore, they encouraged and, in some cases, financially supported the ex-directors so that they could establish professional service offices which would supply the occasional demand for these services.[42]

b) *The Period of "Opening" (1985-1988) - Guadalajara:*

During the period of "opening," the situation of Guadalajara's manufacturing sector became more critical than in the previous period of economic crisis (see Figure 6.1). Manufacturing as a whole as well as four of its subsectors stagnated. Additionally, all of them reduced their level of productivity.

Guadalajara's capitalist group had not designed a global strategy to meet the new challenges that emerged with the "opening" of the border: the increase of both imports of manufactured goods and foreign industrial investment. Furthermore, local government, specifically the *Department of Promotion and Economic Development*, had not prepared a strategy to take advantage of the new economic conditions to attract foreign capital and support local industry.[43]

Local industrialists and government were overtaken by the fast and drastic transformations experienced by both the Mexican and local economies. Local entrepreneurs became involved in a new situation in which they had to compete, not only in the international market if they exported, but also in the internal market, important outlets for their manufactured products. Imports of electrical and electronic goods, garments, shoes, toys, plastic goods, food and beverages increased during this period. An entrepreneur described the reaction of local government and industrialists to these changes as an "immediate" response, lacking perspective and knowledge of the global industrial processes, in which they are becoming involved.[44] Guadalajara entrepreneurs did not have the experience in dealing with international markets unlike Monterrey or Mexico City-based industrialists.

Firms in Guadalajara had to change from being producers to distributors as local industries could not compete with the low price of imported manufactured goods, mostly shoes and toys from South Asia.

Industrialists stopped producing these goods and started distributing them in the local and regional markets.[45] This is not only a local tendency, but also a national one. Three out of ten small and medium-scale industries changed from production to distribution.[46]

Another important change during this period was the drastic increase of direct foreign investment in the state of Jalisco, particularly in Guadalajara, from US$ 154.8 million in 1984 to US$ 795.2 million in 1987.[47] This direct foreign investment has been heavily concentrated in the manufacturing sector, from maquiladoras for export to high technology plants. By 1991, the following enterprises had established themselves in Guadalajara: Kodak, Unisys, Motorola, IBM, General Instruments, Shizuki Electrónica, Quimi Kao, Hewlett Packard, Wang, Ciba Geigy, Cyanamid, Goodrich Euzkadi, Dodge de México, Mitel de México, Corn Products, Philip Morris, and Anderson Clayton. This is reflected in Guadalajara's remarkable growth in capital and durable goods during this period. However, growth in these modern and large-scale enterprises was not enough to counterbalance the decline of small and medium-scale enterprises in the subsector.

During the period of "opening," Guadalajara's service sector continued to show a moderate growth as it had in the previous period, despite the expansion of producer and personal services (see Figure 6.3). During the "opening" period, manufacturing was restructured and grew slowly in terms of employment. In contrast, the service sector continued as a source of employment in Guadalajara as in the whole country, mostly in producer, personal and distributive services. Figure 6.6 clearly depicts this national trend.

As the economy opened, the import of manufactured goods to Guadalajara increased dramatically, which promoted commercial activity in small businesses. During this period three new commercial areas emerged around the traditional "Mercado de San Juan de Dios," which distributes both imported and locally produced goods. Each of these three commercial areas contained approximately 400 registered commercial establishments, which traded retail and wholesale goods.[48] Much of the western region, Guadalajara in particular, obtained goods in these commercial areas. Another part of Guadalajara's population, mostly higher income groups, shopped in the malls, where prices tended to be higher than in the three commercial areas mentioned above.

Figure 6.6.
Service Subsectors by Economic Performance
in Mexico

	75-80	80-85	85-88
Expansion	Distributive Producer Social Personal Total Service		Distribution Producer Social Personal Total Service
Moderate Growth		Distributive Producer Social Personal Total Service	
Stagnant			

Source: See Under Fig. 6.1.

Monterrey:

In Monterrey manufacturing sector and intermediate goods continued to stagnate during the "opening" period (see Figure 6.4). Basic goods switched from being a subsector in expansion to a moderate growth subsector. Capital and durable goods also continued as a moderate growth subsector. However, it is important to note that all manufacturing subsectors increased their levels of productivity. This suggests that all manufacturing subsectors reduced employment and number of establishments, but they became restructured and more modern so that they could produce more value added than in the previous period. Manufacturing in Monterrey was partially able to overcome the effects of the economic crisis and restructuring and in a way became a more productive sector.

Medium and large-scale enterprises continued to be closed during this period. This contrasts with the situation in Guadalajara where mostly micro and small-scale industries were closed. This tendency is observed in core countries as well, where smaller enterprises can more easily incorporate new technology and implement flexible employment practices. [49]

Part of the restructuring of the manufacturing sector was encouraged by the arrival of direct foreign industrial investment, which either directly or in association with local capital, contributed to the reindustrialization of Monterrey during the second half of the 1980s. Direct foreign investment in the state of Nuevo León increased from US\$ 606.3 million in 1984 to US\$ 1,234.7 million in 1987, and was concentrated mainly in Monterrey. [50] The dramatic increase in the number of maquiladoras for export was largely attributed to the arrival of direct foreign industrial investment in Monterrey. The number of such maquiladoras in Nuevo León reached 73 during the 1986-1989 period. Approximately 80 percent of these maquiladoras were located in Monterrey, including the four largest: Motoi with 1,178 employees, Compañía de Motores Domésticos with 534 employees, Ensamble de Cables y Componentes with 1,100 employees and Rogers Electronics with 513 employees. All of these were U.S.-owned and produced electrical and electronic goods. [51]

Additionally, local capitalists paid off 62 percent of their debt and started joint ventures with foreign capital. VITRO associated with Whirlpool and in 1989 became the majority owner of Anchor Glass, the second most important glass company in the United States. Other entrepreneurial groups such as CEMEX bought the most important cement industries in Mexico as well as the following four U.S. industries: Gulf Coast Portland Cement Co., Houston Shell and Concrete Co., Houston Concrete Products Inc., and Aggregate Transportation Inc. [52] CEMEX became the leader in this industry producing 85 percent of Mexican cement exports. [53]

The service sector unlike manufacturing increased its relative importance in Monterrey's economy during the period of "opening." Additionally, in Monterrey all service subsectors expanded, except for producer services (see Figure 6.5). The expansion of services is explained, in part, by the continuing transfer of labor from Monterrey's manufacturing sector to this sector. All expanding service subsectors experienced a substantial growth in value added, which suggests that these services were provided in modern and large establishments. In general, the local economy was modernized through the creation of specialized services in institutions such as the *International Business Center* and *Pro-Export*.

c) Change in Urban Specialization

The index of dissimilarity (ID) is a useful technique to identify the largest transformations at the subsector level and to assess the transformations in the manufacturing and services subsectors in both cities.[54] In addition, I have created a total ID, which is based on the three indexes of dissimilarity for each indicator.[55] Based on the latter index, Monterrey's economy has experienced a deeper and faster restructuring, with a total ID of 10.7, than that of Guadalajara, whose total ID is only 7.6. The greater transformation in Monterrey, in contrast to Guadalajara, is essentially based on changes in employment, given that both cities have a similar ID in the number of establishments and in value added. Table 6-1 depicts these similarities and differences quite well. In regard to employment, Monterrey has an ID more than twice the size of Guadalajara. This reflects the fact that in Monterrey approximately 6.2 percent of the labor force was transferred from the intermediate goods manufacturing subsector to distributive, producer, and personal services. It appears that economic restructuring has had greater implications for Monterrey's labor force than for Guadalajara's.

In terms of urban specialization, Guadalajara remains specialized in the subsector of basic goods production and in distributive services. Social services also show slight increase in this city in contrast to Monterrey. However, in Guadalajara urban specialization in basic goods had declined in importance by 1988. There was a decline in basic goods production during economic restructuring, and a decrease in the number of small-scale enterprises, while the number of medium and large-scale ones increased. Basic goods production and small-scale enterprises in this city became highly related.

In contrast, urban specialization in Monterrey changed because of the drastic decline of the intermediate goods subsector, while the distributive service subsector increased spectacularly during the period of economic restructuring. However, the relative importance of producer and personal services increased faster in Monterrey than in Guadalajara. By 1988, Monterrey had become specialized both in distributive services and intermediate goods, in contrast to a pronounced urban specialization in intermediate goods during the import-substitution period. Both Guadalajara and, to a greater extent, Monterrey have intensified their service specialization. Moreover, they have both reduced their specialization as manufacturing centers, although this tendency is more pronounced in Monterrey. This trend is similar to that reported in the larger cities of core countries, where economic restructuring brought about an intensification of urban specialization in services and a decline in manufacturing production.[56] However, the level of economic significance reached by producer and social services in semi-peripheral cities is smaller than the trend observed in core cities.

Concluding Remarks

The impact of economic restructuring on the Mexican economy has been more pronounced in Monterrey than in Guadalajara. This comparative study indicates that the following factors play an important role in the way urban economic restructuring takes place: the relative homogeneity of the city's capitalist group, the degree of modernization and concentration of the industrial structure, the dependence of the local industrial base on international markets for industrial inputs and for outlets of industrial production, and the geographical location of the city. In this way, economic restructuring at global and national levels is redefined, to a certain extent, by the specificities of local factors.

The change and intensification of urban specialization in Guadalajara and Monterrey as service centers is important since it suggests that the Mexican urban system is changing during economic restructuring. Under import-substitution, the economy's orientation was centripetal. There was a strong centralization of manufacturing, service activities and population in Mexico City, which made the high primacy characteristic of the Mexican urban system more pronounced. This process was also observed in other Latin American countries, such as Argentina and Peru, that adopted similar models of economic development.[57]

Under the new economic dynamic, one that has a centrifugal orientation and emphasizes the integration of Mexico into the world economy, border and port cities are increasing their economic activity, population size, and ties with the international market. Under this economic dynamic, the relative importance of Mexico City as a manufacturing and service center has declined.[58] However, in Guadalajara and Monterrey an opposite tendency is observed; these two

Table 6-1.
Index of Dissimilarity (ID): Guadalajara and Monterrey
(Percent Distribution by Subsector)

ESTABLISHMENTS

Subsectors	Guadalajara		Monterrey		ID 1975-88	
	1975	1988	1975	1988	Guad	Mont
Basic Goods	11.31	6.81	7.62	5.15	2.25	1.23
Intermediate	3.93	3.81	4.46	3.88	0.06	0.29
Cap/Durable	1.20	1.00	2.35	1.95	0.11	0.20
Distrib. S.	52.69	55.49	53.12	57.64	1.40	2.22
Producer S.	3.55	3.75	5.62	4.49	0.10	0.56
Social S.	4.46	5.27	5.18	5.56	0.40	0.19
Personal S.	22.87	23.89	21.66	21.33	0.51	0.17
TOTAL	100.0	100.0	100.0	100.0	4.83	4.90

EMPLOYMENT

Subsectors	Guadalajara		Monterrey		ID 1975-88	
	1975	1988	1975	1988	Guad	Mont
Basic Goods	28.51	24.66	15.67	15.47	1.92	0.10
Intermediate	12.62	12.81	31.89	19.46	0.19	6.21
Cap/Durable	5.92	5.09	12.79	12.18	0.42	0.31
Distrib. S.	31.36	33.18	22.32	29.22	0.91	3.45
Producer S.	3.61	4.19	3.99	7.90	0.57	1.95
Social S.	3.94	5.17	4.30	4.14	0.61	0.08
Personal S.	14.04	14.91	9.04	11.63	0.43	1.29
TOTAL	100.0	100.0	100.0	100.0	5.05	13.39

VALUE ADDED

Subsectors	Guadalajara		Monterrey		ID 1975-88	
	1975	1988	1975	1988	Guad	Mont
Basic Goods	32.60	23.28	16.97	22.09	4.66	2.56
Intermediate	14.58	19.22	39.46	26.36	2.32	6.55
Cap/Durable	7.47	11.19	12.14	17.37	1.86	2.61
Distrib. S.	35.00	31.57	20.48	21.73	1.71	0.62
Producer S.	3.79	3.52	3.87	5.29	0.13	0.71
Social S.	1.78	2.62	2.86	2.20	0.42	0.33
Personal S.	4.79	8.59	4.21	4.97	1.90	0.38
TOTAL	100.0	100.0	100.0	100.0	13.00	13.76

ID TOTAL* = 7.63 (Guadalajara)
ID TOTAL* = 10.68 (Monterrey)

Source: Industrial, Commerce and Services Census, 1975; and Resultados Oportunos del los Censos Económicos de 1989.

Table 6-2.
Concentration of Manufacturing and Services in the
Three Largest Metropolital Areas
(Percentages)

Guadalajara

	Manufacturing			Services		
	Estab.	ELF*	Value Added	Estab.	ELF*	Value Added
1980	4.9	5.9	5.3	3.9	5.2	4.4
1988	4.9	5.9	4.0	4.3	5.2	4.8

Monterrey

	Manufacturing			Services		
	Estab.	ELF*	Value Added	Estab.	ELF*	Value Added
1980	3.6	9.0	10.2	3.0	4.5	5.3
1988	3.6	6.7	9.5	3.4	5.0	7.0

Mexico City

	Manufacturing			Services		
	Estab.	ELF*	Value Added	Estab.	ELF*	Value Added
1980	28.1	41.5	43.3	27.9	33.9	43.2
1988	21.4	31.1	32.1	24.6	27.9	36.1

* Employed Labor Force

Source: Economic Census, 1980; Resultados Oportunos de los Censos Económicos de 1989; Garza, 1991:211; Garza, 1992: Tables #7-9.

metropolitan centers have intensified their urban specialization as service centers. Table 6-2 illustrates these trends. I have attached three more tables (Tables 6-3, 6-4, and 6-5) in the Appendix (A) at the end of this chapter. These tables further describe the details of urban specialization and change in Guadalajara, Monterrey, and Mexico. These data indicate that while the primate city tends to decline, secondary cities become consolidated as regional urban centers which supply a wide range of specialized services formerly accounted for by the primate city. Thus, for large metropolitan areas (over two million inhabitants) a specific niche in the Mexican urban system has emerged, which of course varies by the respective urban and industrial infrastructure, urban services specialization, and on the ability to intensify ties within the region as well as within the national and world economies.

Notes

1. Sassen-Koob (1984). See also Stanback and Noyelle, *Cities in Transition* (1982).
2. McKenzie (1926).
3. Poston, Frisbie, and Micklin M., "Sociological Human Ecology: Theoretical and Conceptual Perspectives," (1983).
4. Berry, B. and Kasarda, J., *Contemporary Urban Ecology* (1977). See Also, Hawley, A., *Urban Society: An Ecological Approach* (1971).
5. Wallerstein, I., *The Modern World System* (1974).
6. Rodriguez, N. and Feagin, J., "Urban Specialization in the World-System," *Urban Affairs Quarterly* (1986). See also Sassen-Koob (1984).
7. Gottdiener (1989). See also Lubeck and Walton, "Urban Class Conflict in Africa and Latin America: Comparative Analisis from A World Systems Perspectives," *International Journal of Urban and Regional Research* (1979).
8. Stanback and Noyelle (1982, 20).
9. Lamarche (1976).
10. Chill Hill and Feagin (1987).
11. Roberts, *Cities of Peasants* (1978). See also Angotti, "Urbanization in Latin America" (1987).
12. Portes and Browning, *Current Perspectives in Latin American Urban Research* (1976).
13. Arias and Roberts (1984).
14. Stanback and Noyelle (1982).

15. Sassen-Koob (1984, 157).

16. Stanback and Noyelle (1982).

17. See Stanback and Noyelle (1982) and Sassen-Koob (1984).

18. The basic goods industrial subsector is made up of food, beverages, tobacco, textile, garments, shoes and leather, wood and printing branches. The intermediate goods subsector encompasses chemicals, rubber, plastic, non-metal and basic metal branches. The capital and durable goods subsector concentrates electric, electronic, machinery, and equipment branches.

19. I do this because of the heterogeneity of the services sector, in terms of the type of services produced and the diverse qualifications of the labor force demanded. See in this regard, Browning, H. and Singelmann, J., *The Emergence of a Service Society: Demographic and Sociological Aspects of the Sectoral Transformation of the Labor Force in the U.S.A.* (1975), Report Presented to the Manpower Administration, U.S. Department of Labor. The authors divided this sector into distributive, producer, social and personal services. Within each subsector, the service branches are gathered in several groups. Wholesale and retail are the two branches of distributive services. Financial and insurance, real estate and professional services are the three groups within producer services. Medical and education are the two main branches within social services. Finally, hotel, restaurants, bars, entertainment, repair, maintenance and miscellaneous personal services are within personal services.

20. Level of productivity is the outcome of the relation between value added and number of employees in a specific subsector. This is a gross indicator that suggests the degree of modernization of the subsector.

21. Frobel, Heinrichs, and Kreye, *The New International Division of the Labor* (1980). See also Gereffi, "Rethinking Development Theory: Insights from East Asia and Latin America," (1989).

22. For a discussion of the periods of Mexico's economic restructuring see Pozos Ponce, *Economic Restructuring, Employment Change and Wage Differentials: The Case of Guadalajara and Monterrey (1975-1989)* (Doctoral Dissertation, University of Texas at Austin, Austin, TX, 1992).

23. Cárdenas, E., "Contemporary Economic Problems in Historical Perspective" (1990).

24. Canak (1989).

25. Plan Nacional de Desarrollo (1983).

26. Cortés and Rubalcava (1992).

27. Zabludosky (1990).

28. Puebla, the next city in the urban hierarchy, only has about one million inhabitants (Mexican Census 1990).

29. Along with Mexico City, Guadalajara and Monterrey became the most industrialized metropolises during import-substitution period, and the cities where manufacturing was most concentrated. By 1970, these three cities

concentrated 37 percent of the total manufacturing establishments, 47 percent of the labor force, and 58 percent of the value added Industrial Census (1970); Garza (1980).

30. Rivière (1973). See also De la Peña (1986); Arias and Roberts 1984; Alba y Kruit (1988).

31. Balán, Browning, and Jelin, 1977, *El Hombre en una Sociedad en Desarrollo* (1977). See also Vellinga (1979).

32. Walton (1977). See also Unikel, Ruiz, and Garza (1976).

33. Dirección General de Estadística, Industrial Census 1970, 1975. See also, INEGI, Resultados Oportunos de los Censos Económicos de 1985 and 1989.

34. Alba, *La Respuesta de la Crisis en dos Metrópolis Regionales de Mexico: los Casos de Monterrey y Guadalajara* (mimeo, 1990).

35. Investment in real estate has helped increase the urban area of Guadalajara from approximately 20,000 hectares to 29,000 between 1980 and 1990 (Data provided by Jalisco's Department of Urbanization and Planning).

36. Alba and Roberts (1990).

37. Alba (1984). See also Durán and Partida (1990).

38. Alba (1986).

39. During the last half of the 1970s, Mexico contracted a large external debt that increased from 20.1 billion dollars in 1975 to 50.7 billion dollars in 1980 (See Weintraub, *A Married of Convenience*, 1990). The Monterrey entrepreneurs also became indebted during this period, which was a period of prosperity in the Mexican economy.

40. Nuncio (1987).

41. Pozas, *Estrategias Empresariales Ante la Apertura Externa* (1990).

42. Information provided by the Monterry's International Business Center.

43. Rather, Nacional Financiera, a national government credit agency, developed a program to support the micro and small-scale industries in the whole country. Specifically, in the case of Guadalajara this agency is emphasizing support for this type of industry because of its importance to the local economy in terms of employment and basic goods supply. Additionally, it is argued that there is a culture of micro and small-scale industrialization in Guadalajara which should be understood and reinforced by credit and development institutions (Information provided by the head of the Nacional Financiera Regional Office in Guadalajara).

44. Information provided by the Jalisco's Regional Chamber of Transformation Industry.

45. Alba and Roberts (1990, 1). See also *El Financiero*, January 29, 1992.

46. *El Financiero*, December 23, 1991.

47. Palacios, *La Inversión Extranjera en Mexico: Políticas Gubernamentales y Evolución Reciente* (mimeo, 1989). See also Alba and Kruijt (1988).

48. Information provided by the Guadalajara National Chamber of Commerce.

49. Fajnzylber (1990).

50. Palacios (1989, 33); Alba and Kruijt (1988, 100).

51. Ramírez and González-Aréchiga (1992).

52. Pozas (1990, 17, 23).

53. *El Financiero*, January 31, 1992.

54. The Index of Dissimilarity is based on the absolute differences between percents at each subsector according to Shryock, H.S., Siegel, J.S. and Associates, *The Methods and Materials of Demography* (London: Academic Press, 1976). Percentages are summed without regard to sign, and one-half of the sum is taken. The general formula is:

$$ID = 1/2 \ [\ r_{2a} - r_{1a} \ ] \ .$$

55. ID Total $= (ID_1 + ID_2 + ID_3)/N$. Where ID_1 = establishments; ID_2 = personnel occupied, and ID_3 = value added; N = Number of ID involved in the equation.

56. Stanback and Noyelle (1982); Sassen-Koob (1984, 157).

57. Portes (1989).

58. Garza (1992). See also Garza, "Dinámica Industrial de la Ciudad de Mexico, 1940-1988" (1991).

APPENDIX A

Table 6-3.

Average Annual Growth Rates of Manufacturing and Service Subsectors in Guadalajara

Sub-sector	Employment			Value Added			Establishments		
	75-80	*80-85*	*85-88*	*75-80*	*80-85*	*85-88*	*75-80*	*80-85*	*85-88*
Basic Goods	4.4	1.5	6.4	3.7	-2.8	-15.3	-1.4	2.2	-1.3
Intermed. Goods	10.2	4.6	-3.2	12.5	0.4	-14.9	1.9	6.0	2.6
Capital/ Durable	7.8	3.2	-2.4	6.8	-13.5	22.0	7.5	4.7	-10.4
Total Manuf.*	6.2	2.6	2.2	6.4	-2.8	-10.1	1.4	2.1	-0.7
Distrib. Services	5.5	6.4	2.9	2.1	-1.3	-7.3	3.1	5.1	4.9
Producer Sevices	9.9	-0.5	10.1	13.5	-24.3	12.9	3.4	3.6	7.0
Social Services	13.8	3.8	0.6	10.0	3.1	-11.5	4.6	5.0	6.6
Personal Services	3.6	6.4	6.3	8.9	-2.8	6.8	2.4	5.8	4.7
Total Services	6.1	5.7	4.0	4.4	-3.1	-4.2	3.0	5.3	5.0

* Includes other manufacturing.

Source: Industrial, Commerce and Service Census, 1980; and Resultados Oportunos del los Censos Económicos de 1986 and 1989.

Table 6-4.
Average Annual Growth Rates of Manufacturing and Service
Subsectors in Monterrey

Sub-sector	Employment			Value Added			Establishments		
	75-80	80-85	85-88	75-80	80-85	85-88	75-80	80-85	85-88
Basic Goods	6.7	2.3	3.0	1.2	4.8	3.5	2.6	2.8	-1.7
Intermed. Goods	9.0	-3.1	-7.8	7.7	-12.9	0.1	7.3	4.2	-3.4
Capital/ Durable	6.3	3.6	0.3	7.9	-0.2	3.9	7.3	5.6	-7.2
Total Manuf.*	7.9	-0.3	-2.6	6.4	-5.6	2.2	4.8	3.7	-3.2
Distrib. Services	6.3	7.6	4.2	3.0	-10.1	18.5	4.5	5.9	5.7
Producer Sevices	13.7	1.5	15.8	21.6	-8.7	-6.2	0.5	2.8	7.6
Social Services	6.7	2.6	1.6	-0.8	-6.7	8.8	5.1	5.9	4.5
Personal Services	5.8	6.2	6.8	5.3	8.6	15.7	3.6	5.7	4.3
Total Services	7.1	6.0	6.1	6.5	-9.3	12.3	4.1	5.7	5.4

* Includes other manufacturing.

Source: Industrial, Commerce and Service Census, 1980; and Resultados Oportunos del los Censos Económicos de 1986 and 1989.

Table 6-5.
Average Annual Growth Rates of Manufacturing and Service Subsectors in Mexico

Sub-sector	Employment			Value Added			Establishments		
	75-80	80-85	85-88	75-80	80-85	85-88	75-80	80-85	85-88
Basic Goods	3.1	2.0	2.2	2.2	-7.4	3.7	-0.4	-1.1	2.4
Intermed. Goods	5.8	0.1	2.1	2.1	-5.2	11.4	3.2	4.1	4.7
Capital/ Durable	7.1	2.5	2.8	8.3	-9.0	9.3	2.8	3.1	-11.9
Total Manuf.*	3.3	2.7	2.4	3.4	-7.0	8.2	0.5	0.3	2.2
Distrib. Services	5.4	3.9	5.3	0.9	-1.4	0.8	3.6	1.6	6.5
Producer Sevices	16.7	4.8	9.5	25.3	-13.5	1.1	8.3	3.5	10.2
Social Services	11.1	4.3	6.6	39.8	-34.4	5.0	8.7	6.2	7.5
Personal Services	4.6	5.0	5.6	8.0	-7.9	6.5	3.1	3.8	5.2
Total Services	6.3	4.3	5.9	8.9	-7.7	2.0	3.8	2.5	6.3

* Includes other manufacturing.

Source: Industrial, Commerce and Service Census, 1980; and Resultados Oportunos del los Censos Económicos de 1986 and 1989.

7

Competing Perspectives on the Latin American Informal Sector*[1]

Alejandro Portes
Richard Schauffler

This chapter reviews the successive conceptualizations of the phenomenon known as the "informal sector" in Latin America, describes the measurement strategies used to study that sector, and examines ways in which the current state of knowledge about the informal sector affects development policies. We first present an overview of the demographic and economic context in which the phenomenon of informality arose. Broadly speaking, the concept refers to various forms of precarious or subterranean employment concentrated in urban areas, chiefly in the developing world. Among

---

* Reprinted with permission of the Population Council, from *Population and Development Review*, vol. 19, no. 1 (March 1993): 33-60.

the various schools of thought on the informal economy there is agreement that a fundamental reason for its emergence was accelerated rural-urban migration and the labor surplus that it generated in the cities.

Following World War II, the population of Latin America grew rapidly. As in other third world regions, the growth was fueled by high birth rates and declining mortality, the latter due primarily to the introduction of basic sanitation and preventive medicine.[2] Regional growth peaked in the five-year period 1960-65, when the annual growth rate averaged 2.9 percent, with figures for Brazil, Costa Rica, Mexico, and Venezuela exceeding 3.0 percent. Consequently, the economically active population (EAP) grew rapidly. Although the natural rate of increase subsequently declined to a regional average of 2.1 percent per year in 1980-90, the growth of the EAP continued at a high pace: 3 percent annually in 1970-80 and 2.8 percent in 1980-85. Figures for Costa Rica, Ecuador, Mexico, and Venezuela exceeded this average.[3]

High labor force growth rates coincided with economic development policies that had a strong urban bias. The model of import substitution industrialization (ISI), promoted during the postwar years by the UN Economic Commission for Latin America (ECLA), sought the rapid development of domestic industry through high tariff protection, heavy state investments in this sector, and domestic terms of trade that favored urban industry over agriculture.[4] The subsequent accelerated industrialization was concentrated in one or two cities in each country because these were the only areas that possessed the requisite infrastructure and provided the only sizable markets. Combined with declining employment opportunities in the countryside, this situation led to a wave of migration toward the few centers where industrial growth and employment were concentrated.[5]

The ISI model was hence strongly centripetal in its consequences for the spatial distribution of the population.[6] The magnitude of this effect in combination with a growing labor force is difficult to exaggerate. In 1950, Lain America was a continent of rural dwellers where more than half of the population lived in the countryside and the majority of the work force consisted of peasants and farm workers. By 1990, three out of four Latin Americans lived in cities, the majority in large urban centers. Table 7-1 illustrates this extraordinary transformation by comparing Latin American urban growth with that of all less developed regions and that of developed countries during the second half of the twentieth century. As seen in the table, the growth rate of the urban

Table 7-1. Estimated and projected growth of the urban population by world region, 1950-2000

Urban Growth Rates[1]	1950-1955 %	1955-1960 %	1960-1965 %	1965-1970 %	1970-1975 %	1975-1980 %	1980-1985 %	1985-1990 %	1990-1995 %[2]	1995-2000 %[2]
Latin America	4.52	4.42	4.38	4.02	3.81	3.49	3.22	2.93	2.63	2.35
Less Developed Regions[3]	4.26	5.25	3.46	3.59	3.71	3.95	4.62	4.53	4.19	3.74
More Developed Regions[4]	2.43	2.45	2.18	1.83	1.52	1.15	1.02	0.81	0.77	0.78

Urban Population[5]	1955 %	1960 %	1965 %	1970 %	1975 %	1980 %	1985 %	1990 %	1995 %	2000 %
Latin America	45.3	49.3	53.3	57.3	61.2	65.0	68.5	71.5	74.1	76.4
Less Developed Regions[3]	19.0	22.1	23.4	24.7	26.4	28.9	32.8	37.1	41.2	45.1
More Developed Regions[4]	57.0	60.5	63.6	66.6	68.8	70.3	71.6	72.3	73.6	74.9

Source: United Nations 1991b. Tables A.1, A.5.

---

1   Average annual percentage.

2   Estimates.

3   Less developed regions comprise all regions of Africa, all regions of Latin America, all regions of Asia (excluding Japan), Melanesia, Micronesia, and Polynesia.

4   More developed regions comprise North America, Japan, all regions of Europe, Australia, New Zealand, and the former USSR.

5   Percentage of total population.

Table 7-2. Demographic trends in Latin America, selected indicators, 1950-90

Country	Period	Population Growth[1] %	Economically Active Pop. Growth[2] %	Urban Pop. Growth %[1]	Total Urban Pop. Growth[3] %
Argentina	1950-60	1.9	1.6	3.0	73.6
	1960-70	1.6	1.5	2.1	78.4
	1970-80	1.4	1.4	2.2	82.7
	1980-90	1.3	1.3	1.8	86.2
Bolivia	1950-60	2.2	2.0	2.5	39.3
	1960-70	2.4	2.3	2.7	40.7
	1970-80	2.6	2.5	3.4	44.3
	1980-90	2.6	2.7	4.2	51.4
Brazil	1950-60	3.1	2.8	5.3	44.9
	1960-70	2.8	3.0	4.9	55.8
	1970-80	2.4	3.1	4.1	67.5
	1980-90	2.2	2.5	3.4	76.9
Chile	1950-60	2.2	2.0	3.7	69.6
	1960-70	2.2	2.3	3.3	75.2
	1970-80	1.7	2.6	2.4	81.1
	1980-90	1.7	2.1	2.2	85.6
Colombia	1950-60	3.0	2.6	5.5	48.2
	1960-70	3.0	3.1	4.6	57.2
	1970-80	2.3	3.3	3.4	64.2
	1980-90	2.2	2.9	2.9	70.3
Costa Rica	1950-60	3.7	3.0	4.5	36.6
	1960-70	3.4	3.8	4.2	39.7
	1970-80	2.8	4.1	3.6	46.0
	1980-90	2.8	3.2	3.7	53.6
Ecuador	1950-60	2.9	2.4	4.6	34.4
	1960-70	3.2	3.2	4.5	40.0
	1970-80	3.0	3.5	4.7	47.3
	1980-90	2.7	3.4	4.4	56.9

[1]   Average annual growth rate.

[2]   Population between 15 and 64 years of age. Average annual growth rate.

[3]   Percentage of total population. Definition of urban varies across countries. Figures are for the year ending the decade.

Country	Period	Population Growth %[1]	Economically Active Pop. Growth[2] %	Urban Pop. Growth %[1]	Total Urban Pop. Growth[3] %
El Salvador	1950-60	2.9	2.3	3.3	38.3
	1960-70	3.3	3.1	3.6	39.4
	1970-80	2.4	2.4	2.9	41.5
	1980-90	1.5	1.7	2.2	44.4
Guatemala	1950-60	3.0	2.6	3.8	35.7
	1960-70	2.8	2.8	3.7	35.7
	1970-80	2.8	2.8	2.9	38.5
	1980-90	2.9	2.9	2.2	42.0
Mexico	1950-60	3.2	2.6	4.8	50.7
	1960-70	3.3	3.0	4.8	59.0
	1970-80	2.9	3.5	4.1	66.4
	1980-90	2.3	3.6	3.2	72.6
Panama	1950-60	2.9	2.8	3.9	41.2
	1960-70	3.0	2.8	4.3	47.6
	1970-80	2.8	3.2	2.9	50.6
	1980-90	2.2	3.1	2.8	54.8
Peru	1950-60	2.5	2.1	5.3	46.3
	1960-70	2.9	2.9	5.0	57.4
	1970-80	2.7	3.2	3.9	64.5
	1980-90	2.2	3.0	3.0	70.2
Uruguay	1950-60	1.3	1.3	1.5	80.1
	1960-70	1.0	0.9	1.3	82.1
	1970-80	0.4	0.3	0.6	83.8
	1980-90	0.6	0.6	0.8	85.5
Venezuela	1950-60	3.9	3.5	6.3	66.6
	1960-70	3.5	3.5	4.3	72.4
	1970-80	3.5	4.4	4.9	83.3
	1980-90	2.7	3.2	3.6	90.5
Latin America	1950-60	2.8	2.5	4.5	49.3
	1960-70	2.7	2.7	4.2	57.3
	1970-80	2.6	3.0	3.7	65.0
	1980-90	2.1	2.8[4]	3.1	71.5

Sources: ECLA 1981; ECLAC 1991, Tables 1,2,3,5,7; United Nations 1991a, 1991b.

[4] Figure is for the period 1980-85.

population in Latin America topped 4 percent between 1950 and 1970, roughly twice as high as that of the more developed countries and generally exceeding the average rate of developing regions. Not coincidentally, this period marked the high point of the influence of the ISI development model.[6] Urban growth declined subsequently, but by 1990 Latin America had already achieved levels of urbanization equal to those of the developed world despite much lower per capita incomes.

Significant country-by-country differences existed around these regional averages. Table 7-2 illustrates these differences by showing average annual rates of growth for the national, urban, and the potential economically active population (those aged 15-64) of 14 countries in Latin america from the 1950s through the 1980s. At the beginning of this period, Argentina, Chile, and Uruguay were already highly urbanized and their population growth rates were relatively low. Urban growth continued in these countries at a pace similar to that of developed world so that by 1990, as is shown in the last column of Table 7-2, more than 85 percent of their inhabitants were living in cities. The speed of demographic transformation was more dramatic in Brazil, Colombia, Mexico, and Peru, where the share of the urban population grew from one-half or less in 1950 to about three-fourths in 1990.

The migrants who gave rise to such rapid rates of urban growth throughout the post-World War II period did not encounter in the cities anything commensurate with their economic aspirations. The nascent ISI-sponsored industries did generate significant labor demand,[7] but the size of that demand was swamped by the sheer number of new migrants. In 1950, modern nonagricultural employment absorbed 26.3 percent of the Latin American labor force. In the subsequent 30 years, employment in that sector grew by an average of 4.1 percent per year. However, the total nonagricultural EAP grew at a similar pace so that, by the end of the period, the proportion employed in the modern urban sector was the same as it had been three decades earlier. Estimates of the excess labor supply in cities during this period ranged from 30 to 60 percent of the urban EAP.[8]

The Concept of Informality

Earlier Theories

The massive labor surplus created by rural-urban migration in major cities of Latin America and elsewhere in the less developed world was noted by demographers as early as the 1940s.[9] By the 1950s and 1960s, a number of concepts had appeared to label the phenomenon and highlight its principal characteristics. A popular terms at the time was "marginality," a concept used by academics of different persuasions to denote the exclusion of the migrant masses from the modern urban economy. Writing from a Marxist perspective, a team of Argentine economists characterized the urban marginal mass as an "excess reserve army" that exceeded the labor reserve requirements of third world economies and hence had no function for economic accumulation.[10] From a more conventional perspective, the economic historian and labor economist Paul Bairoch referred to the phenomenon as an "abnormally swollen, overdistended tertiary sector."[11] The rise of this tertiary sector was, according to Bairoch,[12] a direct effect of excessive urban growth relative to the level of economic development in third world countries, a process that he labeled "hyper-urbanization."

Such conceptualizations flowed directly from the observation of very rapid urban growth and hence the rise in cities of an excess labor supply relative to labor demand in the modern economy. Yet the generally ominous tone of these early theories failed to acknowledge the apparent ability of millions of rural migrants to adapt to the urban environment and survive in it. Shantytowns were growing, to be sure, but seldom were they the site of mass starvation or mass rebellion, outcomes that could be anticipated given the assumed idleness and desperation of the "marginal mass."[13] A breakthrough in the understanding of this anomaly came after a study of urban labor markets in Ghana sponsored by the International Labor Office (ILO). At a conference at the University of Sussex in 1971, the anthropologist Keith Hart described the "formal" and "informal" income opportunities that he observed in Accra, equating the first with salaried jobs and the second with self-employment. He highlighted the notable dynamism of self-employed entrepreneurs whose activities went well beyond those of "shoeshine boys and sellers of matches."[14]

This characterization was then adopted by the ILO mission to Kenya,[15] which defined informality as an urban "way of doing things" whose distinguishing marks included: low entry barriers to entrepreneurship in terms of skill and capital requirements; family ownership enterprises; small scale of operation; labor-intensive production with outdated technology; and unregulated and competitive markets.[16] Hart's analysis changed the way in which the problem of urban excess labor supply was conceptualized. The gloomy portrayals of a swollen tertiary sector or an inert marginal mass gave way to a more dynamic view of popular entrepreneurship in which lack of capital resources was compensated by the ingenuity and motivation of the people involved. More importantly, the proliferation of small informal sector enterprises provided an explanation for the puzzle left unanswered by earlier theories, namely how the migrant poor managed to adapt and survive within the constraints of peripheral urban economies.[17]

In Latin America, the concept of the informal sector was readily adopted by the ILO's Regional Employment Program, known by its Spanish acronym PREALC. Program staff proceeded to elaborate the concept, defining it in terms of "rationality" of production different from that of the modern capitalist economy. According to this view, the economic goal of informal enterprises is to ensure the survival of the individual and his or her immediate family in contrast to the goal of capitalist enterprise, which is to generate and accumulate profit.[18] This distinct rationality of the informal sector was closely tied to its other characteristics, such as little capital use, intensive use of family labor, and activities at the edge of the law.[19]

The writings originating from PREALC on the informal sector preserved Hart's original insight about the mechanisms that allowed the migrant poor to survive in cities, but failed to echo his dynamic characterization of the phenomenon. Informal enterprises were not depicted as a diverse and promising manifestation of popular ingenuity but were interpreted as a simple survival mechanism. The emphasis on the distinct economic "rationalities" in the two sectors gave PREALC writings a strong dualistic bent. Informality became the term of reference for activities excluded from the modern sector and hence was seen as synonymous with poverty. This view came close to earlier portrayals of the urban "marginal" mass and gave rise to numerous conceptual and empirical anomalies.

An Alternative Theory

The heritage of Keith Hart was rescued in a novel way by the Peruvian economist Hernando De Soto during the 1980s. Where PREALC and marginality theorists had seen survival activities employing surplus workers, De Soto saw efficient production and trade organized by small entrepreneurs. He did not acknowledge past research and theorizing on the informal sector, including those of PREALC, but proceeded to an entirely different conceptualization. In his book *The Other Path*,[20] he attributed the origins of informality not so much to excess labor supply as to excess regulation of the economy. According to this view, the "mercantilist" Latin American state survives by granting the privilege of legal participation in the economy to a narrow elite. Informality is the popular response that successfully breaks down this legal barrier.

According to De Soto, popular disregard for legal restrictions leads to de facto deregulation of the economy. Hence, more than a survival mechanism in response to insufficient job creation, informality also represents the irruption of "real" market forces in an economy straitjacketed by mercantilist regulation. From this perspective, the informal entrepreneur is not a low-productivity marginal actor, but something of an economic hero who manages to survive and even prosper despite state oppression.

For De Soto, the massive population shifts from the countryside to the cities in the decades before 1980 provided the demographic base for the informal economy. The dominant urban elites were hostile to the migrants because "each person who migrates to the capital is in some way a potential competitor and it is a natural inclination to try to avoid "competition."[21] Rural migrants to Peru's cities were transformed into informal workers less by their numbers than by the legal barriers to their participation in the mainstream economy. Informal economic activity was originally a survival mechanism, but gradually it expanded in response to the rigidities and limitations of the mercantilist state. Informal provision of goods and services proved to be a cheap and efficient method, leading, in Peru, to the conversion of unregulated enterprise into the real economic core of many industrial and service activities. This view of informality is reflected in De Soto's elaboration of a series of stages (10 for housing, 13 for trade, and 17 for transport) that mark "the steady advance of informal over formal society and the latter's corresponding retreat."[22]

This alternative conceptualization proved immensely influential in policy circles, in part because of its overlap with the shift in mainstream economic thought from Keynesian to neoliberal and supply-side doctrines. De Soto's call to dismantle state regulatory barriers so that popular entrepreneurship could flourish found a receptive audience in a number of international development agencies, some of which made his views their own.[23] Yet this optimistic portrayal also gave rise to empirical and theoretical contradictions that, to some extent, were the obverse of those created by PREALC's analysis. Whereas the latter overemphasized the marginal character of urban informal activities and the associated poverty, De Soto's analysis leaned in the opposite direction. We shall return to examine the conceptual difficulties associated with each approach after summarizing the empirical material in support of their respective positions.

Measurement Strategies

Because of its very nature, informality is difficult to measure since it consists of activities generally unrecorded in official statistics. For this reason, all measurement strategies attempted so far suffer limitations. PREALC analysts, for example, have had difficulty operationalizing the different "rationalities" of production that distinguish formal from informal activities. In the absence of measures to fit the theory, PREALC's research has relied on proxies available in national censuses and in household surveys. The approach consists of designating entire occupational categories as informal on the basis of their presumed correspondence with the conceptual definition.

Thus the self-employed and their unremunerated family workers have been consistently classified as "informal" on the assumption that they engage in low-productivity, low-pay activities. Domestic servants were similarly so classified in earlier estimates, though, for reasons that are not clear, they came to be excluded from more recent figures. Conversely, owners and salaried workers in small enterprises were absent from earlier estimates concerning the informal sector, but are included in recent ones. The definition of "small enterprise" also varies across countries and years, ranging from businesses employing "less than 20" workers to "less than 5." Albeit marred by such changes and inconsistencies PREALC is the only agency that has prepared estimates of the informal sector for every country in Latin America. Summary figures reflecting the evolution of these estimates between 1960 and 1989 are presented in Table 7-3. According to PREALC, during this period approximately 30 percent of the Latin American urban EAP was employed informally. The virtual constancy of this estimate over the 30-year period is noteworthy given both the important changes in Latin American economies and the shifting occupational categories included in PREALC's definition of the informal sector. Variations by country are much greater, both across levels of development and over time. The estimated share of persons in the informal sector within the total urban labor force ranged during the period from a low of approximately 20 percent in the more developed countries such as Costa Rica, Uruguay, and Venezuela to approximately 60 percent in Bolivia and Ecuador. The steep drop in this share in Bolivia between 1980 and 1989 is largely a statistical artifact reflecting changes in the occupational categories included in the definition of this sector.[24]

The organization created by Hernando De Soto, the Institute for Liberty and Democracy (ILD), has not produced similar regionwide estimates, but has concentrated on documenting the extent of informality in metropolitan Lima. In his book, De Soto[25] defines the informal sector in terms of the illegal pursuit of legal economic ends, focusing on three sectors: housing, transport, and petty commerce. The choice combines a subsistence activity (creating housing for self) with two market-oriented ones, while excluding manufacturing. ILD estimates that, in 1982, some 43 percent of all housing in Lima was built informally, providing shelter to 47 percent of the city's population. The replacement cost of this housing was calculated at US$8.3 billion. In commerce, over 91,000 street vendors supported an estimated 314,000 people and generated gross sales of US$322 million per year. In addition, according to ILD, 39,000 other informal merchants built 274 street markets with an estimated value of US$41 million, supporting 125,000 people. In transport, informal entrepreneurs controlled over 90 percent of urban public buses. The 1984 replacement value of their fleet was estimated at US$620 million. The value of the related infrastructure (gas pumps, repair shops, etc.) was estimated at US$400 million.

Other estimates by De Soto and his associates include the claim that in the mid-1980s 61.2 percent of total work hours in Peru were dedicated to informal activities; that 48 percent of the economically active population was engaged in informal activities; and that the latter

Table 7-3.

Latin America: estimates of urban informal employment as a percent of the urban economically active population, 1960-89

Country	1960	1970	1980	1989
Argentina	21.1	19.1	23.0	28.7
Bolivia	62.2	56.0	56.5	27.0
Brazil	27.3	27.9	27.2	28.6
Chile	35.1	23.9	27.1	30.0
Colombia	39.0	31.4	34.4	27.3
Costa Rica	29.3	22.6	19.9	22.0
Ecuador	35.2	58.0	52.8	n.a
El Salvador	42.6	39.5	39.9	n.a
Guatemala	51.6	43.5	40.0	n.a
Mexico	37.4	34.9	35.8	34.8
Panama	25.3	26.5	35.6	n.a
Peru	46.9	41.0	40.5	39.0
Uruguay	18.6	20.7	23.1	19.0
Venezuela	32.3	31.4	20.8	23.3
Latin America	30.8	29.6	30.2	31.0

Sources: PREALC estimates given in García and Tokman 1981, Table 1; García 1991, Tables 5,7,9; Infante and Klein 1990, Tables 2, 4.

accounted for 38.9 percent of gross domestic product (GDP), a share projected to rise to 61.3 percent by the end of the century.[26] The prima facie value of these estimates has been questioned by two British economists, who argued that they are invalid due to: inappropriate use of monetary measures of transactions counted in the GDP; poorly specified models; and mishandling of econometric methods.[27]

More general conceptual difficulties with this measurement approach will be examined below. It is worth noting that De Soto's definition of the informal sector coincides roughly with the definition of the "underground" economy in developed societies, although methods for measuring the latter have not been applied systematically in Latin America. Underground activities are defined as those that take place outside the existing legal framework, and their aggregate value, in terms of relative proportion of the GDP, is estimated by macroeconomic methods.[28] It is possible that failure to apply these methods to the Latin American context, despite the similarity of definitions, stem from the lack of suitable data. For the more advanced Latin American countries, however, this difficulty is not insurmountable.[29]

The Center for Economic Research of the Private Sector (CEESP) in Mexico estimated the size of the country's underground economy between 1970 and 1985 on the basis of two macroeconomic methods. The first, adapted from Tanzi,[30] estimates the currency in circulation required for the operation of the aboveground, or legal, economy and then subtracts this figure from the actual monetary mass. The difference multiplied by the velocity of money provides an estimate of the magnitude of the underground economy. The ratio of that figure to observed GDP then gives the proportion of the national economy represented by these activities. The method depends on the identification of a base period in which the informal economy is assumed to be insignificant.

Table 7-4 presents estimates of the Mexican underground economy based on the monetary method and on the "physical input" method. In the latter method, the ratio of some physical input of wide use such as electricity consumption calculated for the base period and then extrapolated to the present. Assuming a relative constant ratio of electricity consumption to GDP, it is possible to calculate the expected GDP for each year following the base period. The difference between observed and expected GDP is attributed to the underground economy. As seen in Table 7-4, these methods yield estimates of the informal

Table 7-4.

Mexico: Estimates of the "subterranean" economy as a percent of the official gross domestic product calculated by two methods, 1970-1985

Year	Monetary Method	Physical Input Method
1970	13.5	8.0
1971	13.8	13.5
1972	15.4	15.4
1973	15.2	14.7
1974	20.1	18.7
1975	27.3	19.4
1976	25.6	22.3
1977	27.4	28.5
1978	28.0	30.9
1979	24.9	28.6
1980	33.2	23.6
1981	29.1	25.1
1982	39.3	20.6
1983	29.4	30.1
1984	28.0	33.5
1985	25.7	38.4

Source: CEESP 1987, Table 10.

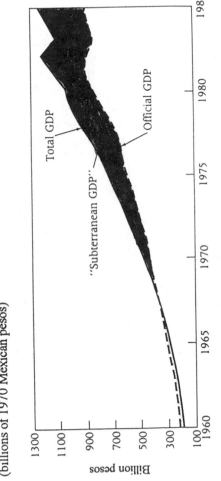

FIGURE 7.1 Mexico: Estimates of the gross domestic product (GDP), 1960-85 (billions of 1970 Mexican pesos)

NOTE: Figure for 1985 is estimated.

SOURCE: CEESP (1987, Table 9).

sector ranging from 20 to 40 percent of the GDP in the 1980s. Eliminating the "anomalous" year 1982 marked by the Mexican debt moratorium, the estimates stabilize in a narrower band of 25 to 38 percent. CEESP notes that both methods show the magnitude of underground activities as increasing steadily. Figure 7.1 portrays this growing gap between the total and official GDPs, based on the physical input method.

The macroeconomic estimates have been criticized on various grounds. The most serious is that they do not differentiate between criminal activities and informal activities proper. The latter involve goods and services that are otherwise licit, but whose production and sale are irregular.[31] Hence the huge estimates of informality that are sometimes reached through these methods may be inflated---for instance, by a large drug underground whose operations are of a nature and size different from those of microentrepreneurs and artisans in the informal sector proper. Despite these limitations, macroeconomic methods provide the best available approximations of the relative weight of unregulated activities in national economies. Their application in Latin America is still rare.

Anomalies and Contradictions

As noted previously, the definition of the informal sector adopted by ILO/PREALC preserves Hart's original insight about the mechanisms that allow migrant poor to survive in the cities, but loses his characterization of this sector as dynamic and flexible. Dubbing all participants in the informal economy "underemployed" or "low-productivity" workers[32] follows from a simple reading of the consequences of the urban labor surplus: migrants are unable to find employment in formal enterprises and, hence, must survive through invented marginal jobs. Although plausible on the surface, this straightforward interpretation confronts a number of conceptual and empirical anomalies.

First, empirical research has uncovered considerable heterogeneity of economic situations within the occupational categories defined by PREALC as informal. Microentrepreneurs consistently earn more than informal workers and self-employed, while the relative earnings of the latter two categories vary across countries. More importantly, surveys conducted in major cities of Latin America find that owners of microenterprises and some of the self-employed earn significantly more than salaried workers in the formal sector. The average ratio of micro entrepreneurial earnings to those of formal workers is approximately 2 to 1, while that to informal workers' earnings is 4 to 1.[33] Roberts,[34] analyzing earnings in the Mexican urban economy, concludes that "entrepreneurs of all types, except the unregistered self-employed, earn more than employed workers, even those in large enterprises."

This economic advantage of microentrepreneurs accounts for a common pattern observed in past fieldwork, namely the decision of formal-sector workers to quit their jobs in order to establish informal enterprises.[35] Skills learned in formal industry are transferred to the new mini-firms, which are often capitalized by severance pay to which formal workers are entitled. This pattern is clearly at odds with accounts of the informal sector as consisting entirely of marginal workers. At minimum, two distinct class positions must be distinguished: informal microentrepreneurs with access to some capital and labor resources; and unprotected workers and the self-employed. PREALC staff have belatedly recognized the internal heterogeneity of the informal economy and the potential for accumulation of some of its enterprises,[36] but their basic conceptualization continues to give rise to other anomalies.

Second, PREALC's definition leaves little room for analysis of interactions between informal activities and the rest of the economy. Contrary to the characterization of informal activities as "traditional," studies in a number of Latin American countries have found them to be quite modern in terms of their technology and their markets. Repair services of all kinds, residential construction, production of garments and footwear, and local and long-distance motorized transport are just some of the activities in which informal entrepreneurs engage.[37] The dynamism of informal enterprise and its manifold connections with larger firms are central issues entirely missed by an analysis that defines the sector as consisting of survival activities engaged in by a surplus labor force.

A third problem relates to the measurement of informality. The assignment of workers to the formal or informal sector on the basis of broad occupational categories is empirically inaccurate because in the context of peripheral economies, workers frequently alternate between different forms of employment or combine them during the same workday. Formal employees commonly moonlight as oddjobbers or establish informal enterprises as sidelines.[38] These complex combinations are lost by a rigid classification of individuals in either the formal or the informal sector.

Fourth, the implicit equation of small enterprises with informality does not square with empirical facts, insofar as large private firms also hire workers casually, "off the books," and under various subcontracting arrangements. These forms of employment are, of course, not reported to the authorities and hence do not figure in the official statistics. Field research has consistently uncovered their existence, however, indicating that wages and work conditions of these supposedly "formal" workers can be more precarious than those in the categories labeled "informal" by PREALC. This is especially true when the comparison involves informal entrepreneurs.[39]

The final anomaly is that the PREALC definition renders its analyses incommensurate with those of the informal economy in other world regions. Elsewhere, the consensus is that activities are informal if they take place outside the pale of regulation to which they should legally be subject.[40] Such a definition encompasses both activities of low productivity and low earnings and those that are not. Indeed the original reason for coining the concept of informality and the present justification for its analysis lie in its distinctness from sheer poverty. If the two were equivalent, there would be no reason for inventing a new term. The PREALC identification of informality with poverty discourages analysis of the complex forms of this phenomenon and prevents systematic comparison of the Latin American data on the phenomenon with empirical results for other parts of the world.

The definition of informality by De Soto---the illegal pursuit of legal economic ends---is in line with the international consensus. The principal conceptual problem in this case stems from the analysis of the origins of informality and the assumed dynamics of the formal-informal relationship. For De Soto and his followers, the origins of the phenomenon lie in the extensive regulation of the economy. If this were the case, other highly regulated economies such as those of northern Europe would have spawned informal sectors, but they have not. The policy solution advocated by De Soto's definition---removing all state regulation of economic activity---is similarly problematic. At the extreme, it would lead to the elimination not of the informal economy, but of the capitalist market. As noted by a long tradition of economic analysts, modern markets are highly regulated institutions.[41] State agencies must oversee transactions and guarantee the observation of contracts. Otherwise, there would be no rational basis for long-term capitalist investment and planning. The formal or regulated economy is hence the proper realm of modern capitalism. Eliminating it through removal of state controls would not give rise to market-led development, but to the disarticulation of orderly economic activity.[42]

Second, De Soto and his followers portray the formal-informal relationship as adversarial insofar as unregulated enterprise represents the popular reaction to the elitist, state-protected enclave. On this point, this school converges with PREALC in viewing Latin American economies as segmented between those "in" and "out" of the modern sector. Reality is more complex. Not only are many informal activities modern, as noted above, but they are often initiated with the support and sponsorship of formal firms. Instead of the Trojan Horse that will ultimately break down the fortress of "mercantilist" privilege, the informal sector in fact represents part of the routine operation of capitalism as it is presently organized in Latin America. Research material illustrating this formal-informal articulation will be presented below.

The principal criticism of De Soto and the ILD concerning measurement is their failure to estimate the magnitude of informality for all of Latin America. Even the figures offered for Lima and for all of Peru are of dubious value because of obscure data sources and the ad hoc character of some estimates. ILD measures are designed to highlight the massive scale of informality in Peru, but they are not easily replicable---either because sources are not given or because the estimating models are poorly specified.[43]

An Alternative Approach: Structural Articulation

The difficulties encountered with the two principal conceptualizations of the informal sector in Latin America have given rise to a third perspective. It evolved in dialogue with the earlier work by Hart and ILO experts and subsequent analysis of the phenomenon by PREALC. In agreement with definitions of informality in other world regions, it characterizes the phenomenon as income-earning activities unregulated by the state in contexts where similar activities are so regulated.[44] This approach is similar to that of De Soto in emphasizing the role of the state in the emergence and growth of the informal economy but differs in that it does not see this sector as isolated from the formal economy or as composed exclusively of microentrepreneurs. In place of the dualistic images of Latin American urban economies proposed by the other perspectives, this third approach describes unified systems encompassing a dense network of relationships between formal and informal enterprises.[45]

The nature of this articulation is not uniform across countries, but varies with the scope of state legislation, the requirements of modern firms, and the size and characteristics of the labor force. This perspective is labeled "structuralist" because its core is precisely the analysis of the structure of formal-informal relationships as facets of the same economic system. This analysis begins by noting that the condition of excess labor supply created by rural-urban migration has had more complex consequences than the survival of the poor at the margins of the urban economy. Two such consequences are particularly important: the functions that informal enterprise plays in support of modern capitalist accumulation; and the creation of new niches in the labor market, corresponding to new positions in the class structure. Each is discussed below.

Functions in the Informal Economy

Contrary to previous prescriptions, the structuralist perspective views informal activities as closely interlinked with activities in the formal sector. A first linkage is the supply of low-cost goods and services for workers in formal enterprises. Unregulated small artisans and merchants engage in the provision of everything from cheap clothing and footwear to auto and residential repairs. Foodstands, urban transport, gardening and landscaping, house cleaning, and the sale of second-hand appliances are services supplied by informal entrepreneurs. The consumption of basic and not-so-basic goods by workers in the formal sector seldom occurs through regulated market channels, but is generally supplied by informal sources. Cheaper informal goods and services increase the consumption "yield" of formal wages, allowing working-class households to make ends meet within the constraint of paltry salaries.[46]

From the standpoint of the economic system as a whole, the existence of an informal market represents a vast subsidy to formal capitalist enterprises, insofar as it makes labor costs lower than they would be if such sources of supply did not exist. Put differently, informal enterprises undergird the profitability of their formal counterparts by allowing the latter to maintain wage levels below the cost of basic needs if these had to be purchased through regulated channels. Not only working-class families, but the urban middle class avails itself of the plethora of informally provided services. The availability of cheap domestic, gardening, and personal services of all kinds is the key factor allowing Latin American upper- and middle-class families to maintain enviable lifestyles.[47]

A still closer interface between the formal and informal sectors is the common practice of large firms to reach down directly into the informal labor pool to allocate a variety of production and marketing tasks. The mechanisms at play are twofold: direct hiring off-workers off the books; and subcontracting of production, input supplies, or final sales to informal entrepreneurs. The incentive for these linkages is the avoidance of legal regulations that increase labor costs and decrease managerial flexibility. To the extent that the costly work force of formal enterprises can be reduced by off-the-books hiring and subcontracting, final profits can be significantly improved.

Because these arrangements skirt legal regulation, managers of firms are careful to conceal them from the authorities. For this reason, they do not appear in the official statistics, leading users of such data to the erroneous conclusion that these linkages do not exist. Structuralist-inspired studies of these interactions have been based instead on first-hand observational studies. Contrary to reports based on official data, most direct observation has reported multiplicity of formal-informal arrangements. Table 7-5 summarizes six recent studies in various Latin American cities documenting the forms this articulation can take.

The most revealing of these studies in terms of the scope of the linkages involve electric appliance homeworkers in Mexico City and garment manufacturing for export in indigenous villages of Guatemala. In the first example, Benería and Roldan[48] were able to document a complex chain reaching from a US multinational firm producing electrical appliances for the Mexican market, to domestic formal suppliers, informal subcontractors, and homeworkers---generally women---who assembled certain parts for a piece rate. At each descending step of the ladder, work conditions became more precarious and wage levels lower. In Guatemala, Pérez-Sáinz and Leal[49] traveled to the indigenous villages surrounding the capital to document the remarkable system organized by agents of several well-known US

Table 7.5. Articulation of the Relationship between Formal and Informal
Activities in Latin America: Selected Examples

Author	Year	Industry	City	Findings
Lomnitz	1976	Construction	Mexico City	Formal construction firms employ informal subcontractors who hire workers on demand in the shantytowns and nearby villages. Subcontractors commonly earn more than engineers or architects in charge of the project, but workers are paid close to the minimum with few or no legal protections. Once a project is finished, workers are dismissed. Most residential and commercial construction in the city is organized in this manner.
Peattie	1982	Footwear	Bogota	The bulk of the industry is small-scale with only five large producers. Subcontracting to informal shops is widespread. Large department stores advance working capital to informal shops or industrial firms, which subcontract in turn part of their production. Thousands of artisanal shops produce for the popular market and for larger firms, such as Bata-Canada, which affixe their own labels. The process of "stitching the uppers" is usually done by women working at home for a piece rate.
Birbeck Fortuna & Prates	1978, 1979 1989	Paper, plastic, and other recyclables	Cali, Montevideo	Garbage pickers supply industry with significant quantities of recyclable inputs at substantial savings. The pickers are industrial outworkers with no job security or benefits.

Author	Year	Industry	City	Findings
Benería & Roldan	1987	Electrical Appliances	Mexico City	A subcontracting industrial chain makes use of informal shops for production of labor-intensive parts used as inputs for formal domestic firms, which are in turn subcontractors of a U.S. multinational. When demand exceeds the informal shops' modest capacity, the excedent is passed down to homeworkers who are paid piece rates below the legal minimum.
Lozano	1992	Jewelry	Santo Domingo	Jewelry production for export and the tourist trade uses local semi-precious stones such as jade. Tourist shops and export houses that control the trade subcontract production to cooperatives of informal artisans. The latter must advance the cost of purchasing the stones from local wholesalers. The slim margin between high input costs and final prices is compensated by use of family labor, but artisans are unable to accumulate enough capital to create their own formal market outlets.
Pérez-Sáinz & Leal	1992	Garments	Guatemala	Indigenous garment producers are subcontracted by U.S. clothing companies to sew various items at a specified rate. The buyers provide the cloth and designs, and the contractors provide the machines and labor, usually female kin. All deals are arranged verbally. Rates paid to contractors are a small fraction of the price at which finished items are sold abroad.

clothing companies. The system, known locally as *maquila*, transformed these villages from traditional producers of handicrafts for the domestic market to informal garment assemblers for export. Indian entrepreneurs are provided with quantities of pre-cut cloth, design patterns, and sometimes low-credit loans for the purchase of sewing machines. Indian village women provide the manual labor, sewing items for a piece rate generally below the minimum wage and without social security protection. Costs of any defects in production are deducted from their wages.

Also revealing is the system through which the activities of garbage pickers, in appearance the most "marginal" of workers, are connected with modern capitalist production. Studies by Birkbeck[50] in Cali and by Fortuna and Prates[51] in Montevideo document how informal garbage collectors are actually disguised workers for large industries, supplying them with significant quantities of recyclable inputs. Paper, plastics, bone, and glass are collected, sorted, and packaged by the collectors; they sell them to informal deposit owners, who, in turn, pass the product to wholesalers that supply the large orders of industrial firms. The firms dictate the final price of recyclables, with each intermediary along the chain taking a share. Collectors receive the lowest share without any form of protection. In this fashion, formal industries avail themselves of the labor of informal workers without assuming any responsibility for them.

These examples illustrate the fact that, contrary to earlier definitions, informal activities are not necessarily traditional or marginal, but can be closely knit into a web of the modern capitalist economy. The same examples also contradict De Soto's characterization of the informal sector as an assemblage of independent entrepreneurs. In reality, they are closely intertwined and dependent on firms within the regulated sector.

Heterogeneity of Class Positions

The second significant consequence of a structuralist analysis is to highlight the fact that the informal sector is internally heterogeneous. The reason lies in the articulation of regulated and unregulated activities, discussed above, which opens opportunities for a number of people to insert themselves as intermediaries. Informal entrepreneurs who perform these intermediary roles commonly earn more than workers in regulated firms. This empirical anomaly is resolved once we realize that the informal economy is more than the simple translation of surplus labor into survival activities.

Structuralists have attempted to systematize this diversity through a typology of informal activities encompassing: direct subsistence activities; informal activities subordinate to production and marketing in the formal sector; and autonomous informal enterprises with modern technology and some capacity for capital accumulation.[52] The third type comes close to De Soto's characterization of the informal sector, but its existence is exceptional in Latin America. It has been documented primarily in other contexts, such as the "industrial districts" of flexible microproducers in Emilia-Romagna and other central Italian provinces.[53]

Empirical work conducted from a structuralist perspective has focused mainly on documenting the relationships between the two sectors of urban economies. For national estimates, this school has relied on secondary figures on the proportion of the economically active population that is not covered by the social security system. Absence of coverage stands as a proxy for unregulated work. Most estimates of social security coverage or exclusion are reported for the total, not urban, economically active population and do not differentiate between workers and microentrepreneurs. Further, coverage by the social security system does not exclude the possibility that workers engage in unregulated activities on the side; hence it underestimates the actual magnitude of informality. Lastly, Mesa-Lago[54] notes in his analysis of Latin American social security systems, the quality of the data is generally poor and does not differentiate between types and levels of coverage.

Despite these limitations, a comparison of the figures on the EAP excluded from legal labor protection and figures on "underemployed" workers, provided by PREALC, is instructive. This comparison is presented in Table 7-6. Except for Brazil, where the extension of some assistance to the entire population led to an official claim of near-universal coverage, the uncovered percentage of the EAP shown here consistently exceeds the PREALC estimates.[55] The range is from a few percentage points to over 50 percent of national EAP. These gaps can be tentatively interpreted as an approximation of the proportion of wage workers who labor under irregular conditions, a category implicitly defined by PREALC as formal and by structuralists as informal. For

Table 7-6. Latin America: Estimates of the informal sector, 1980

Country	% of Nat'l EAP Not Covered by Social Security	% of EAP Under-employed[1]
Argentina	30.9	25.7
Bolivia	81.5	74.1
Brazil	13.0[2]	44.5
Chile	32.7	28.9
Colombia	80.3	41.0
Costa Rica	51.6	27.2
Dominican Rep.	88.7[3]	40.6
Ecuador	78.7	63.3
El Salvador	88.4	49.0
Guatemala	66.9	50.9
Honduras	85.6	49.7
Mexico	59.5	40.4
Nicaragua	81.1	52.1
Panama	47.7	45.5
Peru	62.6	55.8
Uruguay	34.2[4]	27.1
Venezuela	55.8	31.5
Latin America	56.3[5]	42.2

Sources: Mesa-Lago 1985: 342; Mesa-Lago 1991: 50; Portes, et al. 1986: 731; PREALC 1982: 34-81; Wilkie and Perkal 1985, Table 1308; Wilson 1985: 254.

---

[1] Defined by PREALC as the sum of the self-employed minus professionals, unremunerated family workers, domestic servants, and "traditional" rural workers.

[2] Coverage in 1980 is based on selected assistance programs based on universalistic criteria rather than tied to employment. See text.

[3] 1985 figure.

[4] Based on a probability survey of the Montevideo working-class population in 1985. Official figures report near-universal coverage based on selected programs extended to all citizens.

[5] Weighted average.

Table 7-7. Mexico: Estimates of the urban informal economy based on occupational classification and on lack of social security coverage, selected cities, 1989

Informal Employment as % of Urban EAP	Mexico City %	Cities Guadalajara %	Monterrey %	Ciudad Juarez %	Total %
By Occupation:					
(1)*	20.4	22.2	15.6	19.5	19.6
(2)**	38.2	44.1	32.7	32.4	37.6
By Lack of Coverage:***	49.2	54.1	39.6	39.0	46.8
Entrepreneurs	6.7	8.8	6.4	6.8	7.2
Self-employed	14.8	14.5	11.8	14.7	14.0
Workers	27.7	30.8	21.4	17.5	25.6
N	8445	5540	5024	3010	22019

*   Sum of unremunerated family workers and the self-employed.

**   The above two categories plus workers in micro-enterprises and unregistered microenterprises.

*** Entrepreneurs, workers, and the self-employed without Social Security protection.

Latin America as a whole, the difference was approximately 14 percent of the EAP in 1980.

One of the few large data sets that contain reliable information on both employment category and social security coverage is the Mexican governments's Urban Employment Survey of 1989. The survey collected data on a representative sample of some 30,000 adult Mexican workers in seven metropolitan areas, including the four largest cities. As analyzed by Roberts,[56] this survey yields estimates of the proportion of the employed labor force working informally according to the PREALC and structuralist definitions, as well as an internal differentiation of the informal sector by employment categories.

Table 7-7 presents results of our re-analysis of these data for Mexico's four largest cities. The empirical definition of informality commonly employed by PREALC yields estimates that are approximately half of those produced on the basis of lack of social security protection. Inclusion in the PREALC estimates of owners of and workers in microenterprises significantly reduces this difference, but the figures are still lower in each city than those based on lack of coverage. The remaining gap is directly attributable to workers in large firms who do not receive legal protection. The breakdown of the informal sector by employment reveals that microentrepreneurs, the best paid class within the sector, represent between 6 and 9 percent of the employed labor force in each city. The self-employed comprise an average of 14 percent of the urban EAP and 30 percent of those working informally. Unprotected wage workers represent one-fourth of all urban workers and the majority (55 percent) of the informal labor force.

Conclusions: Policies toward the Informal Sector

The topic of informality has received much attention from national governments and international development agencies. In Latin America, numerous programs have been directed to improving conditions in this sector. A great deal of confusion exists, however, about its boundaries, internal dynamics, and needs. Much of the confusion stems from competing definitions of the phenomenon. The critique of the two dominant theoretical perspectives and the outline of the alternative structuralist position above bear directly on the question of policy, since each approach yields different and, at times, conflicting policy recommendations. For the economists in PREALC, the solution to the problem of informal employment is a straightforward derivation of the view of this sector as part of the excess labor supply. Since informals are "excluded" from modern employment, job creation must be expanded as rapidly as possible in order to absorb more labor. This can be achieved through accelerated capital investments in industry and other sectors of the urban economy, either by state or private enterprise.[57]

For the economists and planners assembled by De Soto, the informal sector is not part of the problem of underdevelopment, but part of its solution. It represents the way in which less privileged groups have managed to bypass mercantilist controls. Hence, for Latin American economies to enter a new "path" of development, the state must be removed from the economy so as to give freer rein to the hand of the market. Policies of deregulation and privatization advocated by this approach are closely aligned with those promoted in Latin America by the International Monetary Fund, the World Bank, and other international agencies.[58]

Economists and sociologists grouped under the structuralist label have advanced a third approach that combines elements of the preceding two. Like the PREALC approach, the structuralist approach holds that casual self-employment and other "survival" activities can be reduced through capital investments in the modern industrial and service sectors. This approach notes, however, that rigid legal codes protecting formal workers provide a powerful incentive for firms to avoid expanding their regular labor plants and to make use, whenever possible, of casual labor and subcontracting. In this situation, the informal sector may expand rather than contract in response to increased labor demand.

There is partial agreement between the structuralist position and the policies recommended by De Soto and the ILD. Nevertheless, structuralists stop far short of advocating complete removal of state controls from the labor market. Greater flexibility does require fewer constraints on firms to adjust the size and composition of their labor force in response to economic conditions. However, other protective regulations on wages, work conditions, health and accident insurance, and unemployment compensation should be maintained. Their elimination would lead to a pattern of worker abuse, minimal wages, and disincentives for worker training and technological innovation. The result would not be absorption of workers into the formal sector, but the informalization of the entire economy, as work conditions in larger firms begin to approach those of today's informal enterprises.

For structuralists, removal of state controls would not help the consolidation and growth of microenterprises, as posited by De Soto. Such enterprises exist precisely by taking advantage of interstices in the regulated economy. Lacking much capital or technology, their sole market advantage consists in the ability to escape tax and labor codes. The informalization of the entire economy through removal of these rules would also eliminate the small firms' advantages. The most likely prognosis in this situation would be the disappearance of microenterprises. The typology of informal activities developed by structuralists indicates that there are certain instances where microenterprises have indeed been the engine for sustained economic growth. The experiences of central Italy and Hong Kong are most commonly cited in this regard.[59]

However, there is a large difference between the genesis of these experiences and the policies advocated by De Soto. Every documented instance of the transformation of an informal economy of direct subsistence into an informal economy of growth has been accompanied by the active participation of state agencies in the process, albeit in novel and imaginative ways. In the Italian case, for example, agencies of the provincial governments intervened vigorously to provide the necessary resources and coordination that transformed informal artisanal enterprises into cooperatives of high-tech firms. Without this government assistance, access to the required capital, technical training, and markets would have been impossible.[60]

In synthesis, the goals advocated by both PREALC and the ILD are desirable, but significant gaps exist between such goals and the policies proposed to achieve them. Complete absorption of the labor force into the formal sector is desirable, but it will not occur without relaxation of rigid labor rules. Transformation of subsistence activities into dynamic autonomous small firms is equally desirable, but it will not occur through simple removal of state controls without sustained programs in support of this aim. Policy alternatives stemming from the structuralist perspective combine greater flexibility in existing labor codes with active programs in support of small entrepreneurial development. To work seriously as an entrepreneurial incubator, a program targeted on informal producers should be as flexible as the new firms that it is trying to promote. It should be fully decentralized and adapted to the needs and skills present in local communities. Most importantly, it should pay attention to the social ties and community bonds already present among informal artisans and merchants, a resource commonly neglected by individual-centered programs. Efforts targeted on particular individuals may produce several rags-to-riches stories, but will not lead to emergence of the communities of resilient, technologically advanced firms that constitute the model for policy in this area. Only through a combination of measures grounded on the social dynamics of the informal sector can the energies and entrepreneurial potential of its members be realized.

Notes

1. This is a revised version of a paper written for the Bureau of International Labor Affairs, US Department of Labor. The authors thank Gregory Schoepfle and Jorge Perez-Lopez of the Bureau's staff for their comments on an earlier version. The paper was written while the senior author was a visiting fellow at the Russell Sage Foundation, whose support is gratefully acknowledged.

2. Davis, *World Urbanization, 1950-1970.* Volume 1: *Basic Data for Cities, Countries, and Regions.* Population Monograph Series, no. 4. (1969); Morse, "Trends and Issues in Latin American Urban Research," *Latin American Research Review* (1971).

3. Economic Commission for Latin America (ECLA), *Statistical Yearbook for Latin America* (New York, 1981); Economic Commission for Latin America and the Caribbean (ECLAC), *Statistical Yearbook for Latin America* (New York, 1991).

4. Gereffi, "Rethinking Development Theory: Insights from East Asia and Latin America," (1989).

5. Portes and Walton, *Urban Latin America: The Political Condition from Above and Below* (1976), Ch. 2.

6. Roberts, *Cities of Peasants* (1978).

7. Castells and Laserna, "The New Dependency: Technological Change and Socio-economic Restructuring in Latin America (1989).

8. García, "Growing Labor Absorption with Persistent Unemployment." (1982).

9. García and Tokman, "Dinámica del subempleo en América Latina," (1981); Portes, "Latin American Class Structures" (1985).

10. Davis (1969).

11. Nun, Marin, and Murmis, "La marginalidad en América Latina," (1967).

12. Quoted in Moser, "Informal Sector or Petty Commodity Production: Dualism or Dependence in Urban Development," *World Development* 6 (1978): 1048.

13. Bairoch, *Urban Unemployment in Developing Countries: The Nature of the problem and Proposals for its Solution* (1973).

14. Portes and Walton, *Urban Latin America: The Political Condition from Above and Below* (1976), Ch. 3.

15. Hart (1973, 68).

16. International Labor Office (ILO), *Employment, Incomes and Inequality: A Strategy for Increasing Productive Employment in Kenya* (1972).

17. Peatti, "Living Poor: A View from the Bottom," (1974).

18. Juan Pablo Pérez-Sáinz, *Informalidad urbana en América Latina: enfoque, problematicas e interrogantes* (1992).

19. PREALC (1981); Tokman (1987).

20. Klein and Tokman (1988).

21. De Soto, *The Other Path: The Informal Revolution* (1989).

22. De Soto (1989, 11).

23. De Soto (1989, 75).

24. Bromley (1990).

25. As noted above, PREALC considers the informal economy an exclusively urban phenomenon. But sometimes it provides estimates of the "underemployed" proportion of the total EAP by combining the estimated size of urban informal employment with the labor force in traditional agriculture. For Latin America as a whole, the proportion underemployed by that definition was 42 percent in 1960, 34 percent in 1980, and 37 percent in 1989. See Infante and Klein, "The Latin American Labor Market," *CEPAL Review 45* (1991, Table 2).

26. De Soto, *The Other Path* (1989).

27. De Soto (1989, 12)

28. Rossini and Thomas (1987); Pérez-Sáinz (1992).

29. Feige, "Defining and Estimating Underground and Informal Economies," *World Development* (1990).

30. An important difference between the two definitions is that De Soto's excludes criminal activities, such as the production and sale of drugs. These activities are generally included in estimates of the underground economy.

31. Tanzi (1980, 1982).

32. Castells and Portes (1989).

33. Tokman (1982).

34. Portes, Blitzer, and Curtis (1989).

35. Roberts (1992, 9).

36. Peatti (1982); Fortuna and Prates (1989); Pérez-Sáinz (1992).

37. Infante and Klein (1991).

38. Lomnitz, "Informal Exchange Networks in Formal Systems: A Theoretical Model," (1988); Benería and Roldan, *The Crossroads of Class and Gender* (1987); Fortuna and Prates (1989); Roberts (1992); Lozano (1992).

39. Roberts (1989); Lomnitz (1988); Manigat (1992).

40. Benería and Roldan (1987); Fortuna and Prates (1989); Lomnitz (1988); Portes and Walton (1981), Ch. 3.

41. Feige (1990); Stark, "Bending the Bars of the Iron Cage," (1989).

42. Polanyi, *The Great Transformation* (1957); Granovetter, "Economic Action and Social Structure: The Problem of Embeddedness," (1985); Lie, "The Concept of Mode Exchange," (1992).

43. Evans (1989).

44. Rossini and Thomas (1987).

45. Castells and Portes (1989); Feige (1990).

46. Roberts (1992); Benería (1989); Portes and Benton (1984).

47. Peatti (1974); Roberts (1976).

48. Portes and Walton (1981, 91-94).

49. Benería and Roldan (1987).

50. Pérez-Sáinz and Leal (1992).

51. Birkbeck (1978, 1979).

52. Fortuna and Prates (1989).

53. Portes, Castells, and Benton (1989).

54. Capecchi (189).

55. Mesa-Lago, "Social Security and prospects for Equality in Latin America," (1991).

56. In the 1970s, the Brazilian National Security Institute (INPS) in urban areas and its counterpart FUNRURAL in the countryside extended some assistance programs to most of the population without regard for employment status. This led to an official claim that coverage had leaped from 27 percent in 1970 to 87 percent in 1980. The latter figure is, of course, an overestimate of the proportion of the labor force fully covered by legally mandated protection. On the evolution of Brazilian social security, see Malloy, *The Politics of Social Security in Brazil* (1979).

57. Roberts (1992).

58. García (1982); Infante and Klein (1991).

59. Evans (1989); Bromley (1990).

60. Sabel, *The Division of Labor in Industry* (1982).

61. Similar experiences in Hong Kong and in various European "industrial districts" document the same lesson. The dearth of successful instances in Latin America is attributable to the absence of state intervention, at least in ways that would actively support the capitalization and technological development of high-tech small firms. See Castells and Laserna (1989). Also see Lazerson (1988) and Capecchi (1989).

8

The Informal Sector, the Popular, and Public Policy

Mary C. Froehle

Increasing political interest in the informal sector within Latin America has coincided with processes of democratization. The need for politicians to seek votes from the large and growing popular sectors of the population, and the more democratic environment in which oppositional groups can express their interests have considerably increased the visibility and power of people at the base.[1] One result of this political climate has been a more active approach toward the development of public policy concerning the informal sector. Affinities can be observed between alliances of the state and classes or class segments, the preferred theoretical interpretation of the informal sector, and resulting public policy. The policies adopted tend to more closely favor one or another of the currently debated theories depending on the exact nature of the political climate and the political and economic alliances that have been forged.

At least until quite recently, the PREALC approach was the most widely accepted and utilized theory of informality in Latin American public policy.[2]   The theory has particular appeal in situations of alliance between the state and national capital. Government programs based on this theory typically have two main goals: increasing access to credit through low interest or targeted loan programs and improvements in education and training.[3]   Such policies directly address the issues of imperfect capital markets and low endowments of human capital raised by PREALC theorists.[4]   With relatively little investment, the state can provide jobs and goods for the poor and thereby increase social stability.   From the perspective of national capital, the informal economy is seen as benefitting the development of domestic markets because "profits stay in the country rather than being repatriated to corporate headquarters in New York or being stashed in private bank accounts in Miami."[5] It is widely recognized that the informal sector has developed a highly efficient means for distribution and exchange among some of the most difficult to reach segments of the national market.   Thus public policy incorporates the informal sector in order to "favor the circulation of national production."[6] These policies benefit the informal sector in the short run, however, the underlying intention is toward the eventual absorption of this sector and the expansion of the formal economy.

In light of declining possibilities for domestic industry in many Latin American countries, the increasing acceptance of neoliberal theory may reflect new alliances between relatively weak states and international capital.   International pressures have clearly increased the saliency of the neoliberal agenda to Latin American governments.   Loan policies of the International Monetary Fund and World Bank, as well as international efforts for trade liberalization, have given rather pointed direction to governments concerned with their very survival. Indirectly, such policies are expected to benefit the small entrepreneur. According to neoliberals, informal businesses will have more opportunity for success in markets free of the protectionism that favored the formal sector.[7] Free trade will lead to greater efficiency as businesses unable to operate efficiently fail against the competition.   Since small businesses have already demonstrated their ability to maximize their comparative advantage in labor intensive production, the question becomes one of extending this advantage to the arena of international competition.[8]

In a sense, it is rather contradictory to expect the state to support policies toward informality that severely limit its role. This may explain why the neoliberal agenda has not been adopted wholesale in the form of guaranteed property rights and deregulation. Instead, the state has tended to simply not enforce labor and environmental regulations and other restrictive legislation.[9] There are also seeming contradictions in the state supporting a sector that by its very nature eludes the control of the state, including the non-payment of taxes. However, Pásara cautions against making too much of the facile relationship between the state's interest in revenue and the inability to tax informal activity.[10] Informal activity stimulates economic growth. While taxes may not be collected at the point of production, Pásara points out that tax structures can be altered to focus instead on the taxation of consumption. In this way the state still benefits from the increased economic activity.

Applications of both PREALC and neoliberal theories, in spite of the different alliances between the state and domestic or international capital, have resulted in state policy that has been relatively favorable toward the informal sector. As structural theory suggests, this level of consistency is to be expected because of the importance of the informal sector as a tool of capital, domestic or foreign, against labor. Public policy toward the informal sector is a reflection of the state's responsiveness to capital. Policies of credit and training to encourage women to sew at home, as put forth by adherents of PREALC's theory, or policies overlooking the seizure of land for housing, as proposed by neoliberals, both result in a type of wage-subsidy by the state.[11] This is not to imply that according to structural theory the state does not have its own interests in promoting informal activities. Informality may be a result of the economic processes of global capitalism, but the state can utilize the existence of the informal sector to its own advantage. For example, small amounts of investment in informal activities can placate the disadvantaged and quell unrest. If funnelled judiciously, the same funds can also buy essential political support.[12]

The persistence of informality and its increasingly large share of economic activity, when combined with the democratic state's concern for support among the largest segments of the population and the state bureaucracy's interest in control, suggest another potential alliance. While remote, the possibility of an alliance between the state and the informal sector is more plausible in light of Matos Mar's reflection that it no longer makes sense to speak of the informal sector because the smaller sector is the formal sector.[13] At what share of national production does the informal sector become a source of autonomous power? What is the economic source of power when domestic capital is hobbled and international capital looks elsewhere in the face of debt problems and more pliable labor pools in Southeast Asia? For years Latin American governments have modeled their development strategies on the "successes" of other nations and have continually met with failure. Does the informal sector offer a uniquely Latin American, self-generated alternative for development?

Popular Economy

For PREALC theorists the economic potential of individuals in the informal sector is bleak. Economic growth may eventually absorb surplus labor into the formal economy. However, in the mean time, which appears rather long term, competition in the informal sector relegates individuals to low paying, low productivity enterprises. Neoliberals speak hopefully of the "capitalist entrepreneurs" of the informal sector, but they also make it clear that these entrepreneurs will only reach their potential when significant changes are made in the legal structure. Until then these individuals and society must bear the high costs of informality. For structuralists, informality is a new form of intensified exploitation further squeezing a long suffering working class. Even theories of flexibilization with their optimism for the potential contributions of informality to overall growth recognize that this growth is based on capitalist repositioning designed to only more efficiently extract surplus from its workers. One element all these theories share is an analysis of the effects of the system on individuals without considering how the individuals affected might respond to and alter the system. While the structures of informality may constrain individuals, they do not necessarily determine their prospects. History presents many cases where "...people take conditions that have been thrust on them and out of them create a history and a future."[14] This issue is captured in the idea of the popular economy.

As Levine notes, it is important to begin any consideration of the "popular" with a definition of the concept itself.

> Caution is needed because the term "popular" has connotations in contemporary Latin America which catch North Americans unawares. Its core meaning rests not on popularity (something favored by many), but rather on a sense of what constitutes the *populus* - the central defining characteristics of the population. At a

minimum, "popular" thus involves some notion of subordination and inequality, pointing to "popular" groups or classes.... As used in Latin America today, "popular" also implies a sense of collective identity... reference to "the popular" directs attention to the ideas, beliefs and practices, and conditions of poor people...[15]

This term is sometimes used somewhat loosely to refer to indigenous or traditional cultural practices or even to any aspect of the common culture of the poor. As it is used here, the concept of "popular" also incorporates an understanding of this common culture as it is "rooted in their class situation and giving voice to its contradictions and dilemmas." Only this anchoring in economic relations allows for the use of the term "popular" in speaking of "reflection, organization, and action."[16]

An important contribution made by theorists of the popular economy toward understanding these economic relations is to reject negative classifications such as the "the marginalized" or "the dominated." Traditionally, popular classes have been defined in reference to the centrality of other groups in society. However, theorists of the popular economy make it clear that "the popular is not only need but also contributions."[17]   Another contribution made by this school is the recognition that within any household unit one is likely to find some combination of formal work, informal work, delinquency, use of collective demand, such as community cooked meals or informally organized loan programs, and production for home use.[18]   This blurs distinctions between formal and informal, reduces the explanatory power of formal worker relations in understanding class actions,[19] and displaces some of the focus of class struggle from the workplace. The contradictions between capital and formal workers remain important, but they are mixed "in a sea of other social contradictions which opens a new situation full of unknowns."[20]

While the idea of the popular is tied closely to culture, its implications can be seen in material economic actions. Production and distribution of goods in a popular context can be seen as a form of resistance to labor force control.[21]   The various types of economic activity that the family undertakes outside the sphere of formality may be seen as everyday resistance to the process of proletarianization. Pérez Sáinz refers to this activity in the title of his book, *Silent Responses.* Such "responses" also pose a challenge to the traditionally paternalistic, clientelistic Latin American state.[22]

Not all activities of the popular sectors remain at the level of the cotidian, nor are they quite so silent. In a classic analysis, Hirschman argued that while backward and forward economic linkages can be affected by changes in technology, they are "invariant" to social and political change.[23] Missing from his analysis is a consideration of the potential for social and political forces to alter the development of technology, and therefore the direction of growth. As the popular sectors organize both socially and economically, they look toward technology and productive processes appropriate for the development and expansion of their interests. These interests give

> ...power and sense... to the struggles of the subordinate classes for the usufructuary of scientific-technological progress and for the control of their future way of life and economy.[24]

Initial forays into informality may begin as petty acts of resistance, but the networks of economic exchange and production that have developed within the informal sector increase its power of resistance.[25] The vast array of organizations that make up the popular economy, such as commercial establishments, small production enterprises, associations for collective purchases, associations for the construction of housing, and inter-household trading,[26] all contribute to the cohesion of the popular sectors.

Many countries of Latin America have seen a rebirth of voluntary associations, neighborhood organizations, and combative labor unions. "The people" and "lo popular" return or appear for the first time as actors on the political stage now, not as dependent clients but with a broader-based and radically democratic dimension that is new to the continent.[27]

Those whose work focuses on the popular economy recognize the constraints posed by the larger economic system, but their emphasis is on "the spaces that open between said limits,... that hidden alternative potential that informal experiences might hold as possible support for the task of social transformation."[28] In redefining the content of success and in forging new paths to achieve it, informal activity may alter the context in which social transformation takes place.

As the popular economy expands, the state has compelling interests in an alliance with the informal sector given the sheer number of constituents it represents as well as the economic power it wields. At the same time, the state offers its ability to coalesce the vast daily experiences of the base into organized outcomes benefitting the popular economy. Those daily experiences often take the form of interaction within small organizations, but those organizations represent varied and overlapping interests. Larger, societal level organization responsive to the nexus of organizations at the base must exist for the daily experiences to find a voice in the public sphere. In this regard, Palma argues that "party organizations are indispensable in structuring a complete popular praxis that will be adequate for the constitution of the desired collective subject."[29] In other words, under specific conditions, an alliance between the state and the informal sector may result in the satisfaction of mutual self-interest.

Currently there is no national policy that explicitly favors informal activity over the interests of capital, but there has been increased attention given to the potential contribution of the informal economy to national growth. Flexibility advocates speak of an "infrastructure of small firms that would provide a basis for growth."[30] In theories of flexibilization and industrial restructuring the dominance of capital and its control over flexible arrangements to maximize surplus is clear. However, for theorists of the popular economy, a point exists at which these arrangements, constructed by capital, could themselves propel the economy and not vice versa. Informal economic activity is offered as the much sought after alternative path to growth. Not surprisingly, acceptance of the growth generating potential of the popular economy becomes more likely in crisis situations when traditional alliances lose their salience. One example is Peru. Civil unrest and massive debt have crippled formal production, both domestic and international. In light of such a reality, the striking similarities in the political agenda of groups at different ends of the political spectrum are noted.

Both the "new" right and the "new" left see people in the informal sector not as victims, or a backwater, or a side effect, but as Peru's best and most realistic hope for development. Thinkers on both the right and the left are building a new politics, a sociology, and a macroeconomics upon the idea of the informal sector.[31]

Although the exact nature of public policy rooted in the popular has not yet been fully developed, Portes and Schauffler indicate in the conclusion of their chapter the direction that a reorientation toward the popular might take. They discuss the need for decentralized public policy, attention to the social networks in which microbusinesses function, and a focus on community not the individual. Further, policy toward the informal sector must be "grounded on the real social dynamics of the informal sector."[32] Thus, the first step in developing such a public policy must involve a careful analysis of the daily interactions of individuals, groups, and the processes of production and exchange within the popular economy.

Public Policy and the Venezuelan Informal Sector

While the situation of economic crisis has been more extreme in some countries than others, even the most advantaged nations of Latin America have experienced changing economic relations in recent years. All have faced the processes and politics of informalization. In this regard, resource rich Venezuela provides a valuable case study of evolving public policy toward the informal sector and the nature of the political alliances supporting those policies. Current developments in Venezuela suggest that conditions which may contribute to the creation of public policy are more consciously rooted in experience of the popular sectors.

Although the role of oil in Venezuela's economy distinguishes it from many of its Latin American counterparts, oil has not shielded the country from the recurring economic crises that have affected the continent. Venezuela's economy has been described as a form of rentistic capitalism.[33] Even without taking into consideration the cartel created scarcities of oil, natural limitations on its supply create an economic rent which accrues to its owners. Natural scarcity leads to a price for oil in the market which exceeds the cost of its factors of production thus creating a surplus which can be used for investment in other areas. Through taxation and subsoil property rights, the Venezuelan state has been able to appropriate much of this surplus and direct its reinvestment.[34] This made it appear that Venezuela had better prospects for development than other Latin American countries. However, years of continuous recession and slow economic growth despite the enormous increases in oil prices in 1973 and 1979 have brought this belief into question.

Venezuela has proven itself vulnerable to the same economic forces that have challenged its less well-endowed neighbors throughout Latin America. These include the failure of policies of import substitution, persistent income inequalities, inflation, inability to control export prices, and rapidly increasing indebtedness. Between 1970 and 1979

Venezuela's foreign debt grew from one billion to twenty-three billion dollars. In 1985, as a result of internal tensions and competition, OPEC altered its strategy of tightly constrained oil production. The supply of oil increased and prices fell to half of their previous level.[35] During this same period, the Venezuelan government adopted a tight fiscal policy to reduce deficits.[36] The fall in oil prices combined with reduced government expenditures eventually led to a negative rate of growth of 8.6 percent in 1989, the lowest recorded in Venezuelan history.[37] Growth rates have improved in the last four years, though Gross Domestic Product (GDP) in constant dollars is still below the 1973 level and approximately three-quarters of the highest GDP levels of the late 1970s.[38] Inflation in 1992 was over 30 percent.[39] Oil prices are low and not likely to rise significantly in the near future. Interest payments alone on the national debt now amount to over 15 percent of export income.[40]

While GDP has grown slowly or even declined in recent years, population growth has consistently increased by 2 to 3 percent per year.[41] Thus, economic declines are even more pronounced when GDP per capita is considered. These macro-level declines have translated into significantly reduced real wages and increasing poverty. In 1981, approximately 20 percent of urban Venezuelan households were in poverty. By 1988, 60 percent of urban households were in poverty, a threefold increase in just seven years. In 1981, 4 percent of urban households were in a situation of extreme poverty and could not afford to buy food for an adequate diet. By 1988, that number had risen to 20 percent. Between 1978 and 1988 family incomes rose 50 percent, while prices rose 379 percent.[42]

In light of these statistics, it is not surprising to see growth in informal sector employment. From 1976 to 1989, urban informal sector employment as a percent of total urban employment increased from 20 percent to 33 percent.[43] The growth and increasing importance of the informal sector have not gone unheeded in Venezuelan public policy. Since the 1940s, Venezuelan politics had been characterized by an alliance between domestic capital and the state.[44] International capital played a role in Venezuelan politics, but the state's appropriation of the petroleum rent and subsequent investment in domestic production led to a domestic capitalist class strong enough to contribute to and often dominate political discourse. In turn, passing on part of the petroleum rent to workers in the form of higher wages permitted a social pact to develop between wage labor and national capital.   Under these conditions, Venezuela adopted policies toward the informal sector based primarily on the theories associated with PREALC. The bulk of this policy has focused on efforts to stimulate overall economic activity in order to increase employment opportunities in the formal sector and to improve the levels of human capital in the population in order to reduce both unemployment and informal activity. The most dynamic segments of the informal economy, those considered to have the potential to develop into formal sector businesses, have been the target of many specific governmental programs. "Credit and managerial training are frequently necessary to convert these small enterprises into successful businesses."[45]   That domestic capital sees such a program as in their interests is clear from their support of it.   FEDEINDUSTRIA, an association of artisans, small and medium industry in Venezuela (a subgroup of FEDECAMARAS, Venezuela's most important association of businesses), formed a fund "to develop productivity, quality, competition and technology among micro, small and medium industry... [through] activities of research, promotion, training, information and technical assistance."[46]   They have also signed contracts with the government whereby they promise to provide assistance to small enterprises.

Increasingly attention has turned to the benefits of supporting less dynamic enterprises in order to bolster consumer demand and discourage unrest.[47]   In the past these goals were accomplished through job creation programs financed by the government in concert with domestic capital.   As the economic crisis persists and the government's resources are stretched, a central goal is to increase employment with smaller levels of investment.   Trino Márquez, coordinator of United Nations Development Program (PNUD) in Venezuela, states that while ideally all workers would eventually be absorbed into formal employment, this is an unrealistic expectation in the current economic climate.   "The alternative in light of the structural limitations is to promote productive units that are able to commence production with small investments and that do not demand a highly qualified labor force."[48] The government has consciously adopted this strategy.   As Marisela Padrón, head of the central government's Ministry of the Family during Carlos Andres Pérez' second administration, stated, the small businesses of the informal sector "represent an alternative of valid employment for an important portion of our labor force."[49]

While more attention has been directed toward the informal sector, the changes have not been sweeping and it is evident that the emphasis in public policy remains on formal domestic production. Mauricio Iranzo, director of the Program of Popular Economy of the Ministry of the Family under Carlos Andres Pérez, proposed legislation designed to protect the informal sector, but it has not been acted upon.[50] Development of the informal sector is not specifically considered in the VIII Plan, the current five year Plan for the Nation.[51] Blumenthal estimates that programs related to the popular economy account for only 1/400th of the total investment proposed in the plan.[52] The placement of programs for the informal sector under the Ministry of the Family, as opposed to the government controlled and operated CORPOINDUSTRIA (Corporation for the Development of Small and Medium Industry) is evidence that the informal sector is not seen as a vital component of national economic activity.

Nonetheless, years of economic crisis have taken a toll on domestic capital, and the underlying alliances may well be changing. In the past, the petroleum rent supported relatively high and increasing wages for workers, but the social pact with labor has become increasingly difficult to maintain as real wages have declined.[53] International capital coexisted fairly contentedly with the state and domestic capital when economic prospects were brighter, but now concern for its investments in Venezuela are bringing about an end to the modus vivendi.[54] Increasingly the state is pressured to undertake more restrictive measures and to squeeze the domestic population, thus further reducing the prospects for domestic capital. Free trade, free exchange and reduced government spending have become the contested issues of the current political dialogue. At the same time, pressures from below in the form of social unrest, particularly the nationwide riots of February 1989, have shaken the foundations of contemporary political arrangements.

This changing political situation is reflected in subtle changes taking place in public policy. Plans have been made to rename the Ministry of the Family, which was formerly concerned fundamentally with the provision of social services, the Ministry of Social Development, thus implying a new role for the popular sectors.[55] Within this Ministry a separate department will be established for the popular economy.[56] It remains to be seen whether these are substantive changes or merely cosmetic. What is clear is the development of a new discourse concerning the popular economy. Marisela Padrón, who headed the

Ministry of the Family in the early 1990s, spoke of the possibility of "converting the productive forms of the popular economy into a true alternative for development."[57] The blueprint for such a goal is set forth in Barrante's 1989 proposal for "The Social Policy of Support to the Popular Economy in Venezuela," written under the auspices of the Ministry of the Family and ILDIS (Instituto Latinoamericano de Investigaciones Sociales/Latin American Institute of Social Research). Much of what is outlined concerns the development of bureaucratic structures and governmental interaction with non-governmental agencies, but there are indications of a shift of perspective on the part of the policy-makers.   Policy is to start at the level of the popular, "from the heterogenous practices of the category, 'pueblo.'" Beginning with the practices of the people it will be possible to "embody a project of organization which will guide the tasks of the desired transformation for the popular sectors and possibly for the whole of Venezuelan society."[58]

Public Policy Rooted in the Popular: The Case of Women and Gender Inclusive Public Policy

One of the first discoveries of efforts to understand the "real social dynamics of the informal sector"[59] or the "practices of the category, 'pueblo'"[60] has been the radically heterogeneous nature of the popular economy.   While theoretically convenient, generalizations of the informal sector as a whole mask an enormous depth of variation. Within the informal sector are grouped an astonishingly wide variety of types of economic activity (including production, services and sales), businesses with varying potentials for growth, workers and owners, registered and unregistered activities, women and men.   Effective public policy requires an understanding of the differences as well as similarities of these diverse and overlapping groups within the popular economy.

The study of women within the popular economy provides a rich starting point for understanding the degree and significance of diversity within the informal sector. The process of informalization affects both men and women, but it presents special challenges and opportunities for women due to their unique economic and cultural history. Rakowski has called women in the informal sector "multiply disadvantaged: the disadvantages of being female multiplied by the disadvantages of informality."[61] Yet women continue to struggle, survive, and even succeed within the popular economy. By focusing on women, who face multiple structural disadvantages, one can more readily understand the possibility for all those in the popular economy to find "the spaces that open between said limits."[62] Specifying the policy adaptations necessary to address the unique constraints faced by women in the informal sector is one step in creating policy that adequately addresses the diverse array of everyday experiences and interactions of groups within the popular economy. In developing gender inclusive policy based on the experiences of women in the popular economy, an outline of public policy rooted in the popular begins to emerge.

The changing economic landscape of Third World countries in the last several decades has brought about changes for women and their role in society, the family, and the economy. In 1950, women made up only 17.9 percent of the labor force in Latin America. By the year 2000, they are expected to be 27.5 percent of the labor force.[63] Much of women's increased participation has occurred in the growing informal sector. Lycette and White summarize some of the statistics concerning women's participation in the informal sector.[64]

In Peru, even when domestics are excluded, 40 percent of the informal sector labor force and 61 percent of self-employed workers are women. In comparison only 18 percent of the formal sector labor force is female. Fifty percent of the informal labor force in Brazil is female, and in Ecuador half of the women employed in urban labor markets work in the informal sector.[65] A study of Jamaica found 83 percent of small commercial vendors are women...[66] In La Paz, Bolivia, in 1976 women represented 66 percent of the street vendors, and in 1983 this proportion had grown to 71 percent.[67]

Women's participation in the informal sector is high, frequently as high or higher than their overall labor force participation. In Venezuela, women make up nearly one third of the total labor force, and approximately 30 percent of employment in both the formal and informal sectors. Table 8-1 illustrates this and other characteristics of the Venezuelan labor force.

It is likely that women's participation is even greater than that accounted for in national statistics because most of these are based on individual's primary occupation, typically defined or self-identified by women as "homemaker." Therefore, much of the work performed less than full time in the informal sector, particularly that carried out in the home, is lost in national statistics.[68] According to official statistics in Venezuela, one of every three women is employed in the informal sector. If anything, women's informal work tends to be underreported. According to a study of one urban area in Venezuela, some 21 percent of the women who stated they were not actively employed actually carried out paid activities from their home such as retail sales, laundry, and food preparation.[69]

Table 8-1. Urban Formal and Informal Sector Workers		
Type and Gender of Workers	Total Number	Percent
Total Urban Workers	4,538,489	100.0
Males	3,132,525	69.2
Females	1,405,964	31.0
Formal Sector Workers	2,976,275	65.6
Males	2,018,359	67.8
Females	957,916	32.2
Informal Sector Workers	1,562,214	34.4
Males	1,114,166	71.3
Females	448,048	28.7

Source: Cartaya, 1989: 25, 30.

Men and women are not distributed evenly throughout the informal sector. Males are concentrated in transportation, street vending, repair shops, construction and manufacturing, while females are found mainly in those occupations which have a relation to household tasks, such as cooking, sales from the home, domestic work, washing and ironing, handicrafts, and sewing.[70] Márquez and Portela found that 59 percent of workers in personal services, which includes domestic workers, cooks and launderers, are women.[71] Seventy-five percent of informal textile workers are women while 98 percent of transport workers are men. In general, as is true throughout the economy, women's wages in the informal sector are significantly lower than men's both across and within occupations.[72]

In order to better understand this labor market segmentation and the presence of wage differentials, it is necessary to consider some of the obstacles to employment faced by women, particularly those faced by women in Latin American developing countries such as Venezuela. Gender relations throughout Latin America are characterized by "machismo," a cultural belief in the strength, superiority, and, thereby, justified dominance of men. The effects of this belief are perhaps most clearly seen in relations within the home where women are expected to fill the roles of wife, mother and homemaker and limit their interactions outside the home.[73] The tasks necessary for the survival and reproduction of the family unit are clearly demarcated as either male and female. Men are primarily responsible for the generation of income to support the family, and women for all those daily tasks necessary to transform income into familial consumption.[74] Even when women work outside the home, men are unlikely to share in household chores.[75] While such a situation may not appear greatly distinct from that which persists in the United States, the time consuming and physically demanding nature of household work in developing countries must be taken into consideration.[76] Simply completing the daily tasks of housecleaning, washing, sewing, grocery shopping, carrying water and buying fuel consume a great deal of time.[77] When increased household savings are necessary because real household income is declining, the household tasks typically multiply and become even more labor intensive.

Within this context, women's increased participation in the informal sector can be understood both in terms of supply and demand. On the supply side, women are often able to work in informal sector positions when formal employment would be impossible. Informal work often permits the combination of work and household duties and utilizes skills women have obtained working in the home.[78] The ability to combine household duties and work is of particular importance because in making the decision to enter the labor force, women must calculate the value of their potentially unperformed household work as a cost of working outside the home.[79]   While the value of some household contributions may be difficult to ascertain, much of it can be understood in terms of market prices: the price of child care, the cost of a launderer, or the purchase of prepared foods. These costs tend to be particularly high in societies where the social norm is for women to be in the home because social and economic networks to support working women have not been fully developed. Since women's market wages are already relatively low, if women are unable to combine work and household duties, the costs to employment can easily supersede market wages.

Thus the nature of certain types of informal work allows for a ready supply of female labor otherwise constrained by the demands of household work. The increase in demand for women's informal sector work is due in large part to the direction that has been taken in terms of flexibilization and industrial restructuring in general. Production costs can be lowered either by lowering labor costs through changes in the division of labor, or through technological innovation.[80] Which of these options is selected will depend on relative costs. Given the low relative wages for women in Latin America, companies are able to lower their production costs by utilizing more female labor. Additionally, firms are able to further reduce their cost of production by altering the relations of production through the use of subcontracting, a form of employment that simultaneously overcomes some of the constraints faced by the female labor supply.[81]

Why is it that within this environment the forces of supply and demand in the informal labor market result in an equilibrium characterized by low relative wages for women? A key part of the explanation rests in the existence of segmented labor markets. Women are concentrated in the sectors of service, trade and in the production of food and clothing. They are not found in more productive positions in industry, construction and transport.[82] Women's relatively low reserve of human capital and acquired experience have been offered as reasons for concentration in these categories. In the absence of other barriers it would be expected that over time a more even distribution of human capital would develop as women are attracted to new occupations by higher wages. However, it has been observed that other vulnerable groups in the labor market such as young people, older people, and migrants also tend to concentrate in these same occupations.[83] This suggests that other barriers exist which increase the labor market vulnerability of women and limit their options.

The household demands made on women form perhaps the most formidable barrier.[84] By limiting women to positions that allow for a compromise between household and paid labor, an artificially high labor supply is created in those occupations, and earnings are commensurately lower. The limited number of possible occupations for employment also reduces women's flexibility and alternatives, allowing employers as well as more impersonal market forces to exert downward pressures on earnings within these occupational categories.

Insofar as these occupations remain predominantly female, and the wages therefore considered only supplementary to male employment and income, the normal upward pressure exerted on wages by the need to provide for the reproduction of the labor force is absent, or at least sharply mitigated. Although employers have traditionally used the argument that women do not need to earn as much as men because their earnings are merely secondary income,[85] employers are actually able to pay lower wages precisely because women's income is so important to the household. Since even a marginal increase in family income can make a large difference in a family's prospects, the lower limit for women's wages can approach zero. A woman may tend a homefront store all day, for example, and sell only a few items. Her wages are minimal, but still higher than nothing. Given the absence of other alternatives, and faced with household constraints and economic necessity, she will continue to sell. Employers have been known to arbitrarily lower the piece rate for women doing outwork such as sewing in their homes. Again, given their familial constraints and lack of alternatives, most women have no choice but to work at the lower rate. Thus, while women's wages may be below even minimal subsistence, one nevertheless finds women working in the informal sector for literally "next to nothing."

A women's "place" in the home also creates a spacial barrier to organized action for higher wages. While social norms have always sanctioned male interaction, traditional norms looked down upon large gatherings of women. Although such taboos are less restrictive today, the economic structure of men working outside the home and women in their homes maintains these patterns of social interaction. Thus, a large part of women's vulnerability in the labor market stems from the isolation that their home bound situation involves. Even when women work outside the home, household demands leave little time for organizational activity. Further, the occupations women fill outside the home, such as domestics, launderers, cooks, and vendors, are typically solitary occupations or highly atomized, and serve to reinforce the isolation of the home. Female union participation is low, and most traditionally female occupations are not unionized. If an employer chooses to lower the piece rate or the wage rate, each woman is faced with an individual calculation of cost and benefits because she cannot count on others to reject a similar offer.

As it becomes apparent that women play an increasingly important role in the generation of family income and represent a growing share of all economic activity, governments have begun to reassess current policies and their impact on women's economic participation. Certainly, policies that fail to recognize unique constraints faced by women are unlikely to achieve their desired results. The rather dismal record of general educational, credit, and training programs only confirms this.[86] A move to policy based in the popular would suggest programs rooted in the real experiences of the actors within the popular economy, in this case cognizant of the social dynamic in which women participate. Credit and training programs that give women economic incentives to consider non-traditional employment and business options could lead to a reduction in labor market segmentation. To be most effective, such programs would consider differences in labor force participation over the life course of men and women, particularly in terms of the demands and timing of child rearing. Women's calculations of the costs of employment could be influenced by programs that acknowledge and mitigate the costs associated with foregone household contributions. These might include options such as community kitchens, shared child care, or credit allocations which factor in both household and business expenses. Regulating subcontracting arrangements and providing forums for women to meet could reduce their vulnerability to the downward pressure on wages exerted by larger enterprises.

In the past formulation and adoption of such policies was unlikely. However, as economic and political power shifts, policy rooted in the real experiences of the popular sectors becomes more plausible. The increasing economic importance of the informal sector suggests that addressing the needs of its participants is essential to both policies of social welfare and economic growth. Policies specifically adapted to the social dynamic of the popular economy have the potential not only for generating economic growth but for setting the stage for a new set of actors who will define its direction and goals.

Notes

1. Víctor Tokman, "El imperativo de actuar: el sector informal hoy." *Nueva Sociedad* 90 (1987): 93-105. See pages 95-6.

2. See Portes and Schauffler in this volume for a more detailed summary of the PREALC, neoliberal, and structural theories of the informal sector.

3. See Gustavo Márquez and Carmen Portela, "Los informales urbanos en Venezuela: ¿pobres o eficientes?" (*Simposio IESA: Economía Informal*, October 20 and 21, 1989, Caracas: IESA), p.25. Also see Héctor Béjar, "Reflexiones sobre el sector informal." *Nueva Sociedad* 90 (1987): 89-91.

4. According to PREALC theorists, these are problems related to the influence of international capital. The control of capital by export-producers, as well as interest rates favorable to investment by foreign capital, leads to constraints on capital, overcapitalization, and resulting unemployment of unskilled labor.

5. Sheldon Annis and Jeffery Franks, "The Idea, Ideology, and Economics of the Informal Sector: The Case of Peru" *Grassroots Development* 13 (1): 9-22 (Rossyln, Virginia: Inter-American Foundation), p.11.

6. Silvia Escobar, "El comercio en pequeña escala en la ciudad de La Paz, Bolivia," pp. 97-121 in Marguerite Berger and Mayra Buvinić, eds., *La mujer en el sector informal: trabajo femenino y microempresa en América Latina.* Caracas and Quito: Editorial Nueva Sociedad and ILDIS-Quito, 1988), p.120.

7. Alberto Corchuelo Rozo, "Políticas de internacionalización de la economía y el papel de la microempresa" (paper presented at I Seminario Internacional de Economía Popular: Plenaria I, Posibilidades de desarrollo de la economía popular en el marco de las políticas económicas que se implementan en América Latina. Caracas: Ministerio de la Familia, ILDIS, and PNUD, 1990), p.2.

8. However, Corchuelo Rozo shows that in Chile, where open trade policies have been in place for some time, it is not Chile's comparative advantage in labor that has been exploited, but rather its comparative advantage in natural resources. In this context, it is not the traditionally labor intensive small businesses (such as textiles and shoe making) that have prospered, but those small businesses that have found niches in the national markets as larger domestic companies lose out to international competition (such as in the automotive and metal working industries). The market space left to such small firms does not allow for the kind of expansion predicted for informal sector enterprises. Corchuelo Rozo therefore argues that a more interventionist state policy oriented toward improving technology will be necessary to allow small scale Chilean businesses to compete internationally. See Alberto Corchuelo Rozo, "Políticas de internacionalización de la economía y el papel de la

microempresa" (*I Seminario Internacional de Economía Popular*, Plenaria I: See Ibid.

9. M. Patricia Fernández-Kelly and Anna Garcia, "Informalization at the Core: Hispanic Women, Homework, and the Advanced Capitalist State," pp. 247-264 in Alejandro Portes et al. (eds.), *The Informal Economy: Studies in Advanced and Less Developed Countries*, Baltimore: Johns Hopkins University Press, 1989), p. 254.

10. Luis Pásara, "A Reply from Peru," *Grassroots Development* 13 (1989):23.

11. Douglas Uzell, "Mixed Strategies and the Informal Sector: Three Faces of Reserve Labor" *Human Organization* 39 (1980): 43.

12. Manuel Castells and Alejandro Portes, "World Underneath: The Origins, Dynamics, and Effects of the Informal Economy," pp. 11-37 in Alejandro Portes, et al. (eds.), *The Informal Economy: Studies in Advanced and Less Developed Countries* (1989), p. 26.

13. Manuel Barrera, "El movimiento de los excluidos: desempleo y la nueva informalización," *Nueva Sociedad* 90 (1987): 132.

14. Leith Mullings, "Uneven Development: Class, Race, and Gender in the United States Before 1900," pp. 41-57 in Eleanor Leacock and Helen Safa (eds.), *Women's Work: Development and the Division of Labor by Gender* (Massachusetts: Bergin and Garvey, 1986), p. 46.

15. Daniel Levine, "Religion, the Poor, and Politics in Latin America Today," pp 3-23 in Daniel Levine (ed.), *Religion and Political Conflict in Latin America* (Chapel Hill: The University of North Carolina Press, 1986), p.6.

16. Daniel Levine, "Columbia: The Institutional Church and the Popular" (1986:189).

17. Diego Palma, *La informalidad, lo popular, y el cambio social* (Lima: DESCO, 1987), p. 57.

18. Ibid:65.

19. Juan Pablo Pérez Sáinz, *respuestas silenciosas: proletarización urbana y reproducción de la fuerza de trabajo en América Latina* (Caracas: UNESCO and Editorial Nueva Sociedad, 1989), p. 7.

20. Héctor Béjar, "Reflexiones Sobre el Sector Informal" *Nueva Sociedad* 90 (1987): 90. This is not to say that traditional class analysis loses its relevance. As Pérez Sáinz points out, integration into the wage labor market is still the backbone of most families' strategy for subsistence. See Juan Pablo Pérez Sáinz (1989, 107).

21. See Juan Pablo Pérez Sáinz (1989, 107-108).

22. Cesar Barrantes, "La política social de apoyo a la economía popular en Venezuela: una propuesta en marcha" (Caracas: ILDIS, 1989), p. 15.

23. Albert Hirschman, "A Generalized Linkage Approach to Development, With Special Reference to Staples," *Economic Development and Cultural Change* 25 (Supplement 1977): 67-98.

24. César Barrantes (1989, 16).

25. Ibid:

26. See Mauricio Iranzo, Pedro Sassone and Mireya Vargas, "Líneas estratégias del programa de promoción y apoyo a economía popular: caso Venezuela," (Ministerio de la Familia, Dirección General Sectorial de Promoción y Apoyo a la Economía Popular; I Seminario Internacional de Economía Popular, Caracas: Ministerio de la Familia, ILDIS, and PNUD, 1990), p. 26.

27. Charles Reilly, "Latin America's Religious Populists," pp. 42-57 in Daniel Levine (ed.), *Religion and Political Conflict in Latin America* (1986).

28. Diego Palma (1987, 12).

29. Ibid, 83.

30. Obviously the last three words of this quotation are key to understanding this theoretical perspective. See Lourdes Beneria, "Subcontracting and Employment Dynamics in Mexico City," in Alejandro Portes et al. (eds.), *The Informal Economy: Studies in Advanced and Less Developed Countries* (1989, 184).

31. Sheldon Annis and Jeffery Franks, "The Idea, Ideology, and Economics of the Informal Sector: The Case of Peru," *Grassroots Development* 13 (1989): 19.

32. See the contribution by Portes and Schauffler (Chapter 7) in this volume.

33. Bernardo Mommer, "La distribución de la renta petrolera: el desarrollo del capitalismo rentístico Venezolano" (Unpublished paper, Caracas: ILDIS, 1987).

34. Ricardo Hausmann, "Venezuela 2000: el futuro de la economía no petrolera," pp. 163-182 in José Silva Michelena (ed.), *Venezuela Hacia el 2000: Desafíos y Opciones* (Caracas: Editorial Nueva Sociedad, 1991).

35. Leopoldo Yáñez Betancourt, "La economía Venezolana: problemas y perspectivas," pp. 125-162 in José Silva Michelena (ed.), *Venezuela hacia el 2000: desafíos y opciones* (1991), p.125.

36. Ricardo Hausmann (1991, 172).

37. See International Monetary Fund, *World Economic Outlook: May 1993* (Washington: International Monetary Fund), p. 137 and World Bank, *World Tables 1988-1989 Edition* (Washington: World Bank), p. 36.

38. See United Nations, *Statistical Yearbook: 1990/91* (New York: United Nations, 1993), p. 238. Also see International Monetary Fund (1993, 137) and *World Tables 1988-1989*, p. 36.

39. *World Economic Outlook: May 1993*, p. 145.

40. Inter-American Development Bank, *Economic and Social Progress in Latin America: 1992 Report* (Baltimore: Johns Hopkins University Press), p. 185.

41. *World Development Report 1993*, p.289. Also see IDB, *Economic and Social Progress in Latin America: 1992 Report*, p. 285.

42. Vanessa Cartaya, "La pobreza y la economía informal: ¿casualidad o causalidad?" (*Simposio IESA: Economía Informal*, October 20 and 21 1989, Caracas: IESA), pp. 22-23.

43. Domingo Méndez, "Marco teórico" (Unpublished dissertation proposal, The Hague: Institute of Social Studies), p. 88. Also César Barrantes (1989, 47). It might seem surprising that the informal sector did not grow more given the low, and sometimes negative levels of national economic growth. However, an important aspect of the economic adjustments in Venezuela has been the decline in real wages in the face of inflation, mitigating the process of adjustment through unemployment. Therefore, some of the presumed impetus for informal sector growth is not present. Also, interactions between the formal economy and informal economy are quite complex. Due to the symbiotic nature of these relations, a decline in formal sector economic activity can have deleterious effects on the informal sector.

44. Rafael de la Cruz, "Alternativas frente a la declinación del modelo socioeconómico actual," pp. 247-268 in José Silva Michelena (ed.), *Venezuela hacia el 2000: desafíos y opciones* (1991).

45. Gustavo Márquez and Carmen Portela (1989, 25).

46. Guido Giménez and Vladimir Monslave, "Microempresas y comercialización" (*I Seminario Internacional de Economía Popular*, Mesa 5: Estrategias organizativos de comercialización de insumos y bienes prodJcidos por la microempresa, Caracas: Ministerio de la Familia, ILDIS, and PNUD, 1990), p. i.

47. Vanessa Cartaya, "Relatoría: plenaria 2, impacto de las políticas estatales de apoyo a la economía popular" (*Acta Final del I Seminario Internacional de Economía Popular*, Caracas: Ministerio de la Familia, ILDIS, and PNUD, 1990).

48. Trino Márquez, "El gran mundo de las microempresas." *El Universal* Thursday, November 22, Caracas.

49. *El Nacional*, "Economía popular generó 77.8% de empleos en Latinoamérica." Tuesday, November 27, 1990: Section D, p. 8, Caracas.

50. Pedro González Silva, "Microempresas generan 77.8% de nuevos empleos," *Economía Hoy*, Tuesday, November 27, 1990, Caracas.

51. Leonardo Pizani, "Los microempresarios: un sector del la economía con características propias," *Juntos: La Revista Venezolana de la Acción Popular* January-February (1991): 22-23 (Caracas: CESAP), p. 23.

52. Hans Blumenthal, "Acto de instalación: I Seminario Internacional de Economía Popular" (*Acta Final del I Seminario Internacional de Economía Popular*, Caracas: Ministerio de la Familia, ILDIS, and PNUD, 1990).

53. Domingo Méndez, "Informalización de la fuerza de trabajo en Venezuela: ¿disfunciones en el mercado de trabajo o cambios en la relación salarial?: una investigación histórica para el período 1975-1988," (unpublished master's thesis, The Hague: Institute of Social Studies), p. 12.

54. Rafael de la Cruz (1991, 259).

55. César Barrantes (1989).

56. Leonardo Pizani (1991).

57. Pedro González Silva (1990).

58. César Barrantes (1989, 16).

59. See the chapter by Portes and Schauffler (7) in this volume.

60. César Barrantes (1989).

61. Cathy Rakowski, "Desventaja multiplicada: la mujer del sector informal" *Nueva Sociedad* 90 (July-August 1987): 134-146.

62. Diego Palma (1987:12).

63. Marguerite Berger, "La mujer en el sector informal: introducción," pp. 13-32 in Marguerite Berger and Mayra Buvinić (eds.), *La Mujer en el Sector Informal: Trabajo Femenino y Microempresa en América Latina* (1988).

64. Lycette, Margaret and Karen White. 1988. "Acceso de la mujer al crédito en América Latina y el Caribe," pp. 35-66 in Marguerite Berger and Mayra Buvinić eds. (1988:39).

65. Dikak Mazumbar, "The Urban Informal Sector," *World Development* August 1976 (4).

66. Alicia Taylor, Donna McFarlane, and Elsie LeFranch, "The Higglers of Kingston," pp. 228-240 in Marianne Schmink, Judith Brice and Marylyn Kohn, (eds.), *Learning About Women and Urban Services in Latin America and the Caribbean* (New York: The Population Council, 1986).

67. Silvia Escobar, "La microcomerciante de La Paz, Bolivia: características y necesidades" (Seminario Internacional, La mujer y su acceso al crédito en América Latina, sugerencias para programas de desarrollo, September 12, 1986, Quito).

68. María Cristina Lopéz-Garza, *Informal Labor in a Capitalist Economy: Urban Mexico* (dissertation, Los Angeles: University of California, 1985), p. 118.

69. Vanessa Cartaya (1989, 27).

70. Cathy Rakowski (1987, 140).

71. Gustavo Márquez and Carmen Portela (1989, 17-18).

72. Cartaya (1989).

73. See Ana Silvia Monzón M., "El machismo: mito de la supremacía masculina," *Nueva Sociedad* 93 (January-February 1988): 148-155, especially p. 150.

74. Bethencourt G., "La investigación y la política hacia los populares" (Caracas: Ministerio de la Familia, ILDIS, and PNUD, 1990), p. 9.

75. Neuma Aguiar, "Las mujeres y la crisis Latinoamericana," pp. 11-30 in Neuma Aguiar (ed.), *Mujer y Crisis: Respuestas ante la Recesión* (Río de Janeiro and Caracas: DAWN/MUDAR, Development Alternatives with Women for a New ERA/Mujeres por un Desarrollo Alternativo, and Editorial Nueva Sociedad, 1990), p. 21.

76. One example of life in the extreme absence of labor saving devices is offered by Mona Hamman, "Capitalist Development, Family Division of Labor, and Migration in the Middle East," pp. 158-173 in Eleanor Leacock and Helen Safa, eds., *Women's Work: Development and the Division of Labor by Gender* (Massachusetts: Bergin and Garvey Publishers, 1986), p. 160. It takes at least two Yemeni women just to complete the everyday tasks necessary to maintain an average household, and a third to produce the objects necessary for household use. In such a situation, the possibilities for women's labor market participation are clearly limited.

77. Mónica Lanzetta de Pardo and Gabriel Murillo Castaño with Alvaro Triana Soto, "The Articulation of Formal and Informal Sectors in the Economy of Bogotá, Columbia," in Alejandro Portes et al. (eds.), *The Informal Economy: Studies in Advanced and Less Developed Countries* (1989), p. 103.

78. Cathy Rakowski (1987, 138).

79. Vanessa Cartaya (1989, 32).

80. Harry Braverman, *Labor and Monopoly Capital* (New York: Monthly Review Press, 1974).

81. Lourdes Beneria, "Subcontracting and Employment Dynamics in Mexico City," pp. 173-188 in Alejandro Portes et al. (eds.), *The Informal Economy: Studies in Advanced and Less Developed Countries* (Baltimore: Johns Hopkins University Press, 1989), p. 181.

82. Vanessa Cartaya (1989, 33).

83. Jaime Mezzera, "Abundancia como efecto de la escasez: oferta y demanda en el mercado laboral urbano," *Nueva Sociedad* 90 (July-August 1987): 110.

84. Ana Silvia Monzón M. (1988:148-155). Also see Vanessa Cartaya (1989, 27).

85. Annette Fuentes and Barbara Ehrenreich, *Women in the Global Factory* (New York: South End Press, Institute for New Communications, 1983), p. 12.

86. See Cressida McKean, "Empresas pequeñas and microempresas: su eficacia e implicaciones para la mujer," pp. 145-170 and Rebecca Lynn Reichmann, "Dos programas de crédito para microempresas: los casos de republica Dominicana y Perú," pp. 187-225 in Marguerite Berger and Mayra Buvinić (eds.), *La mujer en el sector informal: trabajo femenino y microempresa en América Latina* (1988).

9

Economic Globalization and the Urban Process: Political Implications for the State in Latin America

Satya R. Pattnayak

For decades Latin American leaders have pursued imported policy recommendations without giving considerable thought to the appropriateness of such models. But against the backdrop of economic globalization and the concurrent urban change, I propose that a modified vision of the state is needed in the context of Latin America. In this chapter, first, I present an overview of the more influential theories of the state to date. In particular, I examine the liberal-pluralist, dependency/world system, and developmentalist views on the state and the extent to which they need to be modified in order to be relevant to the Latin American context. And second, I examine some crucial current trends in state activities and state capacities in the region. By analyzing specific empirical trends, I intend to transcend the ideological battle raised over the "new state" in Latin America.

Theories of the State and State Elite

The current shifts in the direction of a neoliberal model of growth and development in Latin America are geared towards resolving two recurring problems of paramount importance: 1) the inability to produce sustained growth in the industrial sector and 2) dealing with the enormous political and social pressure resulting from the efforts to industrialize.

Of course, Latin American development efforts are inevitably linked to the role historically played by the state elite.[1] The state elite's continued legitimacy rests on the ability to foster rapid and sustainable industrial growth. Selecting policies that ensure such growth should enhance the elite's standing. Even when an elite already enjoys the success of fostering rapid growth, the popular support extended may be conditional upon the ability to produce new growth. With initial growth, new expectations of future development are created, which in turn put pressure on the state elite to continue the process or risk the loss of popular support.[2] Latin American state elites now face such a dilemma. Under these circumstances, the role of the state in general and the question of state efficacy in particular are fundamental.

Since the Great Depression of the 1930s there has been a steady growth in the state's role across the globe. In Western industrialized democracies, emergence of the managerial state to combat the crisis of capitalism has been one of the significant developments of the present century.[3] In addition, growing state regulative and welfare functions since World War II have contributed to an enormous expansion of the state apparatus and corresponding state activities in the industrial and service sectors. The expansion is even greater in the structuring of economic and social systems of Third World countries.[4] Until about two decades ago, there had been a notorious absence of theoretical analyses of the state and the impact of state policies on society. The intellectual traditions embodied in the liberal-pluralist and the dependency/world system approaches to the state have contributed to this absence.

The Liberal-Pluralist Version of the State

The liberal-pluralist approach is concerned primarily with the individuals who make up society. It asserts that individual welfare is achieved when people are free to pursue their own economic and political interests.[5] In this approach "collective interest" for the common good is interpreted as synonymous with the "sum of individual interests." The belief, therefore, is that the pursuit of individual interest will in itself produce the best for the society as a whole. Liberal-pluralists generally prescribe that:

> ...nothing ought to be done or attempted by government. The Motto, or watchword of government...ought to be--Be quiet...with few exceptions, and these not very considerable ones, the attainment will be most effectually secured by leaving each individual to pursue his own maximum enjoyment.[6]

Adam Smith's "invisible hand" mechanism can be considered the model of a self-regulating society. In brief, the state becomes a dependent variable, subjected to individual interest. Smith writes:

> "Every individual in continually exerting himself to find out the most advantageous employment for whatever capital he can command. It is his own advantage, indeed, and not that of society, which he has in view. But the study of his own advantage naturally, or rather necessarily, leads him to prefer that employment which is most advantageous to the society."[7]

However, there is a very crucial, implicit assumption in the liberal-pluralist approach overlooked by many. This assumption concerns the market. The market mechanism is assumed to be self-regulating only if impartial administrative and institutional infrastructure is provided. Capitalism cannot perform well without this kind of infrastructural support.[8] In the Third World --Latin America in particular-- there are not enough private individuals or corporations to maintain the infrastructural framework needed to make capitalism work, so the role of the state becomes all the more important.

It is clear from the liberal-pluralist view that "market" is the pivot. The notion of "market" as the supreme arbiter of economic behavior might have worked in the West, but in the context of Latin America the effective operation of markets too often requires the presence of strong and interventionist states. This scenario undoubtedly was present in the 1940s, 1950s, and 1960s, when most state-led development efforts were undertaken. But scholars have noted market failures in countries where states lack autonomy and adequate bureaucratic capacity. Therefore, the assumption of dual importance of both states and markets became a starting point for many studies of Third World development in the late 1970s and early 1980s.[9]

The Dependency/World System Views of the State

Dependency theorists assume that economic conflict is a zero-sum game.[10] Since the economic structure provides the base for the sociopolitical superstructure, there is no room for a neutral state or even the possibility of the state elite developing their own independent interest. The state becomes the coercive organ of the dominant class.

Most classical dependency theorists, heavily influenced by the Marxist-Leninist intellectual tradition, view the state as a dependent entity---an instrument of oppression serving the interest of the ruling class at the expense of the proletariat.[11] They generally characterize the state in the Third World as an agent of the dominant classes, who in turn serve the economic and political interests of international corporations. Writes Frank:

> "When imperialism accelerated the production and exportation of raw materials in Latin America at the end of the nineteenth century the economic and class structure of the various countries was once more transformed. The Latin American lumpenbourgeoisie became the junior partner of foreign capital and imposed new policies of lumpendevelopment which in turn increased the dependence on the imperialist metropolis."[12]

The World System variation of this perspective adds a twist to the argument and, instead of exclusively focusing on class, gives much importance to the location of the state in the world system.[13] State capacity to facilitate growth or resolve conflict, in this view, depends on structural location. In a hierarchical three tier system, Third World states are likely to be located in the bottom two tiers and, therefore, the state elite do not have the relative autonomy necessary to engage in successful societal transformation. Since there is not much scope for its autonomy, the state is considered a secondary institution by both dependency and world system theorists.

But by the late 1970s and early 1980s, these simplistic views of the state were questioned. Based on the developmental experiences of the earlier decades, scholars began to challenge the validity of the above approaches.[14] The changing international environment, "...which saw the United States and other leading industrial democracies becoming hard pressed in a world of more intense and uncertain economic and political competition perhaps facilitated more seemingly independent state activities worldwide."[15] Skocpol writes...

> "In today's international environment which stretches from geopolitical domination and competition to world economic competition for trade, investment, market, and finance, modern states stand at the intersection between domestic and international borders, which they must manipulate, mold, and maneuver for survival and gaining advantage over others.[16]

Many studies published in the late 1970s and early 1980s have depicted the state as a forceful and a relatively independent actor in the development process. Some have provided reasons why and how modern state elite have formulated and pursued their own goals. Stepan's work on Peru and Brazil and Trimberger's work on Japan, Turkey, and Egypt have amply highlighted the factors that encouraged leading state officials to pursue necessary strategies in the face of strong opposition from more powerful domestic and foreign groups.[17] For example, Stepan's[18] study of the military in Peru and Brazil has shown that the formation of a strong, ideologically motivated, and organizationally solid cadre can ensure relatively independent political order and promote industrial growth. Military leaders in both Brazil and Peru have used state power to neutralize threats from domestically powerful social groups. During 1964-79 in Brazil, for example, partly through electoral engineering and partly through coercion, the military has sought to exclude dominant social groups from attaining any direct control of the state apparatus.[19]

Even in a non-military dominated state apparatus, such as India, depending on the issue of the time, whether it is of land reform, or raising taxes, frequent alliances have been formed with numerically large lower classes. This has been engineered by the state elite in order to ensure mass political support in the parliament in favor of progressive legislation.[20] Bardhan observes:

> If the industrialists at any time overstep in their bargaining (mostly against organized labor), sure enough there will be an uproar in parliament about the anti-people conspiracy of the

monopoly capitalists. Similar invectives against the Kulaks
...will also be aired on appropriate occasions.[21]

In general, these studies argued that the state elite, through clever
manipulation of domestic channels, have managed to keep dominant
class interests on the defensive. State power has been used to
implement socioeconomic reform plans in order to further
modernization, which the state elite saw as a basic prerequisite for
improved international standing.

Those who argued in favor of including the state in cross-national,
comparative research on Third World growth and development were
branded as "state autonomy" theorists.[22] The new emphasis on "state
autonomy" raised a whole new set of theoretical questions: State
autonomy vis-a-vis which social group(s)? Does autonomy lead
automatically to state efficacy? Are autonomy and efficacy mutually
exclusive? These questions suggest complex issues.

To resolve some of these questions, I define "state efficacy" as the
ability and willingness of the state elite to pursue developmental goals
presumed to be in the interest of the majority of people residing within
its legally defined territorial limits. Since economic growth and social
development are our chief concern, state efficacy must contain two
equally crucial elements: capacity and activism. In the 1970s and
1980s, much of state autonomy research assumed some level of state
autonomy that would sustain state efficacy. State elites were expected
to pursue some industrialization goals even at the risk of antagonizing
the powerful domestic and foreign capitalists who thrive on monopoly
profit in the industrial sector.

Unlike liberal-pluralists, state autonomy theorists argue that the
structural, institutional, and attitudinal conditions necessary to foster
industrial growth did not exist in Latin America. The Marshall Plan
succeeded in Europe because the nations already had well-integrated
financial and commodity markets, a highly developed infrastructure and
educated labor force, the motivation to succeed, and above all, a high
level of state efficacy.[23] The last element of "state efficacy" is
extremely important in this context. If a high level of state efficacy
exists in any given country, one can safely translate that efficacy into
important ingredients necessary for successful industrial growth, such
as possessing a well-integrated financial and commodity market, a well-
trained labor force, and a highly developed infrastructure. Reversing
the argument, a country with a relatively less integrated financial and

the argument, a country with a relatively less integrated financial and commodity market, a badly trained labor force, and a less developed infrastructure is more likely to experience a lower level of state efficacy.

In part because of the newly available empirical information, revisions took place among liberal-pluralists and dependency/world system theorists with regard to their views on the state.[24] Many liberal-pluralists, influenced by neoclassical economic analysis, accorded much more importance to the role of the state.[25] Many dependency/world system theorists also conceded that imperialism could stimulate development of the periphery.[26] These scholars argued that the export of capital could under certain conditions greatly accelerate the development of capitalism in the countries to which it is exported. They admitted that since most of the developing countries of today are low wage, low rent, and cheap raw material economies, they make external capital profitable and thus facilitate the elementary conditions necessary for industrial development. Since the 1970s, tremendous growth of manufacturing activities in countries such as Brazil, Mexico, South Korea, Hong Kong, and Taiwan indicate that imperialism might be consistent with certain kinds of development in the periphery or semi-periphery.

In Latin America, this argument is substantiated historically since the state has played a major part in the consolidation of the internal market through adapting the strategy of Import Substituting Industrialization (ISI).[27] Under ISI, active state encouragement and subsidies contributed to an increasing penetration of direct foreign investment, especially in manufacturing. The various state incentives in the form of tariffs, foreign exchange, and imports encouraged foreign multinationals to set up subsidiaries in Latin America.[28]

Indeed, studies have noted the state's crucial role in channeling foreign resources into priority sectors.[29] In the case of direct foreign investment, the state provides the infrastructure and complementary economic activities to make the investment more productive. Of course, how well the state plays its part differs from one country to another and therefore makes a difference in the achieved level of industrial growth.

Some dependency-oriented scholars have entertained the possibility of an alliance of foreign capital and the state elite to foster industrial growth.[30] In some cases, the alliance may incorporate domestic capital. In this line of argument, multinationals collaborate with the state elite to stimulate the industrial sector in the Third World. This helps internationalize domestic markets and marks the beginning of "vertical industrialization." Specifically, unlike the classical form of economic dependency which revolves around extractive and export-oriented activities, the new alliance facilitates diversification throughout the economy. Such industrialization, however, is possible only with the cooperation of the state elite.

To consolidate "state-autonomy" arguments, a few empirical and cross-national studies have examined the mediating role of the state.[31] These studies generally show that state variables considerably modify the relationship between dependency and development. For instance, Rubinson[32] argued that although dependency indicators such as external trade concentration and external debt negatively affect state strength, the state strength itself has a net positive effect on economic growth. This also means that even though external debt or direct foreign investment may have a direct negative effect on economic growth, the effect may get considerably modified if the state strength is included in the model as an intervening variable. Paradoxically, dependency may provide the state elite with resources conducive to economic growth and to the extinction of the dependency itself.

The "Developmental State" Perspective

By the 1980s, a number of East Asian states, such as South Korea, Taiwan, Singapore, and Hong Kong, had experienced dramatic success in combining fast economic growth with relatively egalitarian distribution of income. For example, according to World Bank reports, the manufacturing sector grew at an annual average rate of 10.4 percent in East Asia between 1980 and 1987, whereas the corresponding rate for Latin America and sub-Saharan Africa was 0.6 percent.[33] Most explanations of East Asia's success have either been market- or state-centered. For example, some studies have argued that such tremendous success in East Asia occurred primarily due to a clear emphasis on trade liberalization, private enterprise, and a restricted role of the state.[34] The assertion that the state's role was limited has been challenged by others.[35] The latter studies have maintained that East Asian states through regulatory policy changes and selective intervention in the economy have successfully harnessed domestic and international market forces of national manufacturing development.[36] Notwithstanding the debate about the nature of success of the East

Asian industrialization, it is fair to argue that the developmental state perspective contains a *strong blend* of neo-classical (or liberal-pluralist) and state autonomy ideas. But one thing is certain --the developmental state literature used the case of East Asian development to claim a legitimate place in academic circles as a competing theory of the state.

The main objective of a developmental state is to lead and actively intervene in selected sectors of the economy in order to guide and promote particular developmental goals.[37] State incentives in tax, subsidy, control over credit, and pricing are used to sway the private sector and to help it become more competitive globally.

Most observes note that the developmental state possesses a (1) high level bureaucratic autonomy and (2) closer institutionalized cooperation with private business. In the case of the first characteristic, it bears more in common with "state autonomy" theorists while the second characteristic brings it closer to the neo-classical perspectives. But as far as the non-business elements, such as labor and popular sectors are concerned, the developmental state has been notoriously authoritarian.[38] Although the authoritarian feature seems to be slowly changing in recent years, it still continues to play a major role in the functioning of the developmental state.

How is the Neoliberal State different in Latin America?

The current neoliberal prescriptions for a reduced state in Latin America have largely been inspired by the economic success of the newly industrializing countries (NICs) of East Asia. What is lost in the discussion is the crucial role played by the state elite, in particular the bureaucratic elite, in sustaining a high level of economic growth. For example, scholars have noted that in East Asia, particularly in South Korea, Taiwan, and Singapore, the state elite implemented strategic industrial policies that guaranteed state subsidies in exchange for measurable performances. A select group of industries were chosen to be the lead industries, enjoying enormous amount of advantage over the rest of the industrial sector. These industries became more efficient as they were gradually exposed to foreign competition and markets. But they were effectively supervised by a competent meritocracy, selected from the best available talent in these societies.[39]

It is not necessarily true then that government bureaucracy is incompetent across societies. The bureaucratic structures could be made more productive, if their size was kept small enough to be coherent and they were considerably autonomous of the major power wielders in society. An effective combination of bureaucratic autonomy and strategic implementation of an industrial policy facilitated the East Asian, export-led growth model.[40]

In the case of Latin America these conditions are rarely observed. On the contrary, the magic hand seems to lie in selling off huge public conglomerates at throwaway prices to private monopolists. First, the tremendous amount of public-private cooperation, as was observed in the case of both Taiwan and South Korea, is nowhere to be seen in Latin America. The East Asian model which did promote high levels of economic growth also came at a price: the exclusion of organized labor from the state-corporate negotiations over industrial policy and relevant compensatory packages. Latin America, at least the countries discussed in the book, seems to have satisfied that requirement. In most of the region, organized labor is either being disorganized or is progressively less able (than previously) to defend the interests of its members.[41]

The most important lesson of East Asia is that the relationship between capitalist growth and democratization is at best tenuous. Capitalism and democracy have always had uneasy coexistence. In the developed countries of the West, this tension has largely been neutralized through effective linkages between civil society and the political apparatus, either through political parties or through other lobbying groups and action committees. In the case of Latin America, civic organization is increasing, but still lags and the political linkage is quite weak. In this scenario, when economically unequal people are given equal political rights, it could lead to trouble.

In particular, in the depressing scenario of declining living standards for most of the population and the rise of the informal sector all across this vast region, it is imperative that links be nourished and forged with the vast segments of the civil society who are in need of allies and help. The church groups are doing some of that, but the region needs effort from political parties of all persuasions to forge links between the popular constituencies and larger political structures.[42]

Decades earlier, in the late 1960s and early 1970s the socioeconomic and political tensions generated by dependent capitalist modernization had ushered in regime change in many Latin American countries. Would there be a repeat of the same drama if the current experiments did not succeed? In order to gain more insight on the matter, at least a cursory look at some state activities is necessary.

Table 9-1. Percent of Urban Households Below or On the Poverty
Line, 1980-90, Selected Countries.

Country	1980	1990
Argentina[a]	5	16
Bolivia	--	50
Brazil	30	39
Chile	--	34
Colombia	37	36
Costa Rica	16	22
Guatemala	41	49
Mexico	29	33
Panama	31	33
Paraguay	--	38
Uruguay	9	11
Venezuela	19	32

[a] Greater Buenos Aires only.
Source: CEPAL, Panorama Social (1994).

Emerging Trends in State Activities in Latin America

As has been stated in Chapter 1, certain indicators of poverty and income inequality have depicted a bleak picture for Latin America as a whole. Since the early 1980s, when some of the current neoliberal economic policies were initiated, poverty and income inequality have worsened. For example, according to Table 9-1 the extent of urban poverty has increased in 9 out of 10 countries on which more complete data are available. During 1980-90, in Argentina the relative increase was the most severe, 16% of the urban population being characterized as poor as opposed to 5% in 1980. During the same time period, in the rest of the group the increase has been wide-ranging: in Brazil the percentage of poor in urban areas increased from 30 to 39%; in Costa Rica 16 to 22%; in Mexico 29 to 33%; in Uruguay 9 to 11%; and in Venezuela 19 to 32%. Only in Colombia has it declined (by a percentage point) from 37 to 36. Although there are some indications that in Argentina, Chile, Mexico, Uruguay, and Venezuela the percentage of urban poor has declined slightly by 1992 from the 1990 level, it has remained substantially higher than the 1980 level.

Table 9-2. Percent Variation in per Capita Real Income in Urban Households, Selected Countries

Country	Bottom 40%	Top 10%
Argentina[a]	-13 (1980-92)	13 (1980-92)
Brazil	-19 (1980-90)	5 (1980-90)
Colombia	38 (1980-92)	8 (1980-92)
Costa Rica	-18 (1980-90)	-8 (1980-90)
Mexico	-12 (1980-90)	41 (1980-90)
Panama	-8 (1980-90)	34 (1980-90)
Uruguay	-15 (1980-90)	-11 (1980-90)
Venezuela	-35 (1980-92)	3 (1980-92)

[a] Greater Buenos Aires only. Source: CEPAL, Panorama Social (1994), p. 36.

A decomposition of the total variation in urban household income reveals some interesting trends in Table 9-2. During 1980-90 the percentage variation of per capita real income in urban areas negatively affected the most vulnerable segment of the population: the bottom

Table 9-3. Trends in the Overall Public Social Expenditure,
Selected Countries (in 1985 dollars)

Country	Period	Social Expenditure as % of Total Public Expenditure	Per Capita Public Social Expenditure
Argentina	1980-81	49.0	569.9
	1982-89	39.4	470.8
Bolivia	1980-81	31.0	73.0
	1982-89	23.8	49.2
Brazil	1980-81	46.5	159.6
	1982-89	29.7	157.5
Chile	1980-81	61.7	264.5
	1982-89	49.3	243.7
Colombia	1980-81	33.9	91.4
	1982-89	33.7	97.9
Costa Rica	1980-81	66.1	251.3
	1982-89	51.0	230.8
Mexico	1980-81	31.1	224.8
	1982-89	24.9	163.0
Peru	1980-81	20.6	38.0
	1982-89	15.2	33.1
Uruguay	1980-81	63.6	278.1
	1982-89	50.1	277.2
Venezuela	1980-81	35.9	475.5
	1982-89	27.6	346.5

Source: CEPAL, Panorama Social (1994).

Table 9-4. Evolution of Sectoral Per Capita Social Expenditures,
Selected Countries (in 1985 dollars)

	Education		Health	
	1980-81	1982-89	1980-81	1982-89
Argentina	113.5	103.5	154.0	133.6
Bolivia	48.1	35.6	18.7	10.0
Brazil	16.7	23.9	29.9	34.6
Chile	63.4	52.6	40.0	36.5
Colombia	34.2	36.9	13.2	13.5
Costa Rica	92.0	69.1	111.1	87.0
Mexico	87.6	68.6	94.0	70.9
Peru	25.9	23.9	9.1	8.1
Uruguay	35.9	31.7	18.7	18.2
Venezuela	202.3	161.5	68.2	58.1

	Social Security		Housing	
	1980-81	1982-89	1980-81	1982-89
Argentina	255.8	191.6	46.7	39.5
Bolivia	--	--	1.3	0.5
Brazil	89.4	85.0	23.6	13.9
Chile	110.6	103.0	16.8	15.7
Colombia	35.5	39.3	8.5	8.8
Costa Rica	32.4	49.6	8.6	16.5
Mexico	--	--	--	--
Peru	0.2	0.3	2.7	0.9
Uruguay	218.9	223.4	0.3	0.4
Venezuela	107.7	77.2	97.3	49.7

Source: CEPAL, Panorama Social (1994), pp. 165-166.

40%. This segment of the urban population experienced a decline in per capita income, by as much as 8% in Panama, 12% in Mexico, and 35% in Venezuela. The only exception to this negative trend has been Colombia, where the bottom 40% of the urban population registered a 38% increase. In contrast, the top 10% of urban households registered income gains in 6 of the 8 countries on which data are available. In this category Mexico registered the largest increase at 41% and Brazil the least at 5%. In those countries where the percentage variation in per capita real income was negative, the relative decline in income of the top 10% was much less severe than among the bottom 40% of the urban population. For example, in Costa Rica the bottom 40% suffered a 18% decline in income whereas the top 10% registered a 8% decline. In Uruguay, a similar trend was observed. The bottom 40% of Uruguay's population experienced a 15% decline in real per capita income while the top 10% suffered an 11% decline.

These trends raise serious questions concerning the appropriateness of the current neoliberal model of economic growth. They make it imperative that we re-evaluate social development in light of certain state activities.

Table 9-3 illustrates the trends for two social expenditure indicators between 1980-81 and 1982-89: Social expenditure as a percentage of total public expenditure and per capita public social expenditure. Of the 10 countries under observation, social expenditure as a percentage of total public expenditure registered a decline in all but one; in Colombia it remained about constant. The decline was most severe in Brazil (17 percentage points). Per capita social expenditure declined in the same 9 countries, Colombia again being the exception. In percentage terms the decline was most severe in Bolivia (33%) and Venezuela (27%).

Overall decline may not mean much unless it is decomposed and the sectoral distribution of social expenditure is also examined. Table 9-4 illustrates just that. The public expenditure in education declined (in constant dollars) between 1980-81 and 1982-89 in 8 of the 10 countries observed. Brazil and Colombia registered the only increases. The health expenditures of 8 (out of 10) countries registered a decline. Only Brazil and Colombia recorded an increase in their level of health expenditures between 1980-81 and 1982-89.

Public expenditure in social security registered a decline in 4 out of 8 countries observed. But Colombia, Costa Rica, Peru, and Uruguay registered increases, Costa Rica's being the largest. Public expenditure in housing declined in 6 of the 9 countries observed. Only Colombia,

Costa Rica, and Uruguay noted increases, Costa Rica almost doubling its housing expenditure between 1980-81 and 1982-89.

Based on the overall and sectoral distribution it is possible to establish a link between the decline in public social expenditures and the increase in poverty and income inequality in the urban areas. Colombia stood out as the most notable exception. It is also in Colombia that one notes across the board increases in social expenditure. There is some evidence to support the fact that despite declines at the aggregate level countries such as Brazil managed to increase their educational and health expenditures at the expense of social security and housing. The reverse is true for Costa Rica. Here, despite a decline at the aggregate level, the state opted for increasing social security and housing expenditure at the expense of declines in education and health. Perhaps such sectoral variations can be explained in terms of specific contextual and political factors in the countries under observation.

Since much has been said about the neoliberal state, it would be prudent to examine some trends with regard to specific state characteristics. I shall limit my observation to two areas of state capacity: extractive and coercive. Both these areas have been amply justified in recent scholarship as the two most important areas of state domain.[43]

Table 9-5 illustrates trends in state extractive and coercive capacity in Latin America. There is no consistent trend that I can observe with regard to the state's extractive and coercive capacities. The extractive capacity is measured in terms of central government revenue (as %GDP) and coercive capacity is measured by per capita military expenditure. Between 1980-81 and 1982-89, the revenue generating capacity declined in 4 of the 9 countries on which data are available. It declined in Argentina, Chile, Peru, and Venezuela. Four registered increases and one registered no change. The revenue generation increased in Brazil, Colombia, Costa Rica, and Mexico, whereas in Uruguay it remained constant. It is difficult to discern any regional trend with regard to state extractive capacity.

Total military expenditure per capita increased in 5 of the 9 countries on which data are available. These countries are: Argentina, Brazil, Colombia, Peru, and Venezuela. Notice that not all of these experienced an increase in revenue-generating capacity. Only Brazil and Colombia experienced increases in both revenue generation as well as military capacity. Two (Chile and Uruguay) noted a decline in military expenditure and two (Costa Rica and Mexico) registered no change. There seems to be no relationship between state revenue indicators and military expenditure indicators.

Table 9-5. Central Government Revenue and Expenditure Trends, 1980-89, Selected Countries

	Revenue & Grant as Percent of GDP		Military Expenditure per Capita (in 1991 dollars)	
	1980-81	1982-89	1980-81	1982-89
Argentina	13.8	11.8	166	172
Brazil	23.7	25.5	19	28
Chile	33.5	27.0	75	69
Colombia	11.8	12.2	11	17
Costa Rica	17.8	22.3	10	10
Mexico	14.9	16.9	17	17
Peru	15.7	11.7	123	145[a]
Uruguay	23.0	23.0	130	76
Venezuela	30.3	23.8	28	46

[a] Data for 1982-87 only. Source: The revenue and expenditure figures are from International Financial Statistics Yearbook (1994); the data for the military expenditure are from World Military Expenditures and Arms Transfers, 1991-92.

However, it is possible to draw a link between military expenditure and social expenditure patterns. Of the 5 countries that experienced an increase in military expenditure per capita, all but Colombia noted a decline in per capita public social expenditure. In the case of Colombia, the increase exceeded the corresponding increase in social expenditure. In Mexico, military expenditure remained constant while per capita public social expenditure declined. In Uruguay, the decline in military expenditure was the most severe (42%), whereas its social expenditure declined less than 1%. The largest countries of the region, namely, Argentina, Brazil, Mexico, Peru, and Venezuela noted a relative increase in the coercive capacity and a simultaneous decline in state involvement in social development.

In sum, in this section specific trends in selected social development indicators and state capacities have been analyzed in an effort to link them. In particular, two findings deserve attention: One, public social expenditure seems to be negatively correlated with income inequality; and second, in the larger Latin American countries military expenditure has either increased at the expense of social expenditure or its decline has been disproportionately less than the observed decline in social expenditure. Overall, military expenditure trends do not seem to be correlated with the revenue-generating capacity of the state. The implications of these findings for a paradigm of the new state is previewed in the following section.

Towards a Paradigm of the "New State"

Based on the theories discussed earlier and the evidence collected by other, albeit scattered, sources, there are indications that the state in Latin America is neither a prototypical liberal-pluralist nor a developmental state. Variation in the extent of market-oriented reforms within the region notwithstanding, the state is also not as autonomous today as it was a decade ago. Furthermore, its dependency on foreign capital and foreign markets has intensified. As the domestic market either is stagnant or growing more slowly than expected due to an increase in social inequity (which affects the majority of the population), this dependency is only going to further intensify.

Briefly, then, the "new state" in Latin America possesses a number of hybrid features. First, it is more interventionist than a liberal-pluralist or a neoclassical state in terms of dictating policy changes that facilitate economic globalization. Second, it is an anti-developmental state (in contrast with East Asian states) in the sense that it seems to be more embedded with domestic private monopoly capital as well as foreign capital without the required bureaucratic autonomy to make policies (and implement them) that make sense for most social groups.[44] And finally, there is some evidence that the new state, particularly in the larger countries of the region, has bolstered its coercive apparatus at the expense of incurring declines in many social expenditure patterns. A sustained movement in this direction may negatively affect the level of political legitimacy many regimes seem to command at the present time.

Notes

1. Duvall and Freeman, "The State and Dependent Capitalism," *International Studies Quarterly* 25 (1981): 99-118; Rothstein, *The Third World and U.S. Foreign Policy: Cooperation and Conflict in the 1980* (1981).

2. Rothgeb, "The Contribution of Foreign Direct Investment to Growth in Third World States," *Studies in Comparative International Development* 19 (1985).

3. Dahrendorf, *Class and Class Conflict in Industrial Society* (1959); *Scientific-Technological Revolution: Social Aspects* (1977).

4. Skocpol (1985).

5. Wolin, *Politics and Vision* (1960); Lowi, *The End of Liberalism* (1969).

6. Bentham in Bullock and Schock (eds.), *The Liberal Tradition* (1977, 28-29).

7. Smith, *An Inquiry into the Nature and Causes of the Wealth of Nations* (1937, 398).

8. See Stepan, *The State and Society: Peru in Comparative Perspective* (1978).

9. Evans (1979); Evans and Stephens (1985).

10. Engels (1958, 295).

11. Baran, *Political Economy of Growth* (1957); A.G. Frank, *Latin America: Underdevelopment and Revolution* (1970).

12. A.G. Frank, *Lumpenbourgeoisie: Lumpendevelopment* (1972, 15).

13. Hopkins and Wallerstein (1982); Chase-Dunn (1991).

14. Rubinson (1977); Trimberger (1978); O'Donnell (1979); Delacroix (1980); Bradshaw (1985); Skocpol (1985); Stephens (1985); Evans (1986); Pattnayak (1992).

15. Skocpol (1985, 6).

16. Skocpol (1985, 7).

17. Stepan (1978; also 1988); Trimberger (1978).

18. Stepan, *The State and Society: Peru in Comparative Perspective* (1978); also see his *Rethinking Military Politics* (1988).

19. Flynn, *Brazil, a Political Analysis* (1978).

20. Bardhan, *India's Democracy* (1988).

21. Bardhan (1988, 216).

22. Rubinson (1977); Bradshaw (1985); Evans (1979); and Pattnayak (1992).

23. Todaro, *Economic Development in the Third World* (1981).

24. Little (1982); Galenson (1985); Balassa (1982); for Dependency/world system revisions see Cardoso and Faletto (1978).

25. In particular Balassa (1982).

26. Hobson (1936); Lenin (1966); Cardoso and Faletto (1978).

27. Cardoso and Faletto (1978).

28. Ibid:

29. Bierstaker (1981); I. Frank (1980).

30. Evans (1979, 1986).

31. Delacroix and Ragin (1981); Bradshaw (1985); Rubinson and Holtzman (1981).

32. Rubinson, "Dependence, Government Revenue and Economic Growth," (1977).

33. World Development Report (1989, 167).

34. Little (1982); Woronoff (1986).

35. See White (1988); Haggard and Moon (1990); Gereffi and Wyman (1990).

36. Also see Amsden (1985); Katzenstein (1985); Deyo (1987).

37. Handelman, *The Challenge of Third World Development* (1996).

38. Johnson (1982) and Haggard (1991).

39. Onis, "The Logic of the Developmental State," (1991).

40. Handelman (1996).

41. Pattnayak, "Non-Traditional Trade Unions and Collective Bargaining in Andean America," (1994).

42. Levine (1995); Froehle (1995); Pattnayak (1995).

43. For a review of the literature, see Pattnayak (1994).

44. See Evans, *Embedded Autonomy: States and Industrial Transformation* (Princeton: Princeton University Press, 1995).

10

Economic Growth, Political Legitimacy, and Social Development: An Epilogue

---

Satya R. Pattnayak

There is no doubt that the issues of economic growth and social development lie at the center of the Latin American political economy. The current emphasis on economic globalization cannot be adequately understood without considering its implications for social development and inequality. From the preceding discussion it is abundantly clear that much of the aggregate growth has not facilitated compatible and comparable social development. Thus the assumption of many theories of development that economic growth will automatically lead to the alleviation of poverty is erroneous.[1]

The authors assembled in this collection are of the opinion that economic growth must be complemented by a series of state policies to sustain a positive link with social development. In the current climate of privatization of much of the public sector across Latin America, pursuing such policies is not easy. It is all the more difficult when the alliance formed among international financial agencies, foreign private capital, domestic private capital, and the state elite prescribes a set of policies and activities to subsidize capital, but not labor and other popular sectors. Political leaders, capitalists, international financial agency representatives, and state bureaucrats in charge of the various economic globalization programs must look beyond the euphoria of an idealized market as a potential solution to all social malaise. In a broader view of Latin America, there is an ever expanding informal sector, a major part of which employs some of the most vulnerable and under-represented segments of these societies. Although there are some signs of economic decentralization in favor of the regional urban centers of production, exchange, and distribution (away from the previously dominant primate city), the issue of informal sector growth is likely to be more pressing in the decades ahead. And this sector is important for both economic growth and social development.

Implications for the Theories of Democratization

In order for Latin America to sustain its recent surges towards political democracy, certain safeguards must be created and sustained in favor of the workers in the informal sector. In the absence of such safeguards (to be guaranteed by the state), the forces of social instability are likely to pose grave future challenges to the emerging political democracies in the region.

Although the book did not explicitly address the issues of democracy and democratization, some of the arguments put forth by the authors may be used to develop a more comprehensive understanding of regime sustenance and/or transition.

Latin America has provided basis for many scholarly work that challenge the theories of democratic transition based on the experiences of European and North American capitalist development. For example, starting with the pioneering work of Lipset,[2] much of modernization theory proposed that changes in socioeconomic conditions precipitate regime change, especially from authoritarian to democratic polity.[3] Variables that have received foremost attention are: level of development, level of education among the citizenry, level of urbanization, and the extent of access to communications and media. Because all of the above are strongly and positively correlated with economic development, economic determinants of political fate gained theoretical primacy in the 1950s and 1960s.[4]

This rather simplistic linear projection of the relationship between level of economic development and political regime type was challenged by a series of studies that includes the seminal works of O'Donnell[5] and Linz.[6] In particular, O'Donnell, based on the experiences of southern cone countries, such as Brazil and Argentina, argued that the relationship may very well be nonlinear, meaning the likelihood of an authoritarian regime replacing a more democratic one increases at middle levels of economic development.[7] This line of analysis --popularly known as the bureaucratic-authoritarian thesis-- gained much support in the late 1970s.

Three elements are crucial to understanding bureaucratic-authoritarianism: the phase of industrialization, the activation of the popular sector, and technocratic vision. O'Donnell argued that political transformations arise from the social tensions produced by industrialization and from the changes that subsequently take place in the social structure at both the *elite* and *mass* levels. The deepening of the Import Substituting Industrialization (ISI) requires increasingly high levels of technology, managerial expertise, and capital to succeed with the larger, more efficient, and increasingly capitalized enterprises. Often these enterprises are affiliates of foreign multinational corporations.[8]

The second important point in O'Donnell's analysis concerns the popular sector. For example, a populist coalition in power in Brazil pursued policies that were beneficial to the popular sector from the 1940s onwards. Sustaining such policies became problematic during the more difficult phases of the ISI and in the context of the new priorities to ensure stability and encourage foreign capital. As the rate of economic growth declined in the early 1960s, owing largely to external factors, the consumption and power demands of the popular sector seemed difficult to satisfy.[9] Tensions grew as the popular sector refused to pay the price for the new austerity measures in the face of growing inflation. This, in turn, produced growing gaps between popular demand and the regime's ability to satisfy that demand, which spilled over to the party system. The political parties, however, failed to funnel the social pressure into institutional channels. The continuing social pressure developed into a crisis and facilitated regime change as the economic decline continued throughout the early 1960s.

The third component of the bureaucratic-authoritarian thesis refers to the increasingly important role for technocrats in the private sector as well as in the civilian and military bureaucracies of the state sector.[10] Generally speaking, the technocrats have little patience with the ongoing political and economic crisis. They tend to perceive mobilization of the popular sector as detrimental to economic growth. Within the military, the technocratic orientation is known as the "new professionalism."[11]

This phenomenon in the military was a product of the changing perception of threat to society.[12] Since World War II, the top ranking military officers had, through study and research, developed a distinct notion of development in the southern cone countries. Unlike in the past, the military's notion of development encompassed all aspects of life---economic, political, and social. The Cold War of the 1960s and the rise of insurgent activity elsewhere in Latin America made the military more conscious of its role in society. In brief then, O'Donnell's analysis of the southern cone countries challenged the modernization hypothesis of a linear, positive relationship between economic development and democracy. On the contrary, using O'Donnell's model, one could argue that economic development at middle levels precipitates regime transition to authoritarianism.

Linz's work concentrates more on the domestic political variables.[13] He emphasized factors such as the state elite's failure to solve critical problems which may accentuate the tensions generated by economic development and accompanying income inequality. These tensions are exacerbated if the prevailing political culture fails to diffuse social tension through established linkages. In addition to economic crisis, the importance of societal heterogeneity, the extent of fragmentation in the party system, the prevalence of ideology as opposed to pragmatism, and the exclusion of leaders associated with previous authoritarian governments in building a multi-class coalition may expedite the process of regime transition from democracy to authoritarianism.[14]

Numerous additional qualifiers have been added by scholars in subsequent years. For example, in addition to the economic development and income inequality-related factors, the importance of institutions, colonial legacy, and strategic political mistakes made by the elite have been cited by scholars to be critical in explaining regime change.[15] Others have emphasized a set of world system-related factors, including the nature of economic and political transactions between the core and peripheral countries, to be important in explaining regime transition.[16]

Of course, it is rather difficult to consolidate all of these variables in order to arrive at a parsimonious model of regime sustenance and change. But it may be noted that many of the factors cited by scholars to be important in explaining regime change are present in Latin America in the 1990s. In particular, in some countries there is little indication that the military has moved away from its commitment to new professionalism. In many others, the role of the military is yet to be defined in the context of the new politically liberal climate.[17] Therefore, in the following section I emphasize "political legitimacy" as a critical variable. It is critical in a dual sense. On the one hand, it cannot sustain itself since it is caused by a multiple set of factors. On the other hand, at high levels it can work like magic, enhancing state capacity to address problems that are difficult to deal with during the times of low legitimacy. Hence, I elaborate on its importance in the understanding of regime sustenance and change in light of the arguments developed in the various chapters of the book.

Political Legitimacy as a Critical Variable

The importance of "political legitimacy" goes back to the seminal work of Max Weber.[18] Weber emphasized that the perception that the leadership and institutions can be trusted to address the demands of the citizenry is critical in sustaining a given type of political structure.[19] This is particularly important in hard economic times when the rate of urban poverty has increased all across Latin America.

Political Legitimacy as a "Dependent Variable"

Conceiving political legitimacy as a dependent variable should help us better explain why some Latin American regimes have more of it than others. Petras' account of Latin America in Chapter 2 raises skepticism about the possibility of cultivating high political legitimacy under the current regimes. In particular, state efforts to privatize gains of large private monopolies and socialize debts (through swapping debt in exchange for equity in the public sector companies) have the potential to create a citizenry that feels distant from its government.[20] This does not bode well for cultivating legitimacy. At best, developments such as these suggest that pro-free market policies and political exclusion may have greater mutual elective affinity than posited by others.[21]

Schmidt's analysis in Chapter 3 with regard to the societal tensions generated from the gradual decline of state welfare activities in Mexico and Central America have implications for my emphasis on political legitimacy. If economic globalization efforts undertaken by states continue to be correlated with privatization efforts in the economy in a climate of worsening income inequity, then a popular perception of the state being weak is likely. Such perception negatively affects political legitimacy.

In Chapter 4, Paige cautions about the limited potential of the successor (to the Sandinistas) Chamorro government in Nicaragua for cultivating consensus among competing social groups on the meaning of democratic pluralism. As has been ably discussed in the chapter, for the agrarian bourgeoisie it means representative democracy, whereas for the Sandinista supporters it implies popular organization under a vanguard party. A meaningful consensus is required to sustain legitimacy of the current electoral system.

According to Cavalcanti's discussion of the Brazilian case in Chapter 5, one must hope that the current Cardoso government will be more inclusive than the two administrations it succeeded. Political inclusion facilitates political legitimacy.

Another dimension of this conceptualization of legitimacy is revealed in Chapters 6, 7, and 8. The processes of urban change, some as a consequence of the current emphasis on economic globalization, have contributed to an enormous growth in the size of the informal sector. As the size of the informal sector grows, organizing political constituencies capable of voicing the concerns of the groups employed in the sector is extremely important. The embeddedness of the formal and informal sectors makes it both easy and difficult to organize. It is easy in the sense that some of those who participate in the informal sector are already well-established in the formal sector. Therefore, they have preexisting opportunities to join the various groups which can raise concerns about the issues affecting the informal sector. On the other hand, precisely because they gain, materially or otherwise, from their interaction with the informal sector, they would like it to remain unrepresented. There is a genuine fear that if the workers in the informal sector are organized it would raise the prices of the goods they produce. This particular complexity is indirectly hinted at by Pozos Ponce in Chapter 6. The lack of any viable link between the informal sector and the state could have potentially negative consequences in terms of sustaining political legitimacy of the regime in power.

As Portes and Schauffler in Chapter 7 recommend, state policy needs to be flexible so that it can accommodate the peculiarities of the activities in the informal sector across different neighborhoods. They caution, however, that a total absence of state policy toward the sector could be dangerous. The lack of any state efforts to eliminate worker abuse could generate problems of political legitimacy on behalf of the regime.

Froehle in Chapter 8 exposes a unique problem faced by Latin American states. Because of the electoral needs of the new political system, the informal sector is more important than ever before as it has grown in size. At the same time, under the neoliberal ideological climate a state may not be willing to do much in the way of policy. If this is the dilemma, then, as Froehle argues, state leaders should consider indirect forms of state subsidy. For example, the Venezuelan experiment, where due to active state encouragement *Fedeindustria's* credit activities have recently been expanded to include less dynamic industries in the informal sector, could be a start. Providing various community-specific needs, such as day-care centers in the areas in which most workers are women, would clearly benefit worker life quality. Such subsidies could serve as social control devices as well as enhancers of political legitimacy.

Political Legitimacy as an "Independent Variable"

Once attained consistent efforts are needed to sustain political legitimacy at higher levels. At those levels, it can have independent positive effects on perceived state capacities to address recurring social problems. State activism, direct and indirect, can also be more fruitful if complemented by high legitimacy. Operationalizing the various dimensions of political legitimacy should enable social scientists to predict the probabilities of success of specific state activities aimed at transforming social relations.

Concluding Remarks

Historically, the legitimacy for legal-rational authority has been minimal in Latin America, largely because it has been perceived to have served the interests of either foreign capital or national oligarchy.[22] The court system has long been perceived to be weak and incapable of forcing the rule of law. In this void of authority, then, how can high political legitimacy be cultivated?

Some Latin American scholars have argued that the streamlining of many state activities is intended to modernize the state apparatus.[23] Undoubtedly, waste-making activities need to be curtailed, which could allow states to better function as legal-rational entities. But at the same time, energizing the popular constituencies about the long-term stakes of not maintaining democratic norms is equally important. In other words, given the cultural legacy of organic-statism[24] in Latin America, a combination of charismatic and legal-rational authority types may be the most pragmatic combination needed.

Of course, both the charismatic leadership and the organizations and institutions that link the various constituencies of the civil society with the larger political structures will have to be perceived to be legitimate. This includes in a major way political parties, labor unions, and various popular sector organizations. Thus far, the regimes have functioned primarily on the basis of "negative legitimacy."[25] Negative legitimacy implies that democratic governments are better than the alternatives, most notably civilian or military dictatorships. This is fine in the beginning of the democratization process. But soon it will top out and the process could then devolve. The inculcation of democratic values is primordial. And political parties in particular, regardless of their ideology, can contribute to the process.[26] Moderate ideological polarization is healthy for the political education and participation of the citizenry. Attaining this may be difficult since under the neoliberal ideological climate the traditional left has generally been in retreat. Although it has in most cases accommodated the electoral system as the most viable option for Latin America, it must maintain its policy preferences different and distant from its political competitors. This distance is critical in maintaining moderate levels of polarization. The informal sector, unrepresented workers in particular, may provide new popular grounds for leftist rejuvenation.

In addition, the understanding that the source of political authority lies in the national population is essential. As Lipset[27] notes, distinguishing the agent of authority from its source goes a long way in the institutionalization of democratic norms and cultivation of political legitimacy. But this requires a painstaking process of educating the public. It takes time. But after a decade or so of economic globalization and changing urban processes that have generally produced more poverty and income inequity and growth in the informal sector, the patience of those who have suffered could run out faster than we think.

Notes

1. Sen, "Development: Which Way Now? (1996); Lal, "The Misconceptions of Development Economics" (1995); see all the dependency literature including Galtung (1980); Petras and Morley, *Latin America in the Time of Cholera* (1992).

2. Lipset, "Some Social Requisites of Democracy: Economic Development and Political Legitimacy," (1959).

3. Deutsch (1961); Lerner (1958); Inkles and Smith (1974).

4. Lipset (1992); Diamond, Linz, and Lipset (1988).

5. O'Donnell, *Modernization and Bureaucratic-Authoritarianism: Studies in South American Politics* (1973); "Reflections on the Pattern of Change in the Bureaucratic-Authoritarian State," (1978).

6. Linz, *The Breakdown of Democratic Regimes: Crisis, Breakdown, & Reequilibrium* (1978).

7. O'Donnell (1973); also see Kuznets (1965).

8. O'Donnell (1973, 56-67).

9. Ibid, 70.

10. Ibid, 75-78; also see Stepan (1978, 1988).

11. Stepan, *Rethinking Military Politics* (1988).

12. Ibid; also Dreifuss, *A Conquista do Estado* (1981).

13. Linz (1978).

14. Collier (1979); Muller (1985); Huntington (1991); Mainwaring (1993); Almond (1980); Diamond (1993).

15. Bollen and Jackman (1985); Linz (1994).

16. Jackson and Rosberg (1982); Whitehead (1989).

17. Lowenthal, "Charting a New Course," (1994).

18. Weber (1946); also see Lipset (1979); Diamond et al. (1990).

19. See Linz (1988).

20. See Petras, "The Transformation of Latin America: Free Markets, Democracy and Other Myths," (Chapter 2 in this volume).

21. Ibid: Also see Deyo (1987) in the case of East Asia.

22. See Ackerman(1992); Weiner (1987).

23. Calderón and dos Santos, *Hacia un nuevo orden estatal en América Latina* (Santiago: Fondo de Cultura Económica, 1991).

24. For a brilliant discussion of organic-statism, see Stepan, *The State and Society: Peru in Comparative Perspective* (1978, 26-45).

25. "Negative Legitimacy" implies that the current democratic regimes in many parts of the world have survived not because they have successfully negotiated the society's pressing problems, but largely because the alternatives (which includes military authoritarianism as well as bureaucratic socialism) are unacceptable to most of the population. See Lipset (1994).

26. On political parties see Mainwaring and Scully (eds.), *Building Democratic Institutions: Party Systems in Latin America* (1995).

27. See Lipset, "The Social Requisites of Democracy Revisited" (1994).

Select Bibliography

Ackerman, Bruce. *The Future of Liberal Revolution*. New Haven: Yale University Press, 1992.

Aguilar Zinzer, Adolfo. "Negotiation in Conflict: Central America and Contadora," Pp. 97-115 In *Crisis in Central America. Regional Dynamics and US Policy in the 1980s*, edited by N. Hamilton et al. Boulder: Westview Press, 1988.

Aguilar Camín, Héctor. *Después del milagro*. México: Cal y Arena, 1989.

Alba, C. and B. Roberts. *Crisis, Adjustment, and Employment in Mexico: Manufacturing Industry in Jalisco*. Mimeo, 1990.

____. "La industrialización en Jalisco: evolución y perspectivas." In *Cambio regional, mercado de trabajo y vida obrera en Jalisco*, edited by G. De la Peña and A. Escobar. Guadalajara: El Colegio de Jalisco, 1986.

____. "Jalisco: un caso de desarrollo contradictorio." Paper presented in the *Primer encuentro de investigación Jaliscience*. Guadalajara, 1984.

Allman, T.D. *Unmanifest Destiny: Mayhem and Illusion in American Foreign Policy - From Monroe Doctrine to Reagan's War in El Salvador*. Garden City: Doubleday, 1984.

Almond, Gabriel. "The Intellectual History of the Civic Culture Concept." In *The Civic Culture Revisited*, edited by G. Almond and S. Verba. Boston: Little, Brown, 1980.

American Security Council Foundation. *Attack on the Americas!* Boston, VA: Coalition for Peace through Strength, 1981.

Amsden, Alice. "The State and Taiwan's Economic Development." Pp. 78-106 In *Bringing the State Back In*, edited by P. Evans et al. New York: Cambridge University Press, 1985.

Angotti, T. "Urbanization in Latin America." *Latin American Perspectives* 14 (1987): 134-152.

Arias, P. and B. Roberts. "The City in Permanent Transition: The Consequences of a National System of Industrial Specialization." In *Capital and Labor in the Urbanized World*, edited by J. Walton. Beverly Hills: Sage, 1984.

Bacha, E. "Selected Issues in Post-1964 Brazilian Economic Growth." Pp.17-48 In *Models of Growth and Distribution for Brazil*, edited by Taylor et al. Washington DC: World Bank, 1980.

Baer, M. Delal. "Profiles in Transition in Latin America and the Caribbean." Pp. 47-57 In *Free Trade in the Western Hemisphere*, edited by S. Weintraub. Newbury Park: Sage, 1993.

Baer, W. "The Brazilian Growth and Development Experience: 1964-1975." Pp. 41-62 In *Brazil in the Seventies*, edited by R. Roett. Washington DC: American Enterprise Institute for Public Policy Research, 1976.

Bailey, Norman A. and William Perry. "The Strategic Impact of Hemispheric Free Trade." Pp. 68-80 In *Free Trade in the Western Hemisphere*, edited by S. Weintraub. Newbury Park: Sage, 1993.

Bairoch, Paul. *Urban Unemployment in Developing Countries: The Nature of the Problem and Proposals for its Solution.* Geneva: International Labor Office, 1973.

Balán, J., H. Browning, and E. Jelin. *El hombre en una sociedad en desarrollo.* Mexico, D.F.: Fondo de Cultura Económica, 1977.

Balassa, Bela. "The Lessons From East Asian Development: An Overview." *Economic Development and Cultural Change* 36 (1988): 273-290.

Baran, Paul. *The Political Economy of Growth.* New York: Monthly Review Press, 1957.

Bardhan, Pranab. *India's Democracy.* Princeton: Princeton University Press, 1988.

Benería, Lourdes. "Subcontracting and Employment Dynamics in Mexico City." Pp. 173-188 In *The Informal Economy: Studies in Advanced and Less Developed Countries*, edited by A. Portes, M.

Castells, and L.A. Benton. Baltimore: The Johns Hopkins University Press, 1989.

_____ and Marta I. Roldan. *The Crossroads of Class and Gender: Homework, Subcontracting, and Household Dynamics in Mexico City.* Chicago: University of Chicago Press, 1987.

Berry, B. and J. Kasarda. *Contemporary Urban Ecology.* New York: Free Press, 1977.

Bierstaker, Thomas J. *Distortion or Development?* Cambridge: MIT Press, 1981.

Birbeck, Chris. "Garbage, Industry, and the 'Vultures' of Cali, Colombia." Pp. 161-183 In *Causal Work and Poverty in Third World Cities*, edited by R. Bromley and C. Gerry. New York: John Wiley, 1979.

_____. "Self-Employed Proletarians in an Informal Factory: The Case of Cali's Garbage Dump." *World Development* 6 (1978): 1173-1185.

Bollen, Kenneth and Robert Jackman. "Economic and Noneconomic Determinants of Political Democracy in the 1960s." *Research in Political Sociology* 1(1985): 27-48.

Booth, John. "Socioeconomic and Political Roots of National Revolts in Central America." *Latin American Research Review* 26 (1991): 33-73.

Bradshaw, York. "Dependent Development in Black Africa." *American Sociological Review* 50 (1985): 195-207.

Brasil Nunca Mais (2nd edition). Rio de Janeiro: Vozes, 1985.

The Brasilians. "Brazil Trade Surplus Rises to $ 1.62 billion." August (1992): 7.

_____. "Corruption and Scandals Plus Illegal Transactions." August (1992): 7.

_____. "The Brazilian Privatization Program." August (1992): 16.

_____. "German Experts Say Brazil Needs to Modernize State." September (1992): 4.

_____. "Privatization Continues." October (1992): 1.

_____. "Collor Impeachment: A Light at the End of the Tunnel for Latin America?" October (1992): 2.

_____. "Focus: Hopes and Challenges: New Brazilian President." October (1992): 4.

_____. "State Steel Mill Sold." November (1992): 4.

Bromley, Ray. "A New Path to Development? The Significance and Impact of Hernando de Soto's Ideas on Underdevelopment,

Production, and Reproduction." *Economic Geography* 66 (1990): 328-348.

Bullock, Alan and Maurice Shock (eds.). *The Liberal Tradition: From Fox to Keynes.* Oxford: Oxford University Press, 1977.

Bulmer-Thomas, Victor. "Honduras Since 1930." Pp. 191-225 In *Central America Since Independence,* edited by L. Bethell. New York: Cambridge University Press, 1991.

Canak, William L. "Debt, Austerity, and Latin America in the New International Division of Labor." In *Lost Promises: Debt, Austerity, and Development in Latin America,* edited by W. Canak. Boulder: Westview, 1989.

Capecchi, Vittorio. "The Informal Economy and the Development of Flexible Specialization." Pp. 189-215 In *The Informal Economy: Studies in Advanced and Less Developed Countries,* edited by A. Portes, M. Castells, and L.A. Benton. Baltimore; The Johns Hopkins University Press, 1989.

Cárdenas, E. "Contemporary Economic Problems in Historical Perspective." In *Mexico's Search for a New Development Strategy,* edited by D. Brothers and A. Wick. Boulder: Westview, 1989.

Cardoso, Fernando Enrique et al. *Eight Essays on the Crisis of Development in Latin America.* Amsterdam: CEDLA, 1991.

_____ and Enzo Faletto. *Dependencia y desarrollo en América Latina.* Mexico: Siglo XXI, 1978.

Castells, Manual and Alejandro Portes. "World Underneath: The Origins, Dynamics, and Effects of the Informal Economy." Pp. 11-37 In *The Informal Economy: Studies in Advanced and Less Developed Countries,* edited by A. Portes, M. Castells, and L.A. Benton. Baltimore: The Johns Hopkins University Press, 1989.

CEESP. *La economía subterranea en México.* Mexico City: Editorial Diana, 1987.

Chase-Dunn, Christopher. *Global Formation: Structures of the World Economy.* Cambridge: Basil Blackwell, 1991.

Chill Hill, R. and J. Feagin. "Detroit and Houston: Two Cities in Global Perspective." In *The Capitalist City,* edited by M. Smith and J. Feagin. Oxford: Basil Blackwell, 1987.

Coatsworth, John H. "Pax (Norte) Americana: Latin America After the Cold War." Pp. 159-177 In *Past as Prelude: History in the Making of a New World Order,* edited by M. Woo-Cumings and M. Loriaux. Boulder: Westview Press, 1993.

Cohen, Isaac. "A New Latin American and Caribbean Nationalism." Pp. 36-46 In *Free Trade in the Western Hemisphere*, edited by S. Weintraub. Newbury Park: Sage, 1993.

Coleman, Kenneth M. and George C. Herring. "Conclusion: Toward a New Central American Policy." Pp. 219-228 In *Understanding the Central American Crisis: Sources of Conflict, US Policy, and Options for Peace*, edited by K. Coleman and G. C. Herring. Wilmington: Scholarly Resources, 1991.

Collier, David (ed.). *The New Authoritarianism in Latin America*. Princeton: Princeton University Press, 1979.

Cortés, F. and R.M. Rubalcava. "Cambio estructural y concentración: un análisis de la distribución del ingreso familiar en México, 1984-1989." Paper presented at the Seminar on *Sociodemographic Effects of the 1980s Economic Crisis in Mexico*. Austin: University of Texas at Austin, 1992.

Costa R.V. da. "Uma Ameaça à Democracia." *Veja* 16 December (1981): 146.

Council of the Americas. *Washington Report*. Fall, 1992.

Crabtree, J. "The Collor Plan: Shooting the Tiger?" *Bulletin of Latin American Research* 10 (1991): 19-132.

Dahrendorf, Ralph. *Scientific-Technological Revolution: Social Aspects*. Beverley Hills: Sage, 1977.

_____. *Class and Class Conflict in Industrial Society*. Stanford: Stanford University Press, 1959.

Davis, Kingsley. "*World Urbanization, 1950-1970. Volume I: Basic Data for Cities, Countries, and Regions*. Population Monograph Series, no. 4. Berkeley and Los Angeles: University of California Press, 1969.

De la Peña, G. "Mercados de trabajo y articulación regional: apuntes sobre el caso de Guadalajara y el occidente Mexicano." In *Cambio regional, mercado de trabajo y vida obrera en Jalisco*, edited by G. De la Peña and A. Escobar. Guadalajara: El Colegio de Jalisco, 1986.

De Soto, Hernando. *The Other Path*. New York: Harper and Row, 1989.

Delacroix, Jacques. "The Distributive State in the World System." *Studies in Comparative International Development* 15 (1980): 3-21.

_____ and Charles Ragin. "Structural Blockage: A Cross-National Study of Economic Dependency, State Efficacy, and Underdevelopment." *American Journal of Sociology* 86 (1981): 1311-1347.

"Democratization and Class Struggle." *Latin American Perspectives* 15, Special Issue (1988).

Deutch, Karl W. "Social Mobilization and Political Development." *American Political Science Review* 60 (1961): 493-514.

Deyo, Frederic C. (ed.). *The Political Economy of the New Asian Industrialism*. Ithaca: Cornell University Press, 1987.

Diamond, Larry (ed.). *Political Culture and Democracy in Developing Countries*. Boulder: Lynn Rienner, 1993.

_____ et al. (eds.). *Politics in Developing Countries, Comparing Experiences with Democracy*. Boulder: Lynne Rienner, 1990.

Diniz, E. and R. Boshi. "A Consolidação democrática no Brasil: autores políticos, procesos sociais e intermediação de interesses." Pp. 17-78 In *Modenização e consolidação democrática no Brasil*, edited by E. Diniz et al. Rio de Janeiro: Vértice and IUPERJ, 1989.

Dreifuss, René. *1964: A Conquista do Estado*. Rio de Janeiro, 1981.

Dunkerley, James. "Guatemala Since 1930." Pp. 119-157 In *Central America Since Independence*, edited by L. Bethell. New York: Cambridge University Press, 1991.

Economic Commission for Latin America (ECLA). *Statistical Yearbook for Latin America*. New York: United Nations, 1981.

Economic Commission for Latin America and the Caribbean (ECLAC). *Statistical Yearbook for Latin America*. New York: United Nations, 1991.

The Economist. "Sleight of Hand." 21 April (1990): 46-47.

_____. "The Right Stuff." 9 June (1990): 75-77.

Engels, Frederick. "The Origin of the Family, Private Property, and the State." Pp. 281-299 In *Selected Works, Vol II*, by K. Marx and F. Engels. Moscow: Foreign Language Publishing House, 1958.

Envío. "Trends in US Aid to the Region." December (1990): 18-19.

Epstein, Barbara. "The Reagan Doctrine and Right-Wing Democracy." *Socialist Review* 19 (1989):9-38.

Evans, Peter. *Embedded Autonomy: States and Industrial Transformation*. Princeton: Princeton University Press, 1995.

_____. "Predatory, Developmental, and Other Apparatuses: A Comparative Political Economy Perspective on the Third World State." *Sociological Forum* 4 (1989): 561-587.

____. "State, Capital, and the Transformation of Dependence." *World Development* 14 (1986): 791-808.

____ and John Stephens. "Development and the World Economy." Pp. 739-766 In *Handbook of Sociology*, edited by Neil Smelsor. New Delhi: Sage, 1985.

Fajnzylber, F. *Unavoidable Industrial Restructuring in Latin America.* Durham: Duke University Press, 1990.

Feige, Edgar. "Defining and Estimating Underground and Informal Economies: The New Institutional Economics Approach," *World Development* 18 (1990): 989-1002.

Felix David. "On Financial Blowups and Authoritarian Regimes in Latin America." Pp 85-125 In *Latin American Political Economy: Financial Crisis and Political Change*, edited by J. Hartlyn and S. Morley. Boulder: Westview Press, 1986.

Flora, Jan L. and Edelberto Torres-Rivas. "Sociology of Developing Societies: Historical Bases of Insurgency in Central America." Pp. 32-55 In *Central America*, edited by J. L. Flora and E. Torres-Rivas. New York: Monthly Review Press, 1989.

Fortuna, Juan Carlos and Suzanna Prates. "Informal Sector versus Informalized Labor Relations in Uruguay." Pp. 78-94 In *The Informal Economy: Studies in Advanced and Less Developed Countries*, edited by A. Portes, M. Castells, and L.A. Benton. Baltimore: The Johns Hopkins University Press, 1989.

Frank, Andre G. *Lumpenbourgeoisie: Lumpendevelopment.* New York: Monthly Review Press, 1972.

Frank, Isaiah. *Foreign Investment in Developing Countries.* Baltimore: Johns Hopkins University Press, 1980.

Froehle, Bryan. "Religious Competition in Contemporary Venezuela." Pp. 125-152 In *Organized Religion in the Political Transformation of Latin America*, edited by S. Pattnayak. Lanham, MD: University Press of America, 1995.

Galenson, W. (ed.). *Foreign Trade and Investment: Development in the Newly Industrializing Asian Economies.* Madison: University of Wisconsin Press, 1985.

García, Norberto E. "Growing labor Absorption with Persistent Unemployment." *CEPAL Review* 18 (1982): 45-64.

____. *Reestructuración, ahorro, y mercado de trabajo.* Santiago de Chile: PREALC, 1991.

_____ and Victor E. Tokman. "Dinámica del subempleo en América Latina." In *Estudios e informes de las CEPAL*. Santiago de Chile: CEPAL, 1981.

Garza, G. "Crisis del sector servicios de la ciudad de Mexico." Paper presented at Conference on *Socio-Demographic Effects of the 1980s Crisis in Mexico*. Austin: University of Texas, 1992.

_____. "Dinámica industrial de la ciudad de Mexico, 1940-1988." *Estudios Demográficos y Urbanos* 6 (1991): 209-214.

Gereffi, Gary. "Rethinking Development Theory: Insights from East Asia and Latin America." *Sociological Forum* 4 (1989): 505-533.

_____. "Paths of Industrialization: An Overview." pp. 3-31 In *Manufacturing Miracles: Paths of Industrialization in Latin America and East Asia*, edited by G. Gereffi and D. L. Wyman. Princeton: Princeton University Press, 1990.

_____ and D. Wyman (eds.). *Manufacturing Miracles*. Princeton: Princeton University Press, 1990.

González, M. and A. Escobar (eds.). *Social Responses to Mexico's Economic Crisis of the 1980s*. San Diego: Center for U.S.-Mexican Studies, 1991.

Gottdiener, M. "Crisis Theory and Socio-Spatial Restructuring: The U.S. Case." In *Capitalist Development and Crisis Theory: Accumulation, Regulation and Spatial Restructuring*, edited by M. Gottdiener and N. Komninos. New York: St. Martin's, 1989.

Granovetter, Mark. "Economic Action and Social Structure: The Problem of Embeddedness." *American Journal of Sociology* 91 (1985): 481-510.

Haggard, Stephen and C. Moon. "Institutions and Economic Policy." *World Politics* 42 (1990): 210-237.

Handelman, Howard. *The Challenge of Third World Development*. Upper Saddle River, NJ: Prentice Hall, 1996.

Hodges, Donald. *Intellectual Foundations of the Nicaraguan Revolution*. Austin: University of Texas Press, 1986.

Hagopian, F. and S. Mainwaring. "Democracy in Brazil: Problems and Prospects." *World Policy Journal* 4 (1987): 485-514.

Hart, Keith. "Informal Income Opportunities and Urban Employment in Ghana." Paper presented at a Conference on Urban Unemployment in Africa. Institute of Development Studies, University of Sussex, September 1971. Subsequently published in revised form in *Journal of Modern African Studies* 11 (1973): 61-89.

Hawley, A. *Urban Society: An Ecological Approach.* New York: Ronald, 1971.

Hobson, J. *Imperialism: A Study.* London: Allen & Unwin, 1938.

Hopkins, Terrence and Immanuel Wallerstein. *World System Analysis.* Beverly Hills: Sage, 1982.

Huntington, Samuel. *The Third Wave: Democratization in the Late Twentieth Century.* Norman: University of Oklahoma Press, 1991.

International Labor Office (ILO). *Employment, Incomes and Inequality: A Strategy for Increasing Productive Employment in Kenya.* Geneva: ILO, 1971.

Instituto Nacional de Estadistica, Geografía e Informática (INEGI). *Encuesta nacional de economía informal.* Aguascalientes: INEGI, 1990.

Infante, Ricardo and Emilio Klein. *Empleo y equidad: Desafío de los 90.* Documentos de Trabajo, No. 435. Santiago de Chile: PREALC, 1990.

____. "The Latin American Labor Market." *CEPAL Review* 45 (1991): 135.

Inkles, A. and P. Smith. *Becoming Modern: Individual Change in Six Developing Countries.* Cambridge: Harvard University Press, 1974.

Isto É. "Bússola Calibrada." 3 December (1992): 16-20.

Jackson, Robert and Carl Rosberg. "Why Africa's Weak States Persist: The Empirical and Juridical in Statehood." *World Politics* 35 (1982): 1-24.

Johnson, Chalmers. *MITI and the Japanese Miracle.* Stanford: Stanford University Press, 1982.

Katzenstein, P. *Small States in World Markets.* Ithaca: Cornell University Press, 1985.

Kirkpatrick, Jeane. "Dictatorships and Double Standards." Pp. 15-39 In *El Salvador: Central America in the New Cold War*, edited by M E. Gentleman et al. New York: Grove Press, 1981.

Klein, Emilio and Victor E. Tokman. "Sector informal: una forma de utilizar el trabajo como consequencia de la manera de producir y no vice versa." *Estudios Sociologicos* 6 (1988): 205-212.

Knight, Alan. 'The Peculiarities of Mexican History: Mexico Compared to Latin America, 1821-1992." *Journal of Latin American Studies* 24 (1992): 99-144.

Kuznets, Simon. *Economic Growth and Structure.* New York: Norton, 1965.

Lal, Deepak. "The Misconceptions of 'Development Economics'." Pp. 29-26 In *The Political Economy of Development and Underdevelopment*, edited by K. Jameson and C. Wilber. New York: McGraw-Hill, 1996.

Lamarche, F. "Property Development and the Economic Foundation of the Urban Question." In *Urban Sociology: Critical Essays*, edited by C. Pickvance. New York: St. Martin's, 1976.

Lazerson, Mark H. "Organizational Growth of Small Firms: An Outcome of Markets and Hierarchies?" *American Sociological Review* 53 (1988): 330-342.

Lerner, Daniel. *The Passing of Traditional Society*. Glencoe, IL: Free Press, 1958.

Levine, Daniel. "Religious Change, Empowerment and Power: Reflections on Latin American Experience." Pp. 15-40 In *Organized Religion in the Political Transformation of Latin America*, edited by S. Pattnayak. Lanham, MD: University Press of America, 1995.

Lie, John. "The Concept of Mode Exchange." *American Sociological Review* 57 (1992): 508-523.

Linz, Juan. "Presidential or Parliamentary Democracy: Does It Make a Difference?" In *The Failure of Presidential Democracy, vol 2: The Case of Latin America*, edited by J. Linz and A. Valenzuela. Baltimore: Johns Hopkins University Press, 1994.

_____. "Legitimacy of Democracy and the Socioeconomic System.' Pp. 65-97 In *Comparing Pluralist Democracies: Strains on Legitimacy*, edited by M. Dogan. Boulder: Westview, 1988.

_____. *The Breakdown of Democratic Regimes: Crisis, Breakdown, & Reequilibration*. Baltimore: Johns Hopkins University Press, 1978.

Lipset, Seymour M. "The Social Requisites of Democracy Revisited." *American Sociological Review* 59 (1994): 1-22.

_____. "Some Social Requisites of Democracy: Economic Development and Political Legitimacy." *American Political Science Review* 53 (1959): 69-105.

Little, I.M.D. *Economic Development: Theory, Policy and International Relations*. New York: Basic Books, 1982.

Lomnitz, Larissa A. "Migration and Networks in Latin America." Pp. 133-150 In *Current Perspectives in Latin American Urban Research*, edited by A. Portes and Harley L. Browning. Austin: Institute of Latin American Studies Publication Series, University of Texas, 1976.

_____. "Informal Exchange Networks in Formal Systems: A Theoretical Model." *American Anthropologist* 90 (1988): 42-55.

Lowenthal, Abraham. "Charting a new Course." *Hemisfile* 5 (July/August 1994): 1-2, 11-12.

Lozano, Lucrecia. *De Sandino al triunfo de la revolución*. México: Siglo XXI, 1985.

Lozano, Wilfredo. "La urbanización de la pobreza: economía informal, familia e identidades colectivas en Santo Domingo." Paper presented at Conference on Caribbean Urbanization in the Years of the Crisis. Sponsored by the Latin American Faculty of Social Sciences (FLACSO) and The Johns Hopkins University. Santo Domingo, August, 1992.

Mainwaring, Scott. "Presidentialism, Multipartyism, and Democracy: the Difficult Combination." *Comparative Political Studies* 26 (1993): 198-228.

_____ and Timothy R. Scully (eds.). *Building Democratic Institutions: Party Systems in Latin America*. Stanford: Stanford University Press, 1995.

Malloy, James M. *The Politics of Social Security in Brazil*. Pittsburgh, University of Pittsburgh Press, 1979.

Manigat, Sabine. "L'urbanisation de Port-au-Prince dans les anees 1980: Economie et conditions de vie des Port-au-Princiens." Paper presented at Conference on Caribbean Urbanization in the years of the Crisis. Sponsored by the Latin American Faculty of Social Sciences (FLACSO) and The Johns Hopkins University. Santo Domingo, August, 1992.

McKenzie, R.D. "The Scope of Human Ecology." *American Journal of Sociology* 32 (1926): 141-154.

Mesa-Lago, Carmelo. "Alternative Strategies to the Social Security Crisis: Socialist, Market, and Mixed Approaches." In *The Crisis of Social Security and Health Care*, edited by C. Mesa-Lago. Pittsburgh: Center for Latin American Studies, University of Pittsburgh, 1985.

_____. "Social Security and Prospects for Equality in Latin America." Discussion Papers No. 140. Washington DC: World Bank, 1991.

Moffett, George D. *The Limits of Victory: The Ratification of the Panama Canal Treaties*. Ithaca: Cornell University Press, 1985.

Morse, Richard. "Trends and Issues in Latin American Urban Research, 1965-70." *Latin American Research Review* 6 (1971): 3-52.

Moser, Caroline. "Informal Sector or Petty Commodity Production: Dualism or Dependence in Urban Development?" *World Development* 6 (1978): 1041-1064.

Muller, Edward M. "Dependent Economic Development, Aid Dependence on the United States, and Democratic Breakdown in the Third World." *International Studies Quarterly* 29 (1985):445-470.

Nairn, Allan. "Guatemala: Central America's Blue Chip Investment." Pp. 100-105 In *Guatemala in Rebellion: Unfinished History*, edited by J. L. Fried et al. New York: Grove Press, 1983.

The New York Times. "Brazil's Bishops and Priests Hold a Fast on Plight of the Poor." 12 October (1984).

Nun, José, Juan C. Martín, and Murmis M. "La marginalidad en América Latina." Joint Program ILPES-DESAL Working Paper No. 2. Santiago de Chile, 1967.

Nuncio, A. *Crisis económica y estancamiento político*. mimeo, 1987.

O'Donnell, Guillermo A. *Modernization and Bureaucratic-Authoritarianism: Studies in South American Politics*. Berkeley, Institute of International Studies: University of California press, 1973.

_____. "Reflections on the Pattern of Change in the Bureaucratic-Authoritarian State." *Latin American Research Review* 13 (1978): 3-38.

_____. "Toward an Alternative Conceptualization of South American Politics." Pp. 239-275 in *Promise of Development: Theories of Change in Latin America*, edited by F. Klarén and T. J. Bosset. Boulder: Westview, 1986.

Onis, Ziya. "The Logic of the Developmental State." *Comparative Politics* (1991): 109-126.

Pattnayak, Satya R. (ed.). *Organized Religion in the Political Transformation of Latin America*. Lanham, MD: University Press of America, 1995.

_____. "Non-Traditional Trade Unions and Collective Bargaining in Andean America." Paper presented at the Latin American Studies Association Meeting, Atlanta, 1994.

_____. "External Debt, State Extractive Capacity, State Coercive Capacity, and Industrial Growth in the Third World." *Journal of Developing Societies* 10 (1994): 148-160.

_____. "Direct Foreign Investment, State, and Levels of Manufacturing Growth in Asia and Latin America." *Journal of Political and Military Sociology* 20 (1992): 83-106.

Pereira, L.C.B. "Collar, Zélia, Marcílio e os Planos Econômicos." *The Brasilians* October (1992): 18.

_____ and Y. Nakano. "Hyperinflation and Stabilization in Brazil: The First Collor Plan." Pp. 41-68 In *Economic Problems of the 1990s*, edited by P. Davidson and J.A. Kregel. Hants: Elgar, 1991.

Peatti, Lisa R. "Living Poor: A View for the Bottom." Proceedings of the Colloquium on Urban Poverty: A Comparison of the Latin American and the U.S. Experience. Los Angeles: UCLA School of Architecture and Urban Planning, 1974.

_____. "Anthropological Perspectives on the Concepts of Dualism, the Informal Sector, and Marginality in Developing Urban Economies." *International Regional Science* 5 (1980): 1-31.

_____. "What is to be done with the 'Informal Sector'?: A Case Study of Shoe Manufacturers in Colombia." Pp. 208-232 In *Towards a Political Economy of Urbanization in Third World Countries*, edited by H. Safa. Delhi: Oxford University Press, 1982.

Pérez-Sáinz, Juan Pablo. *Informalidad urbana en America Latina: enfoque, problematicas e interrogantes*. Guatemala: Editorial Nueva Sociedad, 1992.

_____ and Angela Leal. "Percepciones sobre la crisis en el área metropolitana de Guatemala." Paper presented at Conference on Caribbean Urbanization in the Years of the Crisis. Sponsored by the Latin American Faculty of Social Sciences (FLACSO) and the Johns Hopkins University. Santo Domingo, August, 1992.

Philip, George. "The Nicaraguan Conflict: Politics and Propaganda." Pp. 243-249 In *Vital Interests: The Soviet Issue in US Central American Policy*, edited by B.D. Larkin. Boulder: Lynne Rienner Publishers, 1988.

Polanyi, Karl. *The Great Transformation*. Boston: Beacon Press, 1944.

Portes, Alejandro. "Latin American Class Structures: Their Composition and Change During the Last Decades." *Latin American Research Review* 20 (1985): 7-39.

_____ and H. Browning. *Current Perspectives in Latin American Urban Research*. Austin: University of Texas Press, 1976.

_____ and Lauren Benton. "Industrial Development and Labor Absorption: A Reinterpretation." *Population and Development Review* 10 (1984): 589-611.

_____ and John Walton. *Urban Latin America, the Political Condition from Above and Below*. Austin: University of Texas Press, 1976.

_____. *Labor, Class, and the International System.* New York: Academic Press, 1981.

_____, Silvio Blitzer, and John Curtis. "The Urban Informal Sector in Uruguay: Its Structure, Characteristics, and Effects." *World Development* 14 (1986): 727-741.

_____, Manuel Castells, and Lauren Benton. "The Policy Implications of Informality." Pp. 208-311 In *The Informal Economy: Studies in Advanced and Less Developed Countries*, edited by A. Portes, M. Castells, and L.A. Benton. Baltimore: The Johns Hopkins University Press, 1989.

_____. "La urbanización de América Latina en los años de crisis." In *Las ciudades en conflicto: una perspectiva Latinoamericana*, edited by M. Lombardi and D. Veiga. Montevideo: CIESU, 1989.

_____, Jose Itzigsohn, and Carlos Dore-Cabral. "Urbanization in the Caribbean Basin: Social Change during the Years of the Crisis." *Latin American Research Review* 29 (1994): 3-38.

Poston, Dudley, P. Frisbie, and M. Micklin. "Sociological Human Ecology: Theoretical and Conceptual Perspectives." In *Sociological Human Ecology: Contemporary Issues and Applications*, edited by M. Micklin and H. Cholin. Boulder: Westview, 1983.

Pozas, M.A. *Estrategias empresariales ante la apertura externa.* Tijuana, B.C.N.: COLEF-1, 1990.

PREALC. *Sector informal: funcionamiento y politicas.* Santiago de Chile: PREALC, 1981.

_____. *Mercado de trabajo en cifras: 1950-1980.* Santiago de Chile: International Labour Office, 1982.

Programa de Estudios Relaciones México-Estados Unidos. "México en la encrucijada de Guatemala." *Informe Relaciones México-Estados Unidos* Jul-dic (1982): 10-71.

Rivière D'Arc, H. "Guadalajara y su región: influencias y dificultades de una metrópoli Mexicana." In *Regiones y ciudades en América Latina*, edited by J. Piel, et al. Mexico D.F: Sepsetentas, 1973.

Roberts, Bryan R. "The Provincial Urban System and the Process of Dependency." Pp. 133-150 In *Current Perspectives in Latin American Urban Research*, edited by A. Portes and Harley L. Browning. Austin: Institute of Latin American Studies Publications Series, University of Texas, 1976.

_____. "Employment Structure, Life Cycle, and Life Chances: Formal and Informal Sectors in Guadalajara." Pp. 41-59 In *The Informal*

Economy: Studies in Advanced and Less Developed Countries, edited by A. Portes, M. Castells, and L.A. Benton. Baltimore: The Johns Hopkins University Press, 1989.

____. " The Dynamics of Informal Employment in Mexico." Discussion Paper Series on the Informal Sector *#3*. Bureau of International Labor Affairs, US Department of Labor, 1992.

Rubio, Luis. "El talón de aquiles de la reforma económica." *Vuelta* Julio (1993): 36-39.

Rossini, R.G. and J.J. Thomas. "Comentarios al equipo económico de ILD." In *Los fundamentos estadísticos de el otro sendero: debate sobre el sector informal en el Perú. Taller de investigación*, edited by R.G. Rossini et al. Lima: Friedreich Ebert Foundation, 1987.

Rubinson, Richard. "Dependence, Government Revenue and Economic Growth." *Studies in Comparative International Development* 12 (1977): 3-23.

____ and D. Holtzman. "Comparative Dependence and Economic Development." *International Journal of Comparative Sociology* 22 (1981): 86-101.

Sabel, Charles. *The Division of Labor in Industry*. Cambridge: Cambridge University Press, 1982.

____ and Michel J. Piore. *The Second Industrial Divide: Possibilities for Prosperity*. New York: Basic Books, 1984.

Sassen-Koob, S. "The New Labor Demand in Global Cities." In *Cities in Transformation, Class Capital and the State*, Urban Affairs Annual Reviews. Vol 26. Beverly Hills: Sage, 1984.

Schmidt, Samuel. *The Deterioration of the Mexican Presidency: The Years of Luis Echeverría*. Tucson: University of Arizona Press, 1991.

Schneider, B.R. "A Privatização no governo Collor: triunfo do liberalismo ou colapso do estado desenvolvimentista?" *Revista de Economica Política* 12 (1992): 5-18.

Scholk, Richard S. Stabilization, Destabilization, and the Popular Classes in Nicaragua, 1979-1989." *Latin American Research Review* 25 (1990).

Sen, Amartya. "Development: Which Way Now?" Pp. 1-18 In *The Political Economy of Development and Underdevelopment*, edited by K. Jameson and C. Wilber. New York: McGraw-Hill, 1996.

Serra, J. "Ciclos e mudançãs estruturais na economis Brasileira do pós-guerra." Pp. 56-121 In *Desenvolvimento capitalista no Brasil, vol. 1,* edited by L.G Belluzo and R. Coutinho. São Paulo: Brasiliense, 1983.

Skocpol Theda. "Bringing the State Back In: Strategies of Analysis in Current Research." Pp. 3-37 In *Bringing the State Back In*, edited by P. Evans, D. Rueschemeyer, and T. Skocpol. New York: Cambridge University Press, 1985.

Smith, Adam. *An Inquiry into the Nature and Causes of the Wealth of Nations*. Nashville: Pantheon, 1937.

Stark, David. "Bending the Bars of the Iron Cage: Bureaucratization and Informalization in Capitalism and Socialism." *Sociological Forum* 4 (1989): 637-664.

Stepan, Alfred. *The State and Society: Peru in Comparative Perspective*. Princeton: Princeton University Press, 1978.

_____. *Rethinking Military Politics*. Princeton: Princeton University Press, 1988.

_____ (ed.). *Democratizing Brazil: Problems of Transition and Consolidation*. New York, 1989.

Swedish International Development Authority. *Nicaragua: The Transition from Economic Chaos Toward Sustainable Growth*. Stockholm, 1989.

Syrvud, D.E. *Foundations of Brazilian Economic Growth*. Stanford: Hoover Institute, 1974.

Tanzi, Vito. "The Hidden Economy: A Cause of Increasing Concern." *FMI Bulletin* 9 (1980): 34-37.

_____. *The Underground Economy in the United States and Abroad*. Lexington Books, Mass: DC Heath, 1982.

Teichman, Judith A. *Policymaking in Mexico from Boom to Crisis*. Boston: Allen and Unwin, 1988.

Todaro, Michel P. *Economic Development in the Third World*. New York: Longman, 1981.

Tokman, Victor. "El sector informal: quince años despues." *El trimestre económico* 54 (1987): 513-536.

Torres-Rivas, Edelberto. "Central America Today: A Study in Regional Dependency." Pp. 1-33 In *Trouble in Our Backyard: Central America and the United States in the Eighties*, edited by M. Diskin. New York: Pantheon, 1983.

_____. *Repression and Resistance: The Struggle for Democracy in Central America*. Boulder: Westview Press, 1989.

____. "Crisis and Conflict, 1930 to the Present." Pp. 69-118 In *Central America Since Independence*, edited by L. Bethell. New York: Cambridge University Press, 1991.

Trimberger, Ellen. *Revolution from Above*. New Brunswick: Transaction Press, 1978.

Unikel, L. C. Ruiz, and G. Garza. *El desarrollo urbano de México: diagnósticos y implicaciónes futuras*. Mexico: El Colegio de Mexico, 1976.

United Nations. *World Population Prospects*. New York: United Nations, 1991.

____. *World Urbanization Prospects*. New York: United Nations, 1991.

____. *FAO Yearbook: Trade of the United Nations*. FAO Statistics Series 33 (1979) and 44 (1990).

Veja. "Trama ligadíssima." 29 July (1992): 20-26.

____. "O ministerio do Itamar." 14 October (1992): 32.

Vellinga, M. *Industrialización, burguesía y clase obrera en Mexico*. Mexico D.F: Siglo XXI, 1979.

Vianna, L.W. *De um plano Collor a outro*. Rio de Janeiro: Editora Revan, 1991.

Wallerstein, Immanuel. *The Modern World System*. New York: Academic Press, 1974.

Walton, J. *Elites and Economic Development: Comparative Studies on the Political Economy of Latin American Cities*. Austin: University of Texas Press, 1977.

Weber, Max. *From Max Weber: Essays in Sociology*, edited and translated by H.H. Gerth and C.W. Mills. New York: Oxford University Press, 1946.

____. *Basic Concepts in Sociology*. New York: Philosophical Lib., 1962.

____. *Economy and Society: An Outline of Interpretive Sociology*. New York: Bedminister Press, 1968.

Weiner, Myron. "Empirical Democratic Theory." Pp. 3-34 In *Competitive Elections in Developing Countries*, edited by M. Weiner and E. Ozbudun. Durham: Duke University Press, 1987.

White, G. (ed.). *Developmental States in East Asia*. London: McMillan, 1988.

Whitehead, Lawrence. "The Consolidation of Fragile Democracies." Pp. 79-95 In *Democracy in the Americas: Stopping the Pendulum*, edited by R.A. Pastor. New York: Holmes & Meier, 1989.

Wilkie, James W. and Adam Perkal (eds.). *Statistical Abstract of Latin America* Vol. 24. Los Angeles: University of California Latin American Center, 1985.

Wills, Gary. *Reagan's America*. New York: Penguin, 1988.

Wilson, Richard R. "The Impact of Social Security on Employment." Pp. 247-278 In *The Crisis of Social Security and Health Care*, edited by C. Mesa-Lago. Pittsburgh: Center for Latin American Studies, University of Pittsburgh Press, 1985.

Woo-Cumings, Meredith and Michael Loriaux. "Introduction." Pp. 1-7 In *Past as Prelude: History in the Making of a New World Order*, edited by M. Woo-Cumings and M. Loriaux. Boulder: Westview Press, 1993.

World Development Report. World Bank: Washington D.C., 1989.

Woronoff, J. *Asia's Miracle Economies*. New York: Sharpe, 1986.

Zabludosky, J. "Trade Liberalization and Macroeconomic Adjustment." In *Mexico's Search for a New Development Strategy*, edited by D. Brothers and A. Wick. Boulder: Westview Press, 1990.

Contributors

H.B. CAVALCANTI is assistant professor of sociology at the University of Richmond. His articles have previously appeared in *Work and Occupations*, *Review of Religious Research*, and *International Review of Mission*.

MARY C. FROEHLE is doctoral candidate in sociology at the University of Michigan at Ann Arbor.

JEFFERY M. PAIGE is professor of sociology at the University of Michigan at Ann Arbor. His notable book publications include *Agrarian Revolution: Social Movements and Export Agriculture in the Underdeveloped World* and *The Politics of Reproductive Ritual* (co-author). In addition, he has published numerous articles in the *American Sociological Review*, *American Journal of Sociology*, *Latin American Research Review*, and *Journal of Developing Societies*.

SATYA R. PATTNAYAK is assistant professor of sociology at Villanova University. He is the editor of *Organized Religion in the Political Transformation of Latin America*. In addition, his articles have previously been published in the *Journal of Political and Military Sociology*, *International Studies*, *International Review of Modern Sociology*, *Journal of Developing Societies*, and *Sociological Spectrum*.

JAMES PETRAS is professor of sociology at the State University of New York at Binghamton. Petras has authored over 18 books. His notable publications include *Latin America in the Time of Cholera, U.S. Hegemony Under Seige,* and *Latin America: Bankers, Generals, and the Struggle for Social Justice* (Co-author). In addition, he has published articles in the *American Sociological Review, Journal of Political Economy,* and *Journal of Political and Military Sociology.*

ALEJANDRO PORTES is John Dewey Professor of Sociology and International Relations at the Johns Hopkins University. His notable book publications include *City on the Edge: The Transformation of Miami, Immigrant America: A Portrait,* and *The Informal Economy: Studies in Advanced and Less Developed Countries* (co-author). In addition, he has numerous articles previously published in the *American Journal of Sociology, American Sociological Review, Latin American Research Review,* and *Ethnic and Racial Studies.*

FERNANDO POZOS PONCE is professor in the Departamento de Estudios Socio-Urbanos at the University of Guadalajara, Mexico. The author of *Metrópolis en reestructuración: Guadalajara y Monterrey, 1980-1989,* Pozos Ponce has published numerous articles in Latin American journals including *Revista de Sociales, Revista Cuadernos,* and *Frontera Norte.*

RICHARD Y. SCHAUFFLER is a recent Ph.D. from the Johns Hopkins University. His articles have previously appeared in the *International Migration Review, Population and Development Review,* and *Estudios Sociológicos.*

ARTHUR SCHMIDT is Director of Latin American Studies and Associate Professor of History at Temple University. He is the author of *The Economic and Social Effects of Railroads in Puebla and Veracruz, Mexico, 1867-1911.* In addition, he has authored several articles in Latin American journals including *Tendencias.*

Index

DATE DUE
